Basic Python for Data Management, Finance, and Marketing

Advance Your Career by Learning the Most Powerful Analytical Tool

Art Yudin

Apress®

Basic Python for Data Management, Finance, and Marketing: Advance Your Career by Learning the Most Powerful Analytical Tool

Art Yudin
South Amboy, NJ, USA

ISBN-13 (pbk): 978-1-4842-7188-9   ISBN-13 (electronic): 978-1-4842-7189-6
https://doi.org/10.1007/978-1-4842-7189-6

Managing Director, Apress Media LLC: Welmoed Spahr
Acquisitions Editor: Shiva Ramachandran
Development Editor: Matthew Moodie
Coordinating Editor: Jessica Vakili

Distributed to the book trade worldwide by Springer Science+Business Media New York, 1 New York Plaza, New York, NY 100043. Phone 1-800-SPRINGER, fax (201) 348-4505, e-mail orders-ny@springer-sbm.com, or visit www.springeronline.com. Apress Media, LLC is a California LLC and the sole member (owner) is Springer Science + Business Media Finance Inc (SSBM Finance Inc). SSBM Finance Inc is a **Delaware** corporation.

For information on translations, please e-mail booktranslations@springernature.com; for reprint, paperback, or audio rights, please e-mail bookpermissions@springernature.com.

Apress titles may be purchased in bulk for academic, corporate, or promotional use. eBook versions and licenses are also available for most titles. For more information, reference our Print and eBook Bulk Sales web page at http://www.apress.com/bulk-sales.

Any source code or other supplementary material referenced by the author in this book is available to readers on GitHub via the book's product page, located at www.apress.com/978-1-4842-7188-9. For more detailed information, please visit http://www.apress.com/source-code.

Printed on acid-free paper

For my family for always supporting me.

Table of Contents

About the Author ix

About the Technical Reviewer xi

Chapter 1: Getting Started with Python 1

    Installing Python 3

    Variables and Numeric Types 9

    Strings...16

    Your First Program 20

    Logic with If, Elif, and Else 23

    Methods 31

    Lists and Tuples 35

    Indexing and Slicing..41

    Summary...47

Chapter 2: Writing Your Own Python Scripts 49

    Definite Loops 49

    The Range Function 54

    Nested for Loops...57

    Defining Your Own Functions 59

    Structuring a Program 64

    Indefinite Loop 72

    Dictionary..74

    Writing Information into a Text File 81

    Reading Information from a Text File 84

Chapter 3: Data Analysis with Pandas 93

Series 94

DataFrame 100

Constructing a DataFrame 100

Slicing a DataFrame 103

Filtering a DataFrame 114

Logic Operations in Pandas 118

Reading Data from a CSV File 124

Combining Data Sets 139

Concatenating Data Sets 140

Merging DataFrames 145

Groupby 147

Summary 150

Chapter 4: Gathering Data with Python 151

Web Scraping 152

List Comprehensions 165

Web Scraping with Selenium 171

Introduction to Selenium 175

Working with APIs 192

Pandas-Datareader 200

Chapter 5: Data Visualization 207

Matplotlib 207

Line Plot 208

Histogram Plot 216

Scatter Plot 219

Pie Plot 227

Chapter 6: Essential Financial Tasks Done with Python 231

NumPy Financial 231

Future Value fv( ) 233

Present Value pv( ) 234

Net Present Value npv( ) 235

Value at Risk (VAR) 243

Monte Carlo Simulation 253

Efficient Frontier 257

Fundamental Analysis 267

Financial Ratios 274

Chapter 7: Essential Digital Marketing Tasks Done with Python 277

Getting Started with Google API Client 278

Google Analytics with Python 281

Twitter Bot 298

Email Marketing with Python 304

Index 311

About the Author

Art Yudin is a FinTech enthusiast who has a great passion for coding and teaching. Art is the founder and CEO of Practical Programming, a leading training company for aspiring developers and data scientists. Currently, Art develops financial services software and leads classes and workshops at Practical Programming in New York and Chicago. He is the author of several coding publications including "Building Versatile Mobile Apps with Python and REST: RESTful Web Services with Django and React". You can follow Art Yudin on Twitter @artyudin_nyc.

About the Technical Reviewer

Monica CHIȘ is a Freelancer Software IT Consultant and Trainer. She has been working in various roles in different areas: IT industry, research, and university for more than 23 years. She has experience with external audits and with software development quality management, with highlighting the important key points for clear processes.

She was Quality Manager for software projects in Air Traffic Management and telecommunications, Project Manager and Delivery Manager in IT companies. She has worked with various data analysis methods, she has researches in data mining and she has taught statistics. Her experience involves all aspects of a project, product, and software development life cycles. She is a customer-oriented person, and she has worked in multi-cultural competitive environments. She likes working with people from different cultural groups. She is an enthusiast and passionate about technology and the Software Quality Assurance field, and she is promoting agile methodology. She really believes that it is possible to create simple processes for delivering Quality Software Products. She is passionate about the data mining field.

Starting with 2020 she is also a trainer for "SPOR – Școala pentru oameni responsabili" offering a training for Quality Assurance in Software Projects.

CHAPTER 1

Getting Started with Python

When you are finished changing, you're finished.

—Benjamin Franklin

I came to programming relatively late in my life. My job at that time had nothing to do with software development. I was not one of the computer geeks at school and always thought that coding was not for me. Working in the financial industry, I was heavily dependent on Excel and had to do a lot of manual copying and pasting.

One of my routine tasks was to update the budget and email the updated version to the top management. I decided to automate the burden and googled some script that was supposed to perform that duty. At that time, I was not paying any attention if it was Python script or any other code. The result of the enhancement was devastating. Not only my bosses received an empty file, but I had permanently erased the three-year budget project.

The main lesson I learned was if you want to make it right, you have to learn the subject from the bottom up. I had read numerous articles on how Python was used in real life and quickly realized that automation was the future. These days Python is a required knowledge like Excel or email. If you're constantly crunching numbers at work, your career would definitely

© Art Yudin 2021
A. Yudin, *Basic Python for Data Management, Finance, and Marketing*,
https://doi.org/10.1007/978-1-4842-7189-6_1

benefit of productivity and speed that Python has to offer. Having Python under the belt would allow you to write simple scripts or build complex applications.

Compared with other programming languages, Python is user-friendly and has logical and simple-to-learn syntax. With a right approach and regular practice, Python could be picked up in a matter of a couple of months. As my personal experience shows, it is never too late to get started with programming. If you are driven by a motivation to take your business skills to another level and need to evolve, you would never fail in Python.

While learning Python, the main challenge I had faced was excessively technical and sometimes poorly written documentation. It was as if they specifically wanted to confuse nontechnical people with terminology and keep us out of their hi-tech kingdom. That is why many years later after I have conquered the programming world, I have decided to write this book and explain Python programming with plain words for people who never coded before.

I understand that many of you are not planning to work as full-time programmers and need Python as a modern tool to gather, manipulate, and analyze data. That is why this book is structured as an easy-to-follow practical guide. Our main goal here is to get you started with the Python programming language and show you how Python could be used in business life.

I have structured this book based on my extensive teaching experience. We will start with the basics and then gradually move from simple concepts to more complex ones. Many hypotheses and examples we start with in this chapter would evolve and grow into advanced illustrations of how you could use Python to solve complicated cases. By the time you finish the book, you will have a clear understanding of how to apply Python to day-to-day challenges. The most important part is that you will be able to write Python scripts on your own by the end of the exciting journey we are about to embark on.

Installing Python

First things first, we need to install Python. This initial simple step could be confusing for beginners. There are many different versions of Python, and the installation process would vary for Mac and Windows. In order for us to be on the same page and not to depend on various operating systems, I decided to use the highly popular Python distribution platform Anaconda.

Anaconda is a package that comes with the latest version of Python and a bunch of Python extensions we would need later. There are other Python distributions on the market. Nevertheless, Anaconda was specifically designed for people who want to have all data analysis tools in one place. It is very popular and labeled "the birthplace of Python data science."[1]

The installation process itself is very straightforward and would work for any computer. You could google "download Anaconda Individual Edition" or go to the source www.anaconda.com/products/individual and click the **Download** button. At the bottom of that page, you should see Anaconda Installers (Figure 1-1). Choose a **Graphical Installer** for Mac or Windows and download the package. At the time of writing this book, Python 3.9 is the latest version of Python. No worries if later they move to Python 3.10 or even Python 4. The syntax will be the same. Usually, each version comes with some little improvements that would not affect the concepts we will cover in this book.

---

[1] www.anaconda.com

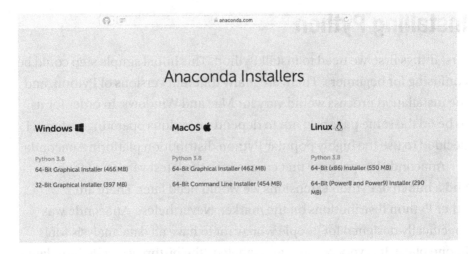

Figure 1-1. *Anaconda Installers at the bottom of the page* (`www.anaconda.com/products/individual`)

After you have downloaded Anaconda, by default it should be in the **Downloads** folder on your computer; click the downloaded installer, and it will start the installation prompt. The installation process is no different than any other application installation. It might offer to install **PyCharm IDE** along the way. We will not be using **PyCharm** in the book, and it is totally optional. If something goes wrong or you would need a step-by-step installation guidance, you could find it here: `https://docs.anaconda.com/anaconda/install/`.

To launch Anaconda on your computer, go to the **Applications** directory; on Mac you'll find it in **Launchpad**, and on Windows go to **Applications** and look for the **Anaconda Navigator** green circle logo or start typing **Anaconda** in the search prompt. After you clicked the **Anaconda Navigator** logo, you should see the **Navigator** menu like in Figure 1-2.

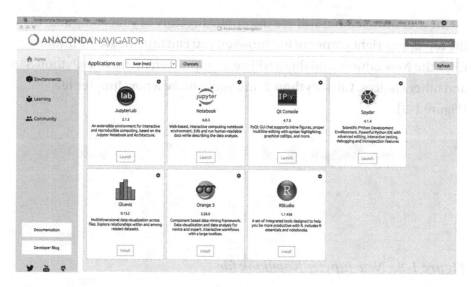

Figure 1-2. *Anaconda Navigator menu*

The **Anaconda Navigator** menu hosts many different apps to run Python – JupyterLab, **Jupyter** Notebook, Spyder, and some others. They are all apps to run Python. In this book, we will be using the **Jupyter Notebook**, simply because it is the most popular app. From now on, I'll refer to it as **Jupyter**. I do not want to go over the pros and cons of all the other apps comparing them. I think you should try all of them and pick the one that would work for you. In my opinion, the main difference among them is the layout. The Python syntax would be the same no matter which one you choose.

To begin with the **Jupyter Notebook**, click the launch button on the bottom of the card. **Jupyter** will launch in the browser running on a local server. That would be a user interface. If you use Mac, you probably noticed that **Jupyter** also launched a Terminal or command prompt window. **Jupyter** has two parts: the user interface, where we write the code, and the Kernel running on a local server, where the code is being executed. If you use Windows, you have the Kernel running quietly under the hood. On Mac, it pops up a Terminal window. We will talk more about the Kernel later.

In your browser, you will see the home directory of your computer. In the top upper-right corner of the browser, you can find the **New** button. Click the **New** button, and there will be a drop-down menu with Python 3 and other choices. Click **Python 3** and you'll make a new **Jupyter** file (Figure 1-3).

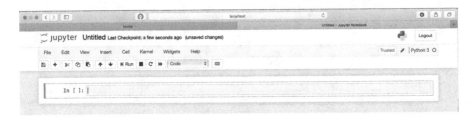

Figure 1-3. *New Jupyter Notebook file*

Untitled is a default name of a file. You could change the default file name if you click it and enter a new file name in the popped up prompt. Unless you save the file in a specific folder by providing a path in the prompt, it will be saved in the home or main directory on your computer with the .ipynb extension. **Jupyter** comes with many great features. We will cover most of them as we move along. One of the features is autosave. Everything is being autosaved every three minutes. Of course, you can save your work manually at any time by clicking the diskette icon (save button) in the toolbar. All actions in the **Jupyter** Notebook can be done with a click of the mouse in the toolbar, or you can find a corresponding shortcut by clicking **help** in the upper menu or pressing the H letter on the keyboard.

In the center, you can see a cell where we will be writing code. If you need more cells, you can always create one by clicking the **plus** icon button in the toolbar. If, on the other hand, you need to remove a cell, you can do it with the **scissors** button. I assume **copy** and **paste** buttons in the menu are self-explanatory.

Before we get to the actual Python coding part, I want to explain how to use **Jupyter**. In the upper cell, write a print() command, like this:

```
print("Hello")
```

Make sure "Hello" is wrapped in quotes. Now, click the **Run play** icon button in the upper toolbar. A couple things just happened. First of all, we got the [1] number in the square brackets on the left of the cell. Second, under the cell, the Hello word was printed (Figure 1-4). The number in the square brackets means that our code was executed in the Kernel. Every time you write code in a cell, you would need to run that cell in order for the code to be executed. It's a little bit annoying to reach for that **Run** button every time you need to run the code. The shortcut for this operation is a simultaneous press of **Shift** and **Enter** keys.

Figure 1-4. *The print() command prints "Hello" when you run the Jupyter cell*

If you run that cell over and over again, you will see that for every operation we get a new number. The number itself is not important. It represents the sequence of operation. What's important is we need to run the cell every time we update the code inside it. For example, let's update our message to

```
print("Hello World!")
```

The output Hello would not be updated unless we run that cell again.
I will run that cell again. In my case, that would be the second time I run
that cell. I'll see the next number in sequence [2], meaning that operation
is in the Python memory, and the output will be changed to Hello World!
(Figure 1-5).

Note   You can see the list of all command shortcuts for **Jupyter** if
you click **Help** and choose **Keyboard Shortcuts** from the drop-down
menu.

Figure 1-5. *The message has changed after we rerun the cell with the*
updated code

The main thing you have to remember is to run or rerun a cell if you
update code or write a new statement. Do not pay too much attention
on numbers in []. Also, numbers in your file do not have to match the
numbers in my file on these figures.

Let me say a couple of words about the Kernel. The Kernel in
Jupyter executes Python code. It quietly does its job in the background.
Sometimes, you might see an asterisk in square brackets after you ran
the cell. The asterisk, [*], means that the Kernel is working. Complex
operations performed on huge data sets might take some time, and it is
normal. However, if it takes too long for a simple operation, that might
indicate that something went wrong, and **Jupyter** is down. To wipe out the

file memory and start from scratch, you would need to click the **Kernel** item in the upper toolbar. The drop-down menu would give options to **Restart** the server or **Restart & Clear Output**. If you choose **Restart & Clear Output**, you would still see your code in the file, but square brackets would be cleared, meaning all operations in memory were successfully wiped out.

We have covered enough of **Jupyter** to get started with coding. Everything else that is needed we would figure out as we go. If at some point you would want to know more about the **Jupyter** Notebook application, I would definitely recommend you to visit their web page at https://jupyter.org.

Variables and Numeric Types

You probably know that computers have two types of memory. There is a long-term memory where you keep your files or store information as a database and a short-term memory, or random access memory (RAM), where your computer runs applications. Although Python is a programming language, it runs in short-term memory.

To store information in Python, we need to use variables. Variables in programming are similar to what we did in school in math. For example, the expression X + Y where X and Y are variables. They are called variables because they could be anything and could hold any values.

The same is true for Python. If we need to save a value to use it later, we would need to declare a variable. Simply put, we would need to come up with a variable name and assign a value. For instance, we can grab randomly picked name x and using an equal sign assign the value 7. In our **Jupyter** cell, it would look like this:

```
x = 7
```

Do not forget to run that cell afterward. You can find all code for this and all other chapters on my GitHub `https://github.com/programwithus/Basic-Python-for-Data-Management-Finance-and-Marketing`. Let's take a closer look at that expression. x is a randomly picked variable name. We could have used anything as a variable name. By the way, "banana" would perfectly do the job. It is really up to us. Later in the chapter, we will discuss the best practices for naming conventions.

However, there are some restrictions. You cannot start a variable name with a number. Also, there are so-called reserved words or keywords that you cannot use. **Jupyter** does a great job identifying words you cannot use as variables. It marks them in bold green. Take a look at the keyword print in Figure 1-5. print is one of the built-in commands and cannot be used as a variable. The one thing you have to remember is that a variable always has to be on the left side followed by an equal sign. An equal sign is defining the variable and assigning some value. A value is where it gets interesting.

The value, 7, we have assigned to variable x has to be stored somehow in the Python memory.

Values would be stored as some **data types**. Many Python tutorials explain data types as the classification of data items. Mostly needed for computers to know how we would intend to use the data in the future. When I heard that explanation for the first time, I found it very confusing. Let me offer my explanation of data types.

Grab a bottle of a simple purified water you can find in any store. The water would be the value, and a plastic bottle is a container. Then suppose you order water in a coffee shop. They would bring you the same purified water in a glass. Obviously, there is a huge difference between a plastic bottle and a glass. For starters, the bottle comes with a cap that won't let the water out of the bottle. A plastic bottle and a glass are different types of containers that are holding the same value – water. We understand that different containers have different features and behave accordingly. The point I am trying to make is that based on your intentions for that value, in our case water, you should choose an appropriate container. If you plan to get into the business of selling purified water, you should choose a plastic bottle or an aluminum can with a flashy label for your value. Contrast that with having a glass of water at a restaurant. Maybe you should store your water in a travel mug or tumbler if you are planning a road trip.

A data type is similar to a container. You should choose an appropriate data type based on how you plan to use your data in the future. "It makes sense with water, but how can you save 7, it's a number," you might ask me. There are three distinct built-in numeric data types in Python: **integer**, **float**, and **complex numbers**. Here, we will use integers and floats.

Integers are whole numbers. For instance, 7, 27, 1,000,000 would be stored as integers, simply because they are whole numbers. Even a negative number as long as it is a whole number would be stored in the memory as an integer.

Floats are numbers with a decimal point. An example would be 7.5 or –2.5. Based on what you are planning to count, you should choose either an integer or a float type. If we talk about money, then we should use floats. People always want to be precise to a penny with money. The contradictory of that would be people. Assuming that your task is to split seven people into two teams, then integers would be an obvious choice. You do not want to end up with three and a half people.

Let's see how this concept works in practice. Under x = 7, add one more statement. Do not forget to run the cell aftewards:

```
y = 5.5
```

Since x and y both hold numeric values, we can do the math. Table 1-1 later in this chapter lists all the arithmetic operators.

```
x + y
```

Keep in mind that Python is case sensitive, and x and y should be lowercase. When you run that cell, 12.5 will be the output (Figure 1-6).

```
In [2]: print("Hello World!")
        Hello World!

In [3]: x = 7
        y = 5.5
        x + y
Out[3]: 12.5
```

Figure 1-6. *The output of the x + y expression*

This time, I did not use the print() command because **Jupyter** by default prints the result of the last operation in a cell. Notwithstanding, if I want to print the result of this operation several times, I would need to use the print() command:

```
print(x + y)
```

Table 1-1. *Arithmetic operators in Python*

Operator	Name	Example
+	Addition	2 + 2 -> 4
–	Subtraction	5 – 2 -> 3
*	Multiplication	2 * 2 -> 4
/	Division	2 / 2 -> 1
//	Floor division	5 // 3 -> 1
%	Modulus (remainder)	5 % 3 -> 2

When you run the cell, make sure your print() command is all lowercase.

We have been using the print() command for quite some time. Now it is time to learn other commands. Python is sometimes called "batteries included" because it comes with a bunch of built-in commands and modules. The commands are called built-in functions. A function is a block of reusable code that performs a task.

You can find the full list of built-in functions here: `https://docs.python.org/3/library/functions.html`. This is the official Python documentation page. Later when you upgrade to the next version of Python at the time it is out, make sure that the documentation matches the version you are running on your machine. In this book, we will learn and use many of built-in functions. If you are serious about Python, bookmark the documentation page to use it as a reference.

One of my favorite functions you can find on that list is `type()`. The built-in function `type()` helps to identify the data type of a value. I'll illustrate how you can use a Python statement in a separate cell and nest a couple statements in one cell. If you run the `type()` function in a separate cell, then you don't need a `print()` function. However, if you place

```
print(type(x))
print(type(y))
```

into the same cell, then you need to wrap each one in a `print()` function (Figure 1-7).

```
In [3]:  x = 7
         y = 5.5
         x + y
Out[3]:  12.5

In [4]:  type(x)
Out[4]:  int

In [5]:  type(y)
Out[5]:  float

In [6]:  print(type(x))
         print(type(y))

         <class 'int'>
         <class 'float'>
```

Figure 1-7. *Running the built-in function type()*

You can see that the output for `type(x)` is an integer because x holds the value of the whole number 7, and `type(y)` prints a float since 5.5 has a decimal point.

How many cells you should use is totally up to you. Usually, I keep separate tasks in separate cells. It would make more sense as we move to more complex tasks.

In my opinion, type() is the most underestimated function. Some people might argue why we would need the function type()? We can clearly see that x holds an integer. That is true. But in real life when data is coming from the Internet in the form of an API (Application Programming Interface), we will discuss APIs later in this book, or you are fetching data from a CSV file, you do not know for sure what data type you are dealing with.

Also, based on my experience, beginners always struggle with and mismatch data types. My advice is run the type function on a variable if you are not sure what data type it holds.

Now let's take a closer look at the x + y expression. Suppose we want to save the result of that operation so we can use it later. To save 12.5 in Python memory, we would need to assign the expression, x + y, to a new variable. Another randomly picked variable total could hold that result. Try this in a new cell (Figure 1-8).

```
x = 7
y = 5.5
total = x + y
total
```

```
In [7]: x = 7
        y = 5.5
        total = x + y
        total
Out[7]: 12.5
```

Figure 1-8. Variable total holding the result of the x + y expression

In some way, it is very convenient to use variable names. Assuming we want to calculate the area of a room. To do that, we would need the length of the room multiplied by the width. We can implement this formula in Python code (Figure 1-9):

```
length = 30
width = 25.5
area = length * width
area
```

```
In [8]:  length = 30
         width = 25.5
         area = length * width
         area

Out[8]:  765.0
```

Figure 1-9. *Calculating the area of a room*

If we want to calculate the area of the next room in a house, we can just reassign the values of length and width and do not have to touch the formula length * width.

We have been using x and y as variable names. However, in real life you would want to use variable names that would reflect the value's purpose. If you used x, y, and z as variables all the time, that would be confusing. Later when you get back to the code, say in a couple of weeks, you would have a hard time remembering what you actually meant by x and y. Also, very often you collaborate with others. It would be much clearer for everyone if variable names represented what information the variable holds. You probably noticed that I do not capitalize my variables. The best practice is to begin a variable with a lowercase letter. Sometimes, you need to use two words to better describe the purpose of a variable. Then use an underscore to connect the two words, such as length_room. This style is called the snake case. Another option would be to start with a lowercase letter and attach the second word capitalized like lengthRoom. Such technique is called the camel case. No matter what style you choose, always stay consistent and never use spaces between words in a variable name.

Strings

Strings are another built-in data type in Python. Any characters or letters wrapped in quotes would be stored in the memory as a string. If we get back to our initial example print("Hello"), Hello in quotes would be regarded as a string by Python.

I think the following example will illustrate the nature of Python strings. In a new cell, try the built-in function ord() (Figure 1-10):

```
ord("a")
ord("A")
```

```
In [9]:    1  ord("a")
Out[9]:  97

In [10]:   1  ord("A")
Out[10]:  65
```

Figure 1-10. *The ord function returns a unique Unicode number for the character*

"A" is the first letter of the alphabet. It makes sense for billions of people using the Latin alphabet. But what if somebody would show you a letter from a foreign alphabet that you have never seen before? Your reaction would be something like "I do not know what that character means." The same is true for computers. Computers do not know the meaning of characters. They store string characters as numbers. If you take a look at how text looks under the hood, you would see a sequence of numbers. In Figure 1-10, the ord() function returns the Unicode integer 97 for the "A" character and 65 for the "a" character. ord() stands for order and provides a corresponding number for a character. Obviously, there is a huge difference between 97 and 65. That proves Python is case sensitive.

The Unicode standard provides a number for each letter, symbol, or emoji. If you are curious, check out the Unicode character table at https://unicode-table.com/en.

You won't be using the ord() function too often in your everyday life, and you do not have to memorize all the numbers. The point I'm trying to make is that a string is a sequence of characters. Computers do not care about the meaning of strings. If I wrote "apple" for us, humans, it would mean some fruit. A computer would just store a bunch of characters in its memory as a sequence of integers.

The number "7" wrapped in quotes would not represent a numeric value, but rather another character. You could give it a try and run the ord() function on "7".

```
ord("7")
```

The result will be 55, a number representing the character 7 in the Unicode table. It means that "7" in quotes cannot be used in arithmetic operations because it would be stored as a string.

Again, think of the analogy of the water stored in different containers. Although "7" looks like a number, in fact it is not a numeric type for Python.

Let me run a couple of examples to illustrate integers, floats, and strings. In a cell, try adding "7" to an integer (Figure 1-11).

```
7 + "7"
```

```
In [11]:  1 7 + "7"

-------------------------------------------------------------
----
TypeError                          Traceback (most recent call l
ast)
<ipython-input-11-62feab9aa80e> in <module>
----> 1 7 + "7"

TypeError: unsupported operand type(s) for +: 'int' and 'str'
```

Figure 1-11. *7 as an integer cannot be added to "7" as a string*

7 + "7" will give us an error message. I would like to stop here and tell you a little more about errors.

I know it could be frustrating to get an error message. Think of it another way. Error messages in Python were created not to judge us but to help us. When you get an error, first of all see where the green arrow is pointing. That is where the problem has occurred. Second, read the message thinkably. Python is telling exactly what went wrong. I know that it might be difficult to comprehend them at first. With experience, you'll be able to understand the types of error messages and how to fix them.

In our case, Figure 1-11, Python is telling us that we cannot mix different data types. It is impossible to add a string to an integer. Literally, it's telling us not to use a plus sign between integers and strings.

There are a couple of things we can do to fix this. We can try to convert one data type into another. Since "7" looks like a number, we can use the built-in function int() to convert it to a numeric data type. If we had a letter or some other character instead of "7", that would not be possible.

```
7 + int("7")
```

```
In [12]:    1 7 + int("7")
Out[12]:    14
```

Figure 1-12. *Using the int() function, we convert a string to an integer*

In Figure 1-12, we can see that the string "7" is being converted to an integer. Integer 7 plus integer 7 expectedly gets us 14. If we had a letter or some other character instead of "7", the conversion to a numeric type would not be possible.

An alternative option would be to convert "7" to a float. Using the function float(), try

```
7 + float("7")
```

```
In [13]:  1 7 + float("7")
Out[13]: 14.0
```

Figure 1-13. *The function float() converts string into a float*

This time, we got **14.0** as a result of integer **7** being added to a float. At the end of the day, the string **"7"** was converted to a float **7.0**. In an arithmetical operation like this, **7 + 7.0**, the float always wins, and the result would be returned as a float.

There is one more option we can do here. We can convert an integer to a string with the help of the built-in function **str()**.

> str(7) + "7"

```
In [14]:  1 str(7) + "7"
Out[14]: '77'
```

Figure 1-14. *Using the str() function, we convert an integer to a string*

In Figure 1-14, you can see that now we have joined or concatenated one string to another. Integer 7 was converted to a string, and the whole operation yielded a new string **"77"**.

The main idea behind these three examples is that the same plus operator brings about different results based on the data type it is applied to. All data types behave differently. In other words, each data type has its own features. This totally makes sense because we understand that a plastic bottle and a cup are two different containers that behave in their own certain ways.

Keep these examples in mind. The behavior of data types is a very important subject. Later, we will move to more advanced objects and learn their features.

Your First Program

I guess we have covered enough to compose your first program. I am a fan of practical examples. What could be more practical than a tax and tip calculator? We all go out, and, in the end, they would bring us a check. For simplicity, we assume that the check is $50. Our task is to calculate the tax and tip in Python and get the bottom-line number. In New York City, the sales tax is 8.875%. To keep numbers small and simple, I'll round it down to 8%. For a tip, I'll use 18%. We have all inputs and can start coding:

```
check = 50
tax_rate = 0.08
tip_rate = 0.18
```

After we defined variables with known values, we would need to calculate the actual dollar amount for the tip and tax.[2] Since we would need to use the tax and tip later, it would be a good idea to assign expressions to corresponding variables:

```
tax = check * tax_rate
tip = check * tip_rate
```

Note that if later we would use a different value for a check, there would be no need to mess with the formula. The final step is to add the tax and tip to the check and print the value:

```
total = check + tax + tip
print("Your total is $", total)
```

---

[2] I know that there are other ways to calculate the tax and tip; however, here I am trying to be as clear as possible.

```
In [15]:    1  check = 50
            2
            3  tax_rate = 0.08
            4  tip_rate = 0.18
            5
            6  tax = check * tax_rate
            7  tip = check * tip_rate
            8  total = check + tax + tip
            9  print("Your total is $", total)

            Your total is $ 63.0
```

***Figure 1-15.** Tax and tip calculator*

I hope your result is 63.0 like I got in Figure 1-15. The comma in the
print() function creates that space where total is printed. Also, a comma
separates a string from a float. We are passing two arguments into the
print() function "Your total is $" and total. Later, I'll introduce the
method format to print nicely formatted strings. If for some reason you
will see NameError: name is not defined, check the spelling of the
variables and make sure they match.

By now you are probably wondering how we can make this calculator
more versatile and use any number as a check. To accept a value from the
user, we would need to use the built-in function input(). The function
input() does two things; first, it would print a message that we want
to pass to a user and then would prompt for a value. I'll replace 50 with
the function input() in the example. Inside the parentheses, I'll pass a
message. A message is optional, but it would be a good idea to guide a user.

```
check = input("How much is the meal? ")
```

Note   After you punched the number, you need to press the **enter**
key on your keyboard. Otherwise, the program would be waiting for
your response and render [*] next to the cell. If that happens, restart
the Kernel as we discussed it before.

If you run the cell with the code as it is, input() would prompt you to enter a value. Suppose you entered 60, the program would throw you the error. The error message would look like the one you can see in Figure 1-16. A crucial part of coding is to debug your own code. Here, I will show you an example of how to debug your code. We would need to start with the error message "can't multiply sequence by non-int of type 'float.'" This is pretty much the same message that we have seen before. It says that we cannot multiply a string by a float. Apparently, the input() function returns any value as a string. Even if it looks like a number. If you read the description of the input() function, it says "converts value to a string".[3] Suppose we did not quite get that message and have not read the documentation. Then we would need to go line by line to identify the bug.

```
In [16]:    1  check = input("How much is the meal? ")
            2
            3  tax_rate = 0.08
            4  tip_rate = 0.18
            5
            6  tax = check * tax_rate
            7  tip = check * tip_rate
            8  total = check + tax + tip
            9  print("Your total is $", total)

How much is the meal? 60

---------------------------------------------------------------
TypeError                              Traceback (most recent call last)
<ipython-input-16-7bb315388f6e> in <module>
      4 tip_rate = 0.18
      5
----> 6 tax = check * tax_rate
      7 tip = check * tip_rate
      8 total = check + tax + tip

TypeError: can't multiply sequence by non-int of type 'float'
```

Figure 1-16. *Error message*

Under the check variable, I'll place a print() statement to inspect the value of the check and its data type:

```
print(check, type(check))
```

---

[3] https://docs.python.org/3/library/functions.html#input

This would get me 60 and a string. Now it is clear, we cannot multiply a string by a float. To fix it, I'll squeeze a new statement to convert the value we received from the input to a float. Also, I'll run the type function on that value one more time to make sure that the type has changed to numeric (Figure 1-17):

```
check = float(check)
print(check, type(check))
```

```
In [17]:   1  check = input("How much is the meal? ")
           2  print(check, type(check))
           3  check = float(check)
           4  print(check, type(check))
           5  tax_rate = 0.08
           6  tip_rate = 0.18
           7
           8  tax = check * tax_rate
           9  tip = check * tip_rate
          10  total = check + tax + tip
          11  print("Your total is $", total)

How much is the meal? 60
60 <class 'str'>
60.0 <class 'float'>
Your total is $ 75.6
```

Figure 1-17. *Tax and tip calculator ready to accept a value from the user*

After we have successfully converted the user's input to a float, our tax and tip calculator works just fine. Print statements on lines 2 and 4 in Figure 1-17 could be removed later. We needed them to find and fix that bug only.

Logic with If, Elif, and Else

To implement logic in Python, we need to use If, Elif, and Else statements. Before we get to them, I want to introduce the **Boolean** data type. There are two Booleans in Python, **True** and **False**. True and False as keywords always should be capitalized. You will see True if you try to evaluate the 2*2 == 4 statement. Consequently, the statement 2*2 == 5 would return False. Let me step back here and explain what a double equal operator means.

When we assign a value to a variable name like x = 7, we use a single equal sign because it defines the variable. A double equal sign is a comparison operator. If we want to compare values, then we would need to use ==. There are more comparison operators you can find in Table 1-2.

Table 1-2. *Comparison operators in Python*

Operator	Name	Example
==	Equal	2 == 2
!=	Not equal	5 != 2
>	Greater than	5 > 2
<	Less than	2 < 5
>=	Greater than or equal	5 >= 2
<=	Less than or equal to	2 <= 5

I'll start with the if statement. The if statement evaluates the expression, and if the result is True, then some conditions would be executed. I think an example with weather conditions will illustrate it. Suppose the weather outside is rainy, and we want to be reminded not to forget an umbrella. We can compose the following Python code:

```
weather = "rainy"
if weather == "rainy":
 print("Take an umbrella")
```

The if condition evaluates weather == "rainy". In order for it to be True, the value of the variable weather has to be identical to the "rainy" string. For Python, "rainy" is a sequence of characters. The computer compares the values character by character. If the weather variable value and "rainy" are perfectly matched, meaning all letters are the same and lowercase, then the condition would return True.

You have probably noticed a colon after the if statement. In short, this is a Python syntax, and you'll have to learn it. The if, elif, and else statements should have a colon at the end. I like to think of that colon as an action trigger. If a condition is true, then do something.

As a rule of thumb, all statements that follow a colon should be indented. An indentation is very important in Python. It is how we bind statements together. We can say that the print("Take an umbrella") statement is in the scope of the if statement. We will talk more about the scope in the next chapter.

The official Python documentation recommends using four spaces for indentation. However, apps like **Jupyter** give you an option to use a tab key on the keyboard to indent. The main rule of programming is always to be consistent. In the same file, you cannot mix spaces and tab as an indentation. You can use whichever you like, but if you use tabs, stick to tabs, or if you choose to indent with spaces, keep doing spaces. One of the common mistakes I have seen is that people would copy somebody's code from the Internet and paste it into their files. This might give you an indentation error because the copied code came with tabs, and you have spaces for indentation in the file. The bottom line you have to remember is never to mix tabs and spaces in one file.

We can try our weather exercises in **Jupyter**, and the output should return Take an umbrella (Figure 1-18).

```
In [18]:   1  weather = "rainy"
           2  if weather == "rainy":
           3      print("Take an umbrella")

        Take an umbrella
```

Figure 1-18. *The if statement prints the "Take an umbrella" message, since weather == "rainy" returns True*

To make our code more versatile, we can replace "rainy" with a familiar function input():

```
weather = input("How is the weather? ")
```

Run your code, and after the input function prompts, "How is the weather?", you type something different than "rainy". Do not forget to press the enter key. The if statement will be evaluated, but would return False in this case, and nothing will be printed.

An if statement can be followed by an else statement. Keep in mind that an if statement is often sufficient by itself. However, most of the time, you would need to have more outcomes.

Let's add an else statement to our weather script:

```
weather = input("How is the weather? ")
if weather == "rainy":
 print("Take an umbrella")
else:
        print("Have a nice day")
```

For the reason that the else statement captures anything else we might get from a user, there is no need for a condition. The else statement is immediately followed by a colon. A rookie mistake is people try to squeeze in some condition after else. That makes no sense at all. In Figure 1-19, you can see how our little program would react if a user entered "windy". Since there is no condition to check for "windy", the else statement catches it and prints "Have a nice day". Keep in mind that our code performs no data validation. If a user for some reason had inputted some abracadabra, the else statement would be triggered and execute whatever code we might have under it.

```
In [19]:   1  weather = input("How is the weather? ")
           2  if weather == "rainy":
           3      print("Take an umbrella")
           4  else:
           5      print("Have a nice day")
```
```
How is the weather? windy
Have a nice day
```

Figure 1-19. *The else statement prints the "have a nice day" message after being executed*

What if we have more conditions than just `"rainy"`? In that case, we would need to begin all other conditions with the `elif` keyword. `elif` stands for "else if" and should be used after opening an `if` statement. Suppose we need another reminder in case it is sunny outside. We can write this additional condition as

```
weather = input("How is the weather? ")
if weather == "rainy":
 print("Take an umbrella")
elif weather == "sunny":
        print("Do not forget your sunglasses")
else:
        print("Have a nice day")
```

The point you have to remember is that you always start decisions with an `if` statement and then use `elif`. You might use a thousand of `elif` statements if needed. In our pattern, we can extend the weather options with another `elif` condition in case there is a blizzard coming:

```
weather = input("How is the weather? ")
if weather == "rainy":
        print("Take an umbrella")
elif weather == "sunny":
        print("Do not forget your sunglasses")
```

```
elif weather == "blizzard":
      print("Stay home")
else:
      print("Have a nice day")
```

Run your code and test all conditions (Figure 1-20).

```
In [20]:   1  weather = input("How is the weather? ")
           2  if weather == "rainy":
           3      print("Take an umbrella")
           4  elif weather == "sunny":
           5      print("Do not forget your sunglasses")
           6  elif weather == "blizzard":
           7      print("Stay home")
           8  else:
           9      print("Have a nice day")

        How is the weather? sunny
        Do not forget your sunglasses
```

Figure 1-20. *Elif triggered by the "sunny" condition*

There is one mistake beginners do over and over again, using an `if` statement instead of `elif`. In some instances, that might work, but I would like to demonstrate why it is so important to use `elif` statements.

Suppose by mistake I had used an `if` statement instead of `elif` for the "sunny" condition. Assuming that a user inputted "rainy" into the prompt, what reminders would we see? You might say "Take an umbrella". This is true. However, we would also see "Have a nice day" (Figure 1-21). Why? Python regards the `if` statement as a beginning of a new set of options and will execute the statement under the `else` after the `if` check for "sunny". In case you expect only one outcome, then you must use an `elif` statement.

In other words, every time Python reads an `if` statement, it takes it as a separate conditional statement or a new decision set. That is why it is very important to follow an `if` statement with `elif` if you want to outline several options and anticipate only one result.

```
In [21]:    1  weather = input("How is the weather? ")
            2  if weather == "rainy":
            3      print("Take an umbrella")
            4  if weather == "sunny":
            5      print("Do not forget your sunglasses")
            6  elif weather == "blizzard":
            7      print("Stay home")
            8  else:
            9      print("Have a nice day")

        How is the weather? rainy
        Take an umbrella
        Have a nice day
```

Figure 1-21. *Wrong example of structuring decision structures*

I guess by now you want to know what we should do if a user enters "Rainy" with a capital "R". The way our code is structured right now, "Rainy" would be captured by the else statement. This is not what we want. As people who write code for others, we would need to think of all possible scenarios. One solution to fix it would be logical operators (Table 1-3). In the course of this book, we will try all of them. We will begin with or.

Table 1-3. *Logical operators in Python*

Operator	Name
and	Two conditions should be True
or	Either condition should be True
not	If a condition is not True
in	If an item is in a sequence
not in	If an item is not in a sequence

We can extend our if statement and use the or operator to give a user more options how to input a weather condition. "Rainy" beginning with a capital letter:

```
if weather == "rainy" or weather == "Rainy":
 print("Take an umbrella")
```

The important part to remember is that you need to outline the whole condition after or. We would need to use the weather variable again. The if statement would not work with just the weather == "rainy" or "Rainy" condition. The if statement would be triggered if either one of the conditions returned True. I'll be honest with you, there is a better way to make sure that the inputted value would match our condition. I'll show it to you later. The current example illustrates the use of the or operator.

Compared to the or operator, and would require a satisfaction of two conditions. To see how it works, we add one more question to our program. The variable season would hold a value like "summer" or "winter":

```
season = input("What season are we in ? ")
```

We will add another elif statement that would require two conditions to be true:

```
elif weather == "cold" and season == "winter":
    print("Dress warmly")
```

Only if two conditions are satisfied and returned True, we would see the "Dress warmly" message (Figure 1-22).

```
In [22]:   1  weather = input("How is the weather? ")
           2  season = input("What season are we in ? ")
           3  if weather == "rainy" or weather == "Rainy":
           4      print("Take an umbrella")
           5  elif weather == "cold" and  season == "winter":
           6      print("Dress warmly")
           7  elif weather == "sunny":
           8      print("Do not forget your sunglasses")
           9  elif weather == "blizzard":
          10      print("Stay home")
          11  else:
          12      print("Have a nice day")

How is the weather? cold
What season are we in ? winter
Dress warmly
```

Figure 1-22. *Elif triggered if two conditions are satisfied and returned True*

Methods

Python is an object-oriented programming language. Object-oriented programming (OOP) is a design method to structure a program. The main concept behind it is to bundle related properties and behaviors as individual objects. In a nutshell, everything in Python is an object. We have briefly touched behaviors of the objects with the water container analogy before.

When I declare variable `season = "summer"`, `"summer"` is stored as an object in Python memory. It is encapsulated as a string, because we have wrapped it in quotes, and `"summer"` is just an instance of a string. Later if we want, we could replace `"summer"` with `"winter"`. `"winter"` would be another instance of a string. Since `"summer"` and `"winter"` are both instances of the string, they would behave similarly and share the same attributes.

There is a command that would show you all built-in methods of an object – `dir()`. A method is similar to a function, which performs a task. The main difference is a method belongs to an object. We will be using `dir()` a lot; as things go more complicated, you will see that the `dir()` function is irreplaceable. Every time you do not know how to do something in Python, I would recommend you start with the `dir()` function. Suppose we need to convert `"summer"` to uppercase `"SUMMER"`. If you have no idea how to do it, always start with the dir() function. Run `dir()` on the object; in this case, run it on `"summer"`. You can pass the instance `"summer"` as an argument into the `dir()` function or a variable name holding that instance. Another option is to pass `str` into the `dir()` function; after all, `"summer"` is an instance of a string.

```
season = "summer"
dir("summer")
or
```

```
dir(season)
```

or

```
dir(str)
```

```
In [23]:    1  season = "summer"
            2  print(dir(season))

['__add__', '__class__', '__contains__', '__delattr__', '__dir__', '__doc__', '__eq__',
'__format__', '__ge__', '__getattribute__', '__getitem__', '__getnewargs__', '__gt__',
'__hash__', '__init__', '__init_subclass__', '__iter__', '__le__', '__len__', '__lt__',
'__mod__', '__mul__', '__ne__', '__new__', '__reduce__', '__reduce_ex__', '__repr__', '__
rmod__', '__rmul__', '__setattr__', '__sizeof__', '__str__', '__subclasshook__', 'capita
lize', 'casefold', 'center', 'count', 'encode', 'endswith', 'expandtabs', 'find', 'forma
t', 'format_map', 'index', 'isalnum', 'isalpha', 'isascii', 'isdecimal', 'isdigit', 'isi
dentifier', 'islower', 'isnumeric', 'isprintable', 'isspace', 'istitle', 'isupper', 'joi
n', 'ljust', 'lower', 'lstrip', 'maketrans', 'partition', 'replace', 'rfind', 'rindex',
'rjust', 'rpartition', 'rsplit', 'rstrip', 'split', 'splitlines', 'startswith', 'strip',
'swapcase', 'title', 'translate', 'upper', 'zfill']
```

Figure 1-23. *String methods*

I know at first what you see in Figure 1-23 looks overwhelming. This is a list of all built-in methods or commands in a string object. Usually, when you want to do something to an object, you want to check all its methods with the function dir(). In the beginning of that list, we see dunder methods. Dunder is short for "double underscores." All these dunder methods have double underscores before and after the method name. Dunder methods are used by Python itself. As an illustration, the function len() would use the dunder method __len__() when called on "winter". Similarly, a plus operator would call the __add__() method if you concatenate two strings (Figure 1-24). Most of the time, you skip dunder methods and start looking for a method you need to use.

```
In [24]:   1  len("winter")
Out[24]: 6

In [25]:   1  "winter".__len__()
Out[25]: 6

In [26]:   1  "winter" + "summer"
Out[26]: 'wintersummer'

In [27]:   1  "winter".__add__("summer")
Out[27]: 'wintersummer'
```

Figure 1-24. *Function len() and "+" act as wrappers for __len__()
and __add__() methods*

After scanning all string methods, we see the upper() method. It is the
second to last on the string method list (Figure 1-23). The name of that
method is self-explanatory. However, there are many others that we do
not know yet and have no idea how to use them. To see a definition of the
method, use the function help() (Figure 1-25). By the way, the function
help() is universal and can be applied to functions too, such as help(len).

```
help("winter".upper)
or
help(season.upper)
or
help(str.upper)
```

```
In [28]:   1  help(season.upper)
           Help on built-in function upper:

           upper() method of builtins.str instance
               Return a copy of the string converted to uppercase.
```

Figure 1-25. *Function help() returns a definition of the function len()*

As we can see from the definition, the method upper() "Return[s] a copy of the string converted to uppercase". Later, we will talk why the method upper() returns a "copy" of an object. Methods are built-in commands into the object itself; that is why we need to use them like this:

```
season.upper()
```
or
```
"winter".upper()
```

Methods are unique to an object. If you run the dir() function on an integer or a float, you won't see the upper() method. That makes sense. Only alphabetical characters can be converted to uppercase.

Beginners always ask me "how would I know which is a function to which I should pass an object as an argument, like len("winter"), or a method that I need to use with a period after an object?" The answer is very simple. You run dir() on an object, and if what you are looking for is in that list, then it is a method, and you should use it with the period, like this:

```
"winter".lower()
```

On the other hand, if it is not in the list, then you cannot run it as a method. A very common mistake is to apply a wrong method to the object. In that case, Python would give you an error message "[type] object has no attribute [name of method]". People do that over and over again. Believe me there is no need to memorize all methods of an object. Sometimes, it is even impossible due to the fact that Python and its extensions are regularly updated. All you have to do is to use dir() to see all available methods of an object.

In our previous example with if and else, we had to use the logical operator or, in case a user would use a capitalized word. With the lower() method, we can convert any incoming string to lowercase and not worry that a user might use different caps and enter something like "suNNy". Keep in mind that we would need to save the copy of the lowercase string, meaning to assign to a variable name. In Figure 1-26, you can see "BLIZZARD" was entered and converted to lowercase on line 3.

```
In [29]:  1  weather = input("How is the weather? ")
          2  season = input("What season are we in ? ")
          3  weather = weather.lower()
          4  season = season.lower()
          5  if weather == "rainy":
          6      print("Take an umbrella")
          7  elif weather == "cold" and season == "winter":
          8      print("Dress warmly")
          9  elif weather == "sunny":
         10      print("Do not forget your sunglasses")
         11  elif weather == "blizzard":
         12      print("Stay home")
         13  else:
         14      print("Have a nice day")

How is the weather? BLIZZARD
What season are we in ? Winter
Stay home
```

Figure 1-26. The function lower converts entered words to lowercase strings

Lists and Tuples

So far, we have learned integer, float, and string types. Here, we will discuss lists and tuples. We will start with the most popular data structure – a list. A data structure is some kind of collection of items or elements. Most of the time, a data structure contains other basic types, like integers or floats. The easiest way to think of data structures is to compare them to containers.

A list is a container that holds items separated by a comma. There is no limit to the number of items in the list. The only limit would be a computer memory.

Usually, I explain a list with a box example. A box is a container where you could put stuff. Later, if needed, you can fetch items from the box. To initialize a list, we have to assign square brackets to a variable. Continuing with a box example, let's define a variable box and assign empty square brackets:

```
box = []
type(box)
```

You could think of this operation as preparing an empty box to put some stuff in. Run the function type(box) to confirm that the box variable holds a list object.

Suppose we needed to add a bunch of numbers to a list object, how would we do it? One option would be to google it; however, the best way would be to see what methods come with the list itself. Remember the function dir() from the previous exercise? Run dir() and pass a variable holding the list object into the function:

```
dir(box)
```

The methods for a list object (Figure 1-27) are completely different from a string or any other data structure.

```
['__add__', '__class__', '__contains__', '__delattr__', '__delitem__', '__dir__', '__doc__', '__eq__', '__format__',
'__ge__', '__getattribute__', '__getitem__', '__gt__', '__hash__', '__iadd__', '__imul__', '__init__', '__init_subcl
ass__', '__iter__', '__le__', '__len__', '__lt__', '__mul__', '__ne__', '__new__', '__reduce__', '__reduce_ex__', '__
_repr__', '__reversed__', '__rmul__', '__setattr__', '__setitem__', '__sizeof__', '__str__', '__subclasshook__', 'ap
pend', 'clear', 'copy', 'count', 'extend', 'index', 'insert', 'pop', 'remove', 'reverse', 'sort']
```

Figure 1-27. *The list methods*

Our goal is to add numbers one by one to the list object. If we take a closer look at the list methods, we would see two commands that sound like we can use them to add data to the list. They are append() and insert() in Figure 1-27. If you want to know the difference between them and how to use them, run the help() function:

```
help(box.append)
```

and

```
help(box.insert)
```

The main difference between these two is that the append() method literally appends an item to the end of a list. The insert() method on the other hand requires not only the item to be inserted but also a location in the form of an index. We will review indexing later in this chapter, and for that reason we will start with the append() method. In a cell, try to append random numbers to the list:

```
box.append(70)
box.append(30)
box.append(50)
box.append(10)
box.append(20)
```

Keep in mind that every time you run the cell, you will see the same number appended to the list again. I am going to run the cell once. After that operation, my list, box, holds all numbers I have appended separated by a comma (Figure 1-28).

```
In [30]:    1  box = []
            2  type(box)
            3  dir(box)
            4
            5  box.append(70)
            6  box.append(30)
            7  box.append(50)
            8  box.append(10)
            9  box.append(20)
           10  box

Out[30]:  [70, 30, 50, 10, 20]
```

Figure 1-28. *The list of numbers*

I hope a box analogy helped you to understand how a list object works. Now it is time to give you a more formal definition of a list data structure. A list is a sequential data structure that can be ordered in ascending or descending order. It is a versatile container. You can add items to a list or remove items from a list. The main thing I want you to understand about a list data structure is that you do not use a list just to store the data.

For that, you would use a file or would write data into a database. But you would choose to use a list because you want to do something with the items in the container down the road. For example, you initialize a list and append numbers to it because you want to sort them. There is a built-in method sort() (Figure 1-29):

```
box.sort()
box
```

```
In [31]:    1  box.sort()
            2  box

Out[31]:  [10, 20, 30, 50, 70]
```

Figure 1-29. *Sorted list in ascending order*

A list data structure is being sorted in place; that means within the object itself. That is why there is no need to assign a box.sort() operation to a variable. This behavior of a list is called mutability. Mutability is a very important concept in programming. It means if the object can be or cannot be changed. A list is mutable, and we can add more items with the append() method or using the remove() method get rid of unwanted items from it:

> box.append(800)
>
> box.remove(10)
>
> box

As a result of these operations, we have added 800 and dropped 10 from our list (Figure 1-30).

```
In [32]:    1  box.append(800)
            2  box.remove(10)
            3  box

Out[32]:  [20, 30, 50, 70, 800]
```

Figure 1-30. *We have appended 800 and removed 10 from the list*

A tuple on the other hand is immutable, meaning it cannot be changed. We can create a tuple with round brackets:

t = (1,2,3,4,5)
type(t)

Run the function type() on t, and you can see that now we deal with a tuple. A tuple is similar to a list. It is also an ordered data structure that can hold elements separated by a comma. However, if you run dir(t), you can see that besides dunder methods there are only two other methods that we can use – count() and index(). The main difference between a list and a tuple is mutability. Again, a list is mutable, and a tuple is immutable.

Sometimes, people in my classroom would ask "do we really need to go so deep in programming concepts like mutability, we just want to use Python." The answer is "Yes." This is important especially if you are planning to work with huge data sets. The general principle is immutable objects tend to be faster than mutable. You can think of list and tuple data structures as an open box and a sealed box. In the case of an open box, you can put more stuff in it or may remove something from it. So, if later you want to review what you have in an open box, it might take some time. In the case of a sealed box, there is no need to waste any time on checking. It is sealed and has a label on it saying what's in it. There will be no new items because it is sealed.

How would you choose a right data structure? Obviously, if we're talking about a carton box and a plastic box, you would choose the one suitable for a job based on the box attributes. In programming, it is pretty much the same. Allow me to demonstrate it with a simple example. Assume we need to write a program that reads a letter from a user. If a user enters a, e, i, o, or u, the program should print "This letter is a vowel". If a user enters any other letter of the alphabet, the program should say "This letter is a consonant". For simplicity's sake, let's assume that "y" is always a consonant.

One approach that quickly comes to mind is to use the or operator and chain all possible conditions like this:

```
letter = input("Give me a letter ")
if letter == "a" or letter == "e" or letter =="i" or
letter == "o" or letter == "u":
print("This letter is a vowel")
```

The solution with a bunch of or operators is valid, but it is not the most efficient one. We can put all vowels into a list and use the in operator from Table 1-3:

```
letter = input("Give me a letter ")
if letter in ["a","e","i","o","u"]:
  print("This letter is a vowel")
```

The solution with the list is neat. However, the set of vowels would never change. On the ground of that, we could use an immutable tuple to pack a constant set of the vowel letters:

```
letter = input("Give me a letter ")
if letter in ("a","e","i","o","u"):
    print("This letter is a vowel")
```

Of course, you will not feel a high rate on a tuple with just five elements (Figure 1-31). Nevertheless, any tuple would be faster than a list, and you can see that difference on a list with more than 10,000 of items.

```
In [33]:   1 letter = input("Give me a letter ")
           2 letter = letter.lower()
           3 if letter in ("a","e","i","o","u"):
           4     print("This letter is a vowel")
           5 else:
           6     print("This letter is a consonant")

Give me a letter a
This letter is a vowel
```

Figure 1-31. *The program to check if a letter is a vowel or a consonant*

Before you start writing a code, you should ask yourself a question, "would I need to add or remove something?" If the answer is yes, then you go with a list. Elseways, you can use a tuple. Also, a list structure can be converted to a tuple with a built-in function tuple(). Vice versa, a tuple object can be converted to a list with a list() function. We will try them later in this book.

We will use lists and tuples extensively in this book, and as we move along, we will discuss other characteristics of them.

Indexing and Slicing

Lists and tuples are ordered collections of elements. That means they retain items in order. Each item in a list or tuple can be accessed by its index. To understand this concept, imagine an apartment building. Tenant Mark lives in apartment number 1, and his neighbor John occupies apartment 2. Mary resides in apartment number 3 and so on. If I want to send a letter to Mark, I will need to include his apartment number in the address. The letter would be delivered to Mark since he occupies apartment 1. Later, Mark moves to another building, and my letter, if it was late, would be delivered to another tenant currently living in apartment number 1. The point is no matter who lives in the apartment, you can always reach out to that person by the apartment number, and every building has apartment numbers 1, 2, and 3. That is why sometimes local businesses would send their flyers addressed to the "current resident" of apartment number 1 or 2 or whatever, hoping to pick up clients no matter who occupies them.

Our example can be translated to Python. We have the list stored with the variable building. The list contains names of building residents:

```
building = ["Mark", "John", "Mary"]
```

The major thing to remember is in Python we start a count at zero. The first element of a list or a tuple or a string would always have an index of zero. To see who occupies the first "apartment," we need to fetch it by index 0:

```
building[0]
```

The building[0] statement gets us "Mark". Consequently, building[1] will retrieve "John" and building[2] expectedly "Mary" (Figure 1-32).

```
In [34]:   1  building = ["Mark", "John", "Mary"]
           2  building[0]
Out[34]:   'Mark'

In [35]:   1  building[1]
Out[35]:   'John'

In [36]:   1  building[2]
Out[36]:   'Mary'
```

Figure 1-32. *Fetching elements from the list by an index*

Again, no matter what is the first element, we can always grab it by index 0. Remember there is a method insert() that requires an index to add an element to a list. Using this method, we can add a new element at a specific location. We will insert "Jackson" at the beginning of the list:

```
building.insert(0,"Jackson")
```

After this operation, the first element in the list is "Jackson" (Figure 1-33).

```
In [37]:   1  building.insert(0,"Jackson")
           2  building
Out[37]:   ['Jackson', 'Mark', 'John', 'Mary']
```

Figure 1-33. *Method insert() adds an element based on the index*

If I have asked you to get me the last element from the list, you would say that we need to count all elements and pass the index of the last element into square brackets, like this:

```
building[3]
```

Although `building[3]` would get us "Mary" which is true, most of the time you do not want to count. A list could hold a gazillion of elements which would make it difficult to count. The golden rule is the first element in a sequence has an index of 0, and the last element in a sequence is always a –1 index. Using this logic, we can access the last element using the –1 index:

```
building[-1]
```

`building[-1]` gets us "Mary" again. You could see in Figure 1-34 we are consequently fetching elements from right to left by a negative index.

```
In [38]:    1  building[-1]
Out[38]:  'Mary'

In [39]:    1  building[-2]
Out[39]:  'John'

In [40]:    1  building[-3]
Out[40]:  'Mark'
```

Figure 1-34. *A negative index would fetch elements from right to left*

The easiest way to remember the syntax would be to think of the direction. The positive sign of an index would take you from left to right. If you want to move from right to left, you should use a negative index, starting at –1 (Figure 1-35).

The indexing concept could be applied to a string. All characters in a string have an index. You can try to grab the first character of "apple" by index 0:

```
word = "apple"
word[0]
```

Indexing helps us to grab one element or character at a time. What if we need to get two or more? Then we need to slice the sequence. The syntax is quite simple; we need to provide indexes for locations of characters where we want to start and where we want to stop:

```
object[ start_index : stop_index ]
```

For example, if we want to grab "pp" out of "apple", we would need to indicate the index for the first "p", which is 1, and the index for the second "p" plus one, 2+1. I know it sounds a bit confusing at first. Remember in Python the stop point is always excluded. For that reason, we would need to add one to the index of the last character of the sliced substring:

```
word[ 1:3 ]
```

This statement would get us the sliced substring "pp" (Figure 1-36). Logically, if we wanted to slice off the last two characters "le", we would write it as word[3:5]. The index of "e" is 4; since the stop is excluded, we would need to go with 5. This is correct, and word[3:5] would get us "le". However, there is no index 5 in the five-letter word "apple". Thereby people would skip the stop index, like this:

```
word[3: ]
```

This syntax means that we want to start at index 3, letter "l", and get all remaining characters. No matter how many is there (Figure 1-37). Skipping the stop index is totally normal if you need to go all the way and fetch all the characters in a sequence after the start point.

In fact, there is one more hidden index in slicing – step. A step index indicates intervals, how you want to move through the sequence. By default, a step index is 1. It is not required if you want to go by every character in a string or element in a list.

```
object[ start : stop : step ]
```

Using the defaulted step index like this:

```
word[0 : : 1]
```

would not do much and return the whole string "apple". The preceding notation simply states that we want to start at the first character and then move one by one letter. Skipping the stop index in the middle means that we do not want to stop anywhere and get all characters no matter how many is there.

In the event that you need to skip a character, you can use 2 as the step index. The word[0 : : 2] statement would return you "ape". Step index 2 is skipping every other letter.

A step index could be negative. To reverse the whole word and read it backward, we would need to use a –1 index as a step:

```
word[-1 : : -1]
```

The first negative index –1 indicates that we want to start at the last character "e". The step index –1 means that we want to get all characters from right to left. The direction example I made earlier makes more sense now. Frankly, the start index is not necessary in this case because a negative step index flips default values for the start and stop. But if the negative start index helps you to reverse strings and lists at first, feel free to include it. Try the negative step:

```
word[ : : -1]
```

The result would be "elppa" as you can see in Figure 1-38.

To to become fluent with slicing, I recommend the very simple exercise. In a new cell, define a string as alphabetical letters:

```
string = "AaBbCcDdEe"
```

Then try to fetch all capital letters starting at "A":

```
string[ 0 : : 2]
```

The start index 0 gets us started at the first letter "A". The step index 2 is getting us every other letter. Since we want to get all capital letters and have no idea how many characters in the string, we can leave the stop index blank.

Right after this, we can get all lowercase letters, `"edcba"`, from right to left. To go backward and jump over every other letter, we would need to use –2 as the step index. Logically, our starting point would be –1 (Figure 1-39):

```
string[ -1 : : -2]
```

Very often, people ask me what the practical use of slicing would be. Believe me, you constantly need to slice or reverse something. The recent example that comes to my mind is mapping clients by the zip code.

A company has very extensive client base and needs to know in what areas the customers are concentrated. To solve this task, they would fetch all client addresses from the database, and each address would look pretty much like this:

```
address = "29 E Madison St., Chicago, IL, 60602"
```

In order to group the customers by areas, we do not need the whole street address. All we need is the zip code. We know that a zip is always five characters at the end of an address. We can slice it with a –5 as a start index:

```
address[-5 : : ]
```

For practice, try to slice the city and the state out of this address. Keep in mind that in Python " " empty space also counts as a character and would have an index.

Summary

I really hope that by the end of this chapter you've caught a Python bug. Believe me, we have just scratched the surface. In the next chapter, we will continue with the introduction to Python programming and approach more advanced examples of everyday Python use. The data type concept we have discussed in the chapter will evolve into more sophisticated data structures in Chapters 2 and 3. If you're still a bit confused about integers, floats, and strings, I would strongly recommend going over the examples we did in the chapter one more time. As I have mentioned before, data types are the cornerstone of any programming language.

CHAPTER 2

Writing Your Own Python Scripts

In the previous chapter, we have covered all the basics of Python. Here, we will take a look at essential control flow statements and will learn how to structure a program. We will learn how to use for and while loops and compose custom functions. Also, we will get familiar with a decisive Python data structure – dictionary.

As we move through the chapter, we will solve a couple of interesting and beneficial challenges. The exercises we are about to take on will demonstrate how to manipulate data with Python. A very necessary skill no matter what field you are in.

Definite Loops

A definite loop or for loop is an essential part of any programming language. Very often, you need to do something many times. For example, you need to send a Christmas greeting to all your friends. The greeting should be personalized and say something like "Merry Christmas {name of your friend goes here}!". The same message should be printed for each of your friends.

© Art Yudin 2021
A. Yudin, *Basic Python for Data Management, Finance, and Marketing*,
https://doi.org/10.1007/978-1-4842-7189-6_2

Let's see how we can do it. For starters, we need to compose a list with names. Creating a list of close friends to greet sounds like a natural task in a holiday season. Translating the task to Python would look like this:

```
friends = ["Mary", "Paul", "John"]
```

Now we need to iterate through the list and grab name by name. The iteration would be possible with a keyword for (Figure 2-1):

```
for name in friends:
    print( "Merry Christmas", name)
```

```
In [1]:   1  friends = ["Mary", "Paul", "John"]
          2
          3  for name in friends:
          4      print("Merry Christmas", name)

          Merry Christmas Mary
          Merry Christmas Paul
          Merry Christmas John
```

Figure 2-1. *For loop iterating through the list of friends*

I want to go step by step and explain this example. Let's start with the anatomy of a for loop. for is a keyword and will be highlighted in **Jupyter**. You have to start with the keyword for to repeat the task multiple times. After for, you need to use some variable. Often, in my class people would ask me how Python knows we are dealing with names of friends. In fact, "name" is a variable and can be replaced with any other placeholder. Try to replace "name" with "banana" on lines 3 and 4 in Figure 2-1, and you'll see exactly the same output. Most of the time, in Python tutorials people use the letter i, stands for item, as a variable in the for loop. The choice of a variable is totally up to you. in is an operator, also green. It is referring to the next sequence. In plain words, we want to do the following:

for variable in sequence:

do something to variable

We are going through the list of items and defining the variable with each value. One at a time. In the greetings example, we literally grab a person's name value by value from the list and assign it to the "name" variable (Figure 2-2). That is what's going on behind the scenes.

```
In [2]:    1  friends = ["Mary", "Paul", "John"]
           2
           3  for name in friends:
           4      print("name =", name)

         name = Mary
         name = Paul
         name = John
```

Figure 2-2. *The variable "name" is being defined with each value from the list*

As the definite term implies, a for loop iterates as many times as many elements you have in the sequence. Since the print statement is in the scope of the for loop, it is executed per iteration.

While you iterate, you can perform any operations on the values. We can insert the string method format() to make the output nicer. The format method will place the value of the variable name into curly braces. This method would escape the need to use multiple commas in the print() function and make our code clean:

```
for name in friends:
    print("Merry Christmas {}! and Happy New Year!".
    format(name))
```

Most of the time, you would need to combine a for loop and if, elif, or else. Extending our example, we can say that if Paul is on the list, print the "Please give me a call" message. To check each value in the list whether it is "Paul", the if statement has to be in the scope of the for loop. It will test each value, and assuming that Paul is in the list, the if condition returns True. Logically, another print() function in the scope of the if statement will be triggered (Figure 2-3).

```
In [3]:    1  friends = ["Mary", "Paul", "John"]
           2
           3  for name in friends:
           4      print("Merry Christmas {}! and Happy New Year!".format(name))
           5      if name == "Paul":
           6          print("{}, Please give me a call".format(name))
```

```
Merry Christmas Mary! and Happy New Year!
Merry Christmas Paul! and Happy New Year!
Paul, Please give me a call
Merry Christmas John! and Happy New Year!
```

Figure 2-3. *Using an if statement while iterating through the list*

The most difficult part for beginners is to understand the scope of the for loop and included if statement. All statements in the scope of the for loop will be executed while the for loop iterates (Figure 2-4).

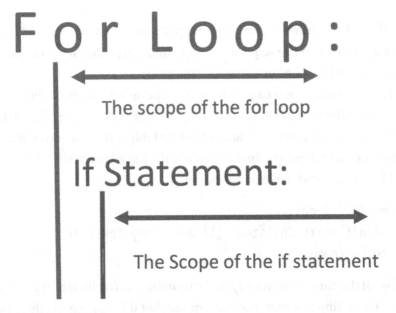

Figure 2-4. *The design pattern for a for loop and an if statement*

Another example to illustrate a for loop would be to iterate over the list of numbers and filter it at the same time. The initial list might look something like this:

```
alist = [1, 5, 2, 5, 3, 5, 4, 5, 6, 5, 7]
```

Our task is to identify the number 5 and add it to another blist. So, let's initialize a new list:

```
blist = [ ]
```

If you do not know where to start, try logically splitting the task into steps. First off, we need to grab each number from the list. This sounds like a for loop job. Then we need to compare each number to 5. Otherwise, how the computer would know we are looking for the number 5. If at some point the comparison returns True, we would need to use the method append() to add that number to blist. All these steps could be translated into code:

```
for number in alist:
    if number == 5:
        blist.append(number)
```

As a result, we would get blist full of 5s (Figure 2-5). On line 6 in Figure 2-5, append() is indented and placed in the scope of the if statement. It would be executed only after the if statement returns True. Indentation is an important part of the Python syntax, and you have to follow the design pattern for a for loop and an if statement (Figure 2-4).

```
In [4]:  1  alist = [1, 5, 2, 5, 3, 5, 4, 5, 6, 5, 7]
         2  blist = []
         3
         4  for number in alist:
         5      if number == 5:
         6          blist.append(number)
         7  blist

Out[4]:  [5, 5, 5, 5, 5]
```

Figure 2-5. *Filtering alist and adding 5s to the blist*

The Range Function

The range function is one of the built-in functions. It generates a sequence of numbers. To use it, we need to specify a start integer (at which number to start a sequence), a stop integer (where to stop), and a step integer (a specific interval) (Figure 2-6). A stop integer is the only required parameter for the function. A stop number is excluded from the generated sequence. By default, the start point is 0, and the step is 1. So, we at least have to provide a stop integer. Do not confuse the range function with slicing. Although the function range() requires similar parameters, start, stop, and step, it has nothing in common with a slice notation.

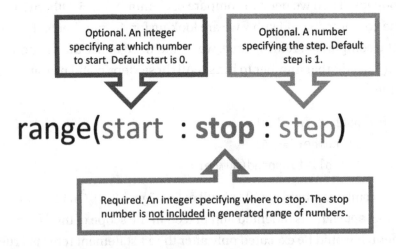

Figure 2-6. *The range function parameters*

Most of the time, the function range() is used with a for loop. Assuming that we want to build a range of numbers from 1 to 5, we can write it like this:

```
for i in range(1,6):
    print(i)
```

The output is numbers from 1 to 5. The stop point is excluded (Figure 2-7). We did not specify the step. It defaults to 1.

```
In [5]:    1  for i in range(1,6):
           2      print(i)
           3

1
2
3
4
5
```

Figure 2-7. *The function range generates numbers from 1 to 5*

So far, pretty simple. What if we want to generate the same range but this time in descending order? Then we would need to start at 5. We cannot use 1 as the stop. If we use 1, we will not see it in the sequence. Zero has to be our stop point. To change the direction, we would use –1 as the step (Figure 2-8).

```
In [6]:    1  for i in range(5,0,-1):
           2      print(i)
           3

5
4
3
2
1
```

Figure 2-8. *The function range generates numbers in descending order from 5 to 1*

You might wonder what the practical use of the range is. Usually, the function range() is used to generate an index. Remember we can access items in a sequence by their indices? Let's get back to the example we used in the previous chapter:

```
word = "apple"
word[0]
```

```
word[1]
word[2]
word[3]
word[4]
```

Using the indexing syntax, we fetch letters by an index. We do not want to do it manually. It would be a much easier task if we can generate an index for any word no matter how long it is. With the help of the function len(), we can get a number of items or characters in any sequence:

```
len(word)
```

The string "apple" has five characters. The function len() always returns an integer. This integer can be used as a stop point in the range() function. Using that as an argument, the function range generates the correct sequence from 0 up to the stop point for any word. We can pass len(word) as the stop argument in range().

i will represent an index of each letter. This index can be used to access a letter, for example, word[0]. In Figure 2-9, you can see that the range has generated a sequence of numbers from 0 to 4. That is exactly what we have expected with the stop point of 5. Then, passing every number into square brackets, we fetched letter by letter from the string.

```
In [7]:   1  word = "apple"
          2
          3  for i in range(len(word)):
          4      print(i, word[i])
          5

0 a
1 p
2 p
3 l
4 e
```

Figure 2-9. *The function range generates numbers that can be used as indices*

In many cases, you would want to get a location of a value in a sequence. That is why we want to know the index of each value. For instance, if we want to replace a value or do something to a value, we would know where the value is stored.

Nested for Loops

The best illustration of nested for loops would be a multiplication table. We all know how a multiplication table looks like. The concept is quite simple; there are two sets of numbers. You take a number from one set and multiply it by the number from another set. The set of numbers from 1 to 10 can be created by range(). The sequence of numbers from 1 to 10 should be printed horizontally. You probably noticed that every time we use the print() function in the for loop, it prints each item on a new line. This behavior of the print() function could be changed. We can see all keyword arguments of any function if we run help() on it:

```
help(print)
```

Apparently, the function print() has a default argument end='\n'. '\n' means a new line. Every time the print() function is executed, it ends a new line character after the printed text. Just for fun, try to replace '\n' with 'ZZ', and it would print 'ZZ' at the end of each statement. For a multiplication table, we would need numbers from 1 to 10 printed horizontally. We can perform it this way:

```
for i in range(1,11):
    print( i, end=' ')
```

Then we would need another set of numbers from 1 to 10. This time, we would use j for a variable:

```
for j in range(1,11):
    print( j, end=' ')
```

Note that as a result of these two for loops, we get 20 numbers. The first for loop iterates and prints ten numbers. So is the second for loop. We can move the second for loop into the scope of the first for loop. This will get us ten js for every iteration of the outer for loop. Next, get rid of the first print statement and multiply i by j in the second print() function:

```python
for i in range(1,11):
    for j in range(1,11):
        print( i*j, end=' ')
```

After we have nested for loops, we get 100 numbers printed. The main message here is that it would take longer to produce 100 operations than 20. By nesting for loops, we have drastically increased the time complexity of our program. In other words, we made our code run slower.

Do not get me wrong. I am not saying that you should never use the nested loops. There are instances where you have to use nested loops. Like a multiplication table. I want you to understand that if you can find a solution without nesting loops, that solution would be faster.

Just before we formalize the multiplication table, we need to add one more print statement at the end. Although this print statement would follow the second for loop, it would be placed in the scope of the outer for loop. That means the last print statement will be executed as many times as the outer for loop iterates. Because the last print statement is in the scope of the outer for loop. We need this print to add '\n' after each set of numbers. It would be easier to understand it if you temporarily place something into that print() function, like "ZZ":

```python
for i in range(1,11):
for j in range(1,11):
    print( i*j, end=' ')
print('ZZ')
```

These little funny labels help you to see what exactly the last print statement does and how many times it is executed. With the added print() function on the bottom, it looks more like a multiplication table. We can add a final touch with a string format method. This format method will help us to space out the numbers with an even interval of four spaces between the numbers. As you may remember, a string method format inserts values into curly brackets. While passing the values, we can format them. In our example, :4 in the curly brackets generates four spaces between numbers:

```
for i in range(1,11):
    for j in range(1,11):
        print("{:4}".format(i*j), end=' ')
    print()
```

In Figure 2-10, you can see the final result. The multiplication table exercise explains the concept of nested for loops very well. For each iteration of the outer for loop, you are getting n iterations of the inner for loop. Next time you decide to use nested for loops, think of a multiplication table and the runtime complexity of your code.

```
In [8]:  1  for i in range(1,11):
         2      for j in range(1,11):
         3          print("{:4}".format(i*j), end=' ')
         4      print()
          1   2   3   4   5   6   7   8   9  10
          2   4   6   8  10  12  14  16  18  20
          3   6   9  12  15  18  21  24  27  30
          4   8  12  16  20  24  28  32  36  40
          5  10  15  20  25  30  35  40  45  50
          6  12  18  24  30  36  42  48  54  60
          7  14  21  28  35  42  49  56  63  70
          8  16  24  32  40  48  56  64  72  80
          9  18  27  36  45  54  63  72  81  90
         10  20  30  40  50  60  70  80  90 100
```

Figure 2-10. *Multiplication table*

Defining Your Own Functions

So far, we have been using Python built-in functions. You however can define your own functions. Before we get to the coding part, we need to understand what a function in Python is. A function is a block of reusable code. The keyword here is reusable. There is a principle in programming – keep your code DRY. DRY means do not repeat yourself. If you want to do something over and over again, wrap it as a function.

Each function is supposed to perform one task and serve a purpose. You do not want to compose the whole program as one long function. Rather, split your code into multiple functions where every step or job would be a separate function. The whole program would consist of multiple functions, blocks of code which you could easily replace or change down the road. Besides, some functions might be used in other programs. It is a common practice to import a function from one module to another.

Let's compose a simple function that sums up two numbers. You start a function with the keyword def. def stands for define. Then you need to come up with some name for a function. Any name will do, but as a best practice, the name of the function is supposed to reflect the purpose of the function. Right after the function name you should place the parentheses with the colon ":".

```
def add():
```

Indentation should follow the colon. All indented statements would be blocked in the scope of the function. Just for now, we will define two variables in the function, a and b, and assign to them values 5 and 6, respectively. Note that variables a and b are defined locally – inside of the function:

```
def add():
    a = 5
    b = 6
```

If you try to use them outside of the function, Python would raise an error message that a and b are not defined (Figure 2-11). That means a and b could be used within the function where they are defined.

```
In [9]:    1  def add():
           2      a = 5
           3      b = 6
```

```
In [10]:   1  a
```

```
--------
NameError                              Traceback (most recent call l
ast)
<ipython-input-10-3f786850e387> in <module>
----> 1 a

NameError: name 'a' is not defined
```

Figure 2-11. *a name is being defined locally within the function*

Our simple function would add a to b, and we save the result with the variable total. Until now we have been using the print() function to see the results of our operations. We, humans, need to see things; computers do not. For that reason, the functions return results. Return is the last statement in a function. You cannot do anything after a return statement. It stops the code. If you need to have a print() function to see the result, you would need to squeeze it in before the return statement:

```
def add():
    a = 5
    b = 6
    total = a + b
    return total
```

If you ran the cell with the function add(), you would see that nothing happened. Except that now the function add() is stored in Python memory. In order to use the function, we would need to call or invoke it:

```
add()
```

In Figure 2-12, you can see the invoked function add() returns the result 11.

```
In [11]:   1  def add():
           2      a = 5
           3      b = 6
           4      total = a + b
           5      return total
```

```
In [12]:   1  add()
```
Out[12]: 11

```
In [13]:   1  c = add()
```

```
In [14]:   1  c
```
Out[14]: 11

Figure 2-12. *The function add() returns 11*

If you want to save the result from the function, you would need to assign the function to a variable name. In Figure 2-12, the result from the function add() is saved with variable c.

To make our function more versatile, we can define a and b as arguments. All we need is to place them inside parentheses after the name of the function and separate by a comma:

```
def add(a,b):
```

Now our function requires any two numbers to produce a result. Calling a function without passing two numbers would raise an error message.

The bottom line is a function takes arguments and returns the result. It is a reusable code you can call over and over again (Figure 2-13). It is a good practice to encapsulate the code based on its purpose. Structuring the code as a set of functions makes it clean.

```
In [15]:    1  def add(a,b):
            2      total = a + b
            3      return total
```

```
In [16]:    1  add(5,6)
```
Out[16]: 11

```
In [17]:    1  add(7,8)
```
Out[17]: 15

```
In [18]:    1  add(2,5)
```
Out[18]: 7

Figure 2-13. *The function add() returns results*

When you work with a team and others would be using your function, it would be a good idea to add a description. The description is called a docstring. Using three single or double quotes on the line below the function definition, write the purpose of the function. The description should not be long. There is no need to explain in detail how your function works. A docstring should outline the purpose of the function. Also, you might specify some values used in calculations.

```
'''
    Return the sum of two numbers
'''
```

If your function has a docstring, people could read it with the help() function (Figure 2-14).

63

```
In [19]:    1  def add(a,b):
            2      '''
            3      Return the sum of two numbers
            4      '''
            5      total = a + b
            6      return total
```

```
In [20]:    1  help(add)
```

```
Help on function add in module __main__:

add(a, b)
    Return the sum of two numbers
```

Figure 2-14. *A docstring can be read with the help() function*

Structuring a Program

It is time to put into practice everything we have learned so far. Here, we will program one of the oldest word games, Pig Latin. The idea behind this exercise is to learn how to manipulate data and structure the code.

If you have never played Pig Latin, the rules are very simple. You ask a user for any word. If a word starts with a vowel, then you need to add "yay" at the end. For example, apple would become appleyay. However, if a word starts with a consonant, you would need to cut off all consonants before the first vowel in the word and add them to the end of the word. Also, you need to append "ay" to a word beginning with a consonant. The word scratch would become atchscray.

If at first the problem sounds too complicated and you have no idea how to approach it, start with a pseudocode.

A pseudocode is an outline in plain words of an algorithm you are about to implement. You can think of it as a road map. On a piece of paper, write all the steps you need to do to accomplish the task. Pretend that you are trying to explain to a kid how to play Pig Latin step by step. The pseudocode code solution for Pig Latin might look like this:

1. Ask a user for a word.

2. Check if the word starts with a vowel.

3. If the word starts with a vowel, add "yay" and save with a variable.

4. If the word starts with a consonant, we need to check all letters and find the first vowel.

5. To remove the letters before the vowel, we need to know the index of the vowel.

6. Store all removed consonant letters using the variable firstpart.

7. Get the rest of the letters and store them with the variable secondpart.

8. Concatenate secondpart with firstpart and add "ay".

The problem broken down into baby steps is easier to solve. If you do not know how to implement a step in Python, you could always google it. OK, now we can start and translate our plan into Python.

For simplicity, I assume that a user has entered the word apple:

```
word = "apple"
```

Now we need to check if the first letter is a vowel. Grabbing the first character from a string sounds like an indexing. The first index is always 0, so the first letter would be word[0]. In the previous chapter, we coded a solution to check if a letter was a vowel. We can use it here:

```
if word[0] in ["a","e","i","o","u"]:
    print("This letter is a vowel")
```

Since "apple" begins with a vowel, according to step 3 we will add "yay" to it. The new Pig Latin word would be saved under the name result:

```
if word[0] in ["a","e","i","o","u"]:
    result = word + "yay"

    print(result)
```

Add a print statement to check the `result's value` and run your code. Make sure the solution works on words that begin with a vowel. The first part was simple to solve. We are halfway there.

For the second half, we would need a word starting with a consonant. Reassign the variable `word` to `"scratch"`. There are only two options: a word either starts with a vowel or not. Logically, it sounds like `if` and `else` statements. So far, we have implemented the `if` part; now we compose the `else` part.

Step 4 in the pseudocode requires testing all letters in a word and finding the first vowel.

To find a vowel, we would need to iterate through the characters of a string or, translating this task into Python, run a `for` loop operation. Step 5 suggests that when we find a vowel in the word, we would need to get hold of the index of the vowel. The function `range()` will be handy to identify an index. Translating steps 4 and 5 into code would look like this:

```
word = "scratch"
if word[0] in ["a","e","i","o","u"]:
    result = word + "yay"
else:
    for index in range(len(word)):
        print(index, word[index])
```

The `print` statement helps us to make sure we are on the right track, and `index` represents the index of each letter in `word`. As you may remember, to fetch a character from a string by an index, we would need to pass it into square brackets as follows: `word[index]`. It would be easy to identify a vowel because we just did it in the first part. We need to replace 0 with `index`:

```
word = "scratch"
if word[0] in ["a","e","i","o","u"]:
    result = word + "yay"
```

```
else:
    for index in range(len(word)):
        if word[index] in ["a","e","i","o","u"]:
            print(index, word[index])
```

The print statement in the scope of the if statement reveals the vowel and its index. In the word "scratch", the index of the vowel is 3. In keeping with the pseudocode, we need to split the word by the vowels' index. We do not want to hardcode it, meaning using 3 explicitly, due to the fact that in another word a vowel might be at a different location. Using slicing, we can grab all consonants in the word "scratch" before the vowel "a". So, step 6 would look in the following way:

```
firstpart = word[0:index]
```

Similarly, we will slice all other letters after the vowel:

```
secondpart = word[index : ]
```

The stop point is left blank because we want to get all characters after the index. The last step in the pseudocode is simple. To be consistent, we will use the same variable result and concatenate secondpart with firstpart and "ay":

```
word = "scratch"
if word[0] in ["a","e","i","o","u"]:
    result = word + "yay"
else:
    for index in range(len(word)):
        if word[index] in ["a","e","i","o","u"]:
        firstpart = word[0:index]
        secondpart = word[index : ]
        result = secondpart+firstpart+"ay"
```

Assign the function input() to word and test your code with different words; make sure it works. One thing is bothering me; the words with two or more vowels are returning the wrong results. If you try the word "brackets", the result will be "etsbeackyay". I believe the rule says we need to identify the first vowel. If we need the code to stop after the first instance of a vowel, we need to conclude the if statement with the keyword break. In Figure 2-15, you can see the whole solution of the Pig Latin challenge.

```
In [21]:    1  word = input("give me a word ")
            2
            3  if word[0] in ["a","e","i","o","u"]:
            4      result = word + "ay"
            5  else:
            6      for index in range(len(word)):
            7          if word[index] in ["a","e","i","o","u"]:
            8              firstpart = word[0:index]
            9              secondpart = word[index : ]
           10              result = secondpart + firstpart + "yay"
           11              break
           12  print("Pig Latin word", result)

           give me a word brackets
           Pig Latin word acketsbryay
```

Figure 2-15. *Pig Latin game programmed in Python*

Our code can be refactored to improve the design and structure. I would start with if statements. The list of vowels is used twice in our code. Wouldn't it be easier and neater if we had a function to tell us whether a letter was a vowel? We can compile a little helper function which would take a letter as an argument and return either True or False. I'll call this function is_vowel:

```
def is_vowel(letter):
    if letter in ["a","e","i","o","u"]:
        return True
    else:
        return False
```

Next, we can wrap the Pig Latin game code as a function. I'll call this function game. The purpose of the function would be to accept any string, we will define it as word, and return the Pig Latin variant:

```python
def game(word):
    if is_vowel(word[0]):
        result = word + "yay"
    else:
        for index in range(len(word)):
            if is_vowel(word[index]):
        firstpart = word[0:index]
        secondpart = word[index : ]
        result = secondpart+firstpart+"ay"
        break
    return result
```

Within the function game, we will be calling the function is_vowel to check if a letter is a vowel. You can test the function game and call it with any word:

```python
game("scratch")
```

We would ask a user for an input in a separate function. For that, we will define a function and name it main. In real life, we would need to validate the user's input. We need to make sure that the input contains no numbers or other non-alphabetical characters, and the length of the input is greater than one letter. There are no one-letter words in English besides a and I. If the input was successfully validated, we would pass it into the function game. After manipulations, the function game would return a Pig Latin word, and we will present the result to a user. If a user's input did not pass our filter, we would return "Invalid input, please try again".

Since is_vowel would work only with lowercase letters, we would need to convert the received word to lowercase before invoking the function game:

```python
def main():
    word = input("give me a word ")
    if word.isalpha() and len(word) .> 1:
    word = word.lower()
    result = game(word)
    else:
    result = "Invalid input, please try again"
    return result
```

You can see the final implementation of the Pig Latin game in Figure 2-16. When we call the function main on the bottom, it prompts us to enter a word. If the filter on line 32 returns True, the function game is called on line 34. The user's input converted to lowercase is passed into game as an argument and assigned to the argument word. On line 15, is_vowel is being invoked with the first letter. In the case of the word "dog", is_vowel returns False, and the program diverted to the else statement. After the second iteration, the function is_vowel is called again, this time with the letter "o". Received True from the is_vowel function lets the code run lines 20–22. The new word is saved under the name result on line 22. Finally, the function game returns the Pig Latin word on line 24. The outcome of the game function is saved on line 34 and returned on line 37 by the main function.

```
In [1]:    1  def is_vowel(letter):
           2      '''
           3      Return True if the letter is a vowel
           4      '''
           5      if letter in ["a", "e", "i", "o","u"]:
           6          return True
           7      else:
           8          return False
           9
          10  def game(word):
          11      '''
          12      Return Pig Latin word by adding a suffix
          13      or by moving the onset to the end of the word
          14      '''
          15      if is_vowel(word[0]):
          16          result = word + "yay"
          17      else:
          18          for index in range(len(word)):
          19              if is_vowel(word[index]):
          20                  firstpart = word[ 0 : index ]
          21                  secondpart = word[ index : ]
          22                  result = secondpart + firstpart + "ay"
          23                  break
          24      return result
          25
          26  def main():
          27      '''
          28      Accept a word and validate it
          29      '''
          30      word = input("give me a word ")
          31
          32      if word.isalpha() and len(word) > 1:
          33          word = word.lower()
          34          result = game(word)
          35      else:
          36          result = "Invalid input, please try again"
          37      return result
```

```
In [2]:    1  main()
```

give me a word dog

```
Out[2]:  'ogday'
```

Figure 2-16. *Refactored code of the Pig Latin game*

Some people might ask why we need so many functions for a simple
task such as the Pig Latin game. The answer is each function has its own
purpose and is responsible for one job. is_vowel is a helper function
that answers just one question, whether a letter is a vowel. If needed,
we can export this function and use it in another file. The function main
is responsible for all user communications. If later you need to alter the
message in the input statement, you could easily get it done without
touching the game function. Communicating with users is a completely
separate task and has nothing to do with Pig Latin code. If we decide to
add more word games to our program, the main function would be the
right place to add a menu and ask users what game they want to play.

Indefinite Loop

There are definite and indefinite loops in Python. We have covered definite for loops; now it is time to take a look at a while loop, an indefinite loop. As you might have guessed from the name, we do not know how many times a while loop iterates. The keyword while requires some condition right after it. If the condition returns True, then the while loop executes statements within its scope. After it is done, the while loop checks the condition again. If the condition is still valid, it iterates again. However, if the condition returns False, the while loop exits. The easiest example would be the work hours. The pseudocode might look like this:

```
while not 6.00pm
        keep working
```

If it is not 6:00 p.m. we would be working. In an hour, we check the time again if it is 6.00pm yet. No, it is not. Keep working. At some point, the while condition is no longer true, because it is passed 6.00pm. We can get out of the loop and stop working. The main rule is the condition should switch to False at some point. Otherwise, you will end up in an infinite loop. In real life, it could be a disaster.

We can construct a simple while loop like this:

```
tally = 0
while tally < 5:
    tally = tally + 1
    print(tally)
```

Before you run this code, make sure you increase tally by 1 with each iteration of the while loop. If accidentally you skip this statement, your while loop will print 0 over and over again. This would be an example of an infinite loop. To exit an infinite loop, you would need to interrupt the Kernel by clicking the stop button in the **Jupyter** upper menu.

The tally = tally + 1 statement in the while loop will increase the value of tally. After five repetitions, the value of tally will be 5, and the condition tally < 5 will return False. The loop will exit (Figure 2-17).

```
In [23]:   1  tally = 0
           2  while tally < 5:
           3      tally = tally + 1
           4      print(tally)

           1
           2
           3
           4
           5
```

Figure 2-17. *A while loop exits if the condition is no longer true*

The key element of a while loop is the condition. The condition has to change at some point to exit the loop.

We can use a while loop in the Pig Latin example. The function main() validates an entered word. If a string contains anything besides alphabetic characters, the code is redirected to "Invalid input, please try again", and the program stops. In reality, we do not want to give up on a user who accidentally entered an invalid word. Using a while loop, we would ask them to try again. Instead of if and else statements, we will use a while loop. The program will be asking a user to enter a word until the right format would be entered. I will add another print statement with a hint that only alphabetic characters can be used:

```python
def main():
    word = input("give me a word ")
    while not word.isalpha() and len(word) > 1:
        print("Invalid input, please try again")
        print("You can use alphabetic-characters only ")
        word = input("give me a word ")

    word = word.lower()
    result = game(word)

    return result
```

The keyword not after `while` makes `word.isalpha()` and `len(word)`
`> 1` filters `False`. This statement literally says `while False`. The `while`
`loop` will be executing `print` statements and asking for `input` over and
over again till a user gets it right. However, if a user enters a word that
can be used, then the `while` statement will not be executed at all, and the
code will go to the `word = word.lower()` line. `word = word.lower()` and
`result = game(word)` statements are outside of the `while loop`. They
will be executed in two cases. The first case would be if the `while loop`
never gets triggered. The second situation would be if the `while loop` was
executed and then terminated.

As you can see, there is a conceptual difference between a `while loop`
and a `for loop`. The `while loop` heavily depends on a condition. The `for`
`loop` contrarily iterates for every item in a sequence.

Dictionary

A dictionary is a very important and widely used data structure. I will be
referring to a dictionary many times as we move along. Understanding a
dictionary will help us to comprehend more sophisticated data structures.

A dictionary is an unordered collection of key and value pairs. A key
holds a single value. A phone book would be the best way to explain a
dictionary structure. To initialize a dictionary, we need to use { } curly
brackets:

```
phone_book = {}
```

After we have defined phone_book as a dictionary, we can add a few
phone numbers to it. In order to add a new pair to a dictionary, we need
a key in square brackets and assign a value. Suppose I want to store my
friend's phone number, then John would be the key, and John's number is
the value:

```
phone_book["John"] = 2123458967
```

The key has to be unique. If I had another friend with the same name, I would need to use a different key to store his number. We can add a couple more friends to the dictionary:

```
phone_book["Tommy"] = 5169873456
phone_book["Mark"] = 2015672189
```

Now phone_book should look like in Figure 2-18.

```
In [21]:   1  phone_book = {}
           2
           3  phone_book["John"] = 2123458967
           4  phone_book["Tommy"] = 5169873456
           5  phone_book["Mark"] = 2015672189
           6  phone_book

Out[21]:   {'John': 2123458967, 'Tommy': 5169873456, 'Mark': 2015672189}
```

Figure 2-18. *Python dictionary*

If you want to fetch a value, all you need is a key. To get Tommy's phone number, I need to pass his name as the key (Figure 2-19):

```
phone_book["Tommy"]
```

```
In [21]:   1  phone_book = {}
           2
           3  phone_book["John"] = 2123458967
           4  phone_book["Tommy"] = 5169873456
           5  phone_book["Mark"] = 2015672189
           6  phone_book

Out[21]:   {'John': 2123458967, 'Tommy': 5169873456, 'Mark': 2015672189}

In [22]:   1  phone_book["Tommy"]

Out[22]:   5169873456
```

Figure 2-19. *Fetching a value by a key*

Compared to a list structure, a dictionary would be faster. It took us one operation to get a value from the dictionary. If I stored phone numbers in a list, I would need to iterate to find Tommy's number. Iteration requires many operations. That in any case would take longer than one operation.

Another feature of a dictionary is easy reassignment of the value. Suppose Tommy changes the phone number, we can replace an old value with a new one (Figure 2-17):

```
phone_book["Tommy"] = 2016546765
```

There is no limit on how many times you want to change the value and how often. Easy reassignment of a value makes a dictionary a perfect structure to hold stock prices. The stock symbol would be the key, and the price as the value could be changed many times. Likewise, a dictionary is used to count stuff. The value is updated for every instance of the key. At the end of the chapter, we will count how many times each word appears in a text file using a dictionary.

Since a dictionary is an unordered collection and can hold thousands of elements, how would you find all the keys? As always, we start with the dir() function. If you run dir() on dict or in our case phone_book, you will find the methods a dictionary supports. The method we are looking for is keys().

The keys() attribute will get all the keys from a dictionary. If you see a dictionary for the first time, start with keys(). This command will return an ordered array of all keys from a dictionary (Figure 2-20):

```
phone_book.keys()
```

```
In [23]:    1  phone_book.keys()
Out[23]: dict_keys(['John', 'Tommy', 'Mark'])
```

Figure 2-20. *The method keys() returns all the keys from a dictionary*

The opposite of the keys() method is values(). values() would return all values from a dictionary as a list (Figure 2-21):

```
phone_book.values()
```

```
In [24]:    1  phone_book.values()
Out[24]: dict_values([2123458967, 5169873456, 2015672189])
```

Figure 2-21. *The method values() returns all the values from a dictionary*

Values are less informative for us because we do not know what they are referring to. On the other hand, if we assume that a dictionary holds all stocks traded on NYSE, by values we could see how many companies are gaining or losing.

The method `items()` converts a dictionary to a list of tuples. Each key-value pair would be presented as a tuple structure (Figure 2-22).

```
phone_book.items()
```

```
In [25]:    1  phone_book.items()
Out[25]: dict_items([('John', 2123458967), ('Tommy', 5169873456), ('Mark', 2015672189)])
```

Figure 2-22. *The method items() returns all pairs from a dictionary as tuples*

The method `items()` will come in handy in the case that we need to convert a dictionary into a list. A dictionary is not an ordered structure; therefore, to sort a dictionary by values, you need a list. A list naturally can be sorted. You will see this example in action later in the chapter.

The method `get()`, as you might have guessed, fetches the value by the key. The main difference between this method and the dictionary notation, `phone_book["Tommy"]`, is that get would return a default value if the key is not found. If a user tries to retrieve Mary's phone number and there is no Mary in the dictionary, then `get()` will return `"Not Found"`:

```
phone_book.get("Mary", "Not Found")
```

Returning a default value would be a neater way compared to an error message (Figure 2-23).

```
In [26]:    1 phone_book.get("Mary", "Not Found")
Out[26]: 'Not Found'

In [27]:    1 phone_book["Mary"]

            KeyError                                Traceback (most recent call last)
            <ipython-input-27-6c9435f5d381> in <module>
            ----> 1 phone_book["Mary"]

            KeyError: 'Mary'
```

Figure 2-23. *The method get() returns a default value if a key is not in the dictionary*

By now, you are probably asking the question, is it possible to iterate over a dictionary with a for loop? My approach is if you are not sure or do not know something, try it. At least you will learn why an operation failed from an error message. As a matter of fact, you can loop through a dictionary.

There are a couple of ways to iterate through a dictionary. The first one is straightforward:

```
for i in  phone_book:
    print(i)
```

This method will get you all the keys from a dictionary. By keys, you can get the values:

```
for i in phone_book:
    print(i, phone_book[i])
```

Another iteration technique requires the items() method:

```
for i in phone_book.items():
    print(i)
```

As you can see, the i variable represents a tuple. The method items() has converted phone_book into a list of tuples. Technically, after items() has been applied, we iterate through a list of tuples. Each tuple contains exactly two values what used to be a key and a value. To extract a key and a value, we need to unpack the tuple. One way would be to index the key and the value:

```python
for i in phone_book.items():
    print(i[0], i[1])
```

However, we can assign variables to the first and second elements in a tuple:

```python
key, value =  ("John", 2123458967)
```

If we go with logic, then the for loop would require two variables and will look like this:

```python
for key, value in phone_book.items():
    print(key, value)
```

In Figure 2-24, you can see that the two solutions are producing the same results. It is up to you which technique to use at the end of the day.

```
In [28]:   1  for i in phone_book:
           2      print(i, phone_book[i])

John 2123458967
Tommy 5169873456
Mark 2015672189

In [29]:   1  for key, value in phone_book.items():
           2      print(key, value)

John 2123458967
Tommy 5169873456
Mark 2015672189
```

Figure 2-24. *Iterating through a dictionary with a for loop*

One simple exercise will sum up getting values from a dictionary and adding new keys and values.

Suppose we have a menu in a restaurant stored as a dictionary:

```python
menu = {"Burger": 3.75, "Soda": 0.99, "Nachos": 2.99, "Shake":1.25}
```

Using an input function, we will ask a user for two items from the menu:

```
item_one = input("What would you like?")
item_two = input("What else would you like?")
```

After we get the desired items, we can fetch the price from the dictionary using them as keys:

```
price_one = menu[item_one]
price_two = menu[item_two]
```

Finally, we will calculate and print the total:

```
total = price_one + price_two
print("Your total is ${}".format(total))
```

The next part of the exercise demonstrates how to populate a new dictionary with keys and values. Continuing with the restaurant example, we decided to mark down by 10% all products and store new prices in another dictionary named sale. We need to initialize a new dictionary:

```
sale = {}
```

While iterating through menu, we will decrease a value by 10% and at the same time add food and new prices to the sale dictionary. The built-in function round will round down numbers after a decimal point to 2:

```
for food, price in menu.items():
    sale[food] = round(price * 0.9, 2)
```

After we went through the menu and decreased all prices, our new dictionary sale would look like this:

```
{'Burger': 3.38, 'Soda': 0.89, 'Nachos': 2.69, 'Shake': 1.12}
```

Writing Information into a Text File

As we have discussed before, Python operates in RAM, short-term memory, and files are stored on a hard drive or in a cloud, long-term memory. The built-in function open() reads and writes data from and into a file. open() returns a Python object. Keep in mind that you are not working directly with a file stored on a hard drive but with an object. The function open() takes keyword arguments. We can take a look at the main ones necessary to open a file. For starters, you need to provide a file name and a file path. Next is the mode. A mode specifies your intention for a file. The default is mode='r'. String 'r' stands for read. If your intention is to get information from a file, you should leave it like it is. For writing data into a file, we would need to change the mode to 'w'. Every time you run the code, the open() function will create a new file. Another keyword argument is encoding. For Mac users, it is optional because by default it will encode or decode a file as UTF-8. Remember in the first chapter, we have talked about how computers store strings. In a nutshell text file is a string. UTF-8 is the most popular encoding system for text right now. If you are curious how exactly UTF-8 encoding works and see the table characters and corresponding numbers, you can find it on Wikipedia (https://en.wikipedia.org/wiki/UTF-8). Windows might require the encoding="utf8" argument to encode a file:

```
obj = open("myfile.txt", "w", encoding="utf8")
```

obj holds an object generated by the function open(). Print it and you will see

```
<_io.TextIOWrapper name='myfile.txt' mode='w' encoding='utf8'>
```

That means that we have successfully created myfile.txt. You can look up a new file on your computer. Use find or search for it in the same directory where you keep the **Jupyter** Notebook.

Open the myfile.txt file in any text editor. It is blank. We have not written anything in it yet. Writing mode is a bit tricky. If you rerun the open() function again, "w" mode will delete the existing myfile.txt file and create a new one with the same name. Keep in mind that if you had myfile.txt on your computer before with some existing information, you would have lost it.

Now that we have a file, we can write something into it. Again, we will be manipulating the Python object. Run dir() on obj, and you would see all read and write methods. To add a string to obj, we use the command write(). When we are done, the command close() saves it in the file.

We need a string to write it into the file; make sure you have all your code in the same cell:

```python
string_one = "This pizza is delicious!"
obj = open("myfile.txt", "w", encoding="utf8")
obj.write(string_one)
obj.close()
```

The method close() saves the object as a file. It works in the same way as a save button in Microsoft Word. Your text is not saved until you click the save as button. If there is a power outage and the data you have on the screen was not saved, you might lose it.

After you run all these commands, refresh the myfile.txt file. "This pizza is delicious!" should be in it (Figure 2-25).

```
In [30]:   1  string_one = "This pizza is delicious!"
           2  obj = open("myfile.txt", "w", encoding="utf8")
           3  obj.write(string_one)
           4  obj.close()
```

```
●  ●  ●                  myfile.txt
This pizza is delicious!
```

Figure 2-25. *Writing information in a text file*

In comparison to write mode, append mode will add a string to an existing file. If you already have the file and want to write in additional data, replace "w" in keyword argument mode to "a". We need another string to append it to myfile.txt. The "\n" sign means a new line in Python. It will start a phrase on a new line:

```
string_two = "I love pepperoni pizza!"
obj = open("myfile.txt", "a", encoding="utf8")
obj.write("\n"+string_two)
obj.close()
```

Every time you run this code, it will append "I love pepperoni pizza!" to "myfile.txt" (Figure 2-26).

```
In [35]:  1  string_one = "This pizza is delicious!"
          2  string_two = "I love pepperoni pizza!"
          3  obj = open("myfile.txt", "a", encoding="utf8")
          4  obj.write("\n"+string_two)
          5  obj.close()
```

myfile.txt — Edited
```
This pizza is delicious!
I love pepperoni pizza!
I love pepperoni pizza!
I love pepperoni pizza!
I love pepperoni pizza!
I love pepperoni pizza!
```

Figure 2-26. *Append mode writes information in a text file*

To sum up everything, let's do a simple example. Suppose we have a dictionary with stock prices and need to store them in a text file:

```
portfolio={"IBM":111.90,"AAPL":155.53,"MSFT":216.39}

obj = open("dummydata.txt", "w", encoding="utf8")
for key, value in portfolio.items():
    obj.write("Stock {} Price{}\n".format(key,value))
obj.close()
```

Here, I use "w" mode because we just write data into the dummydata.txt file. The for loop iterates through the dictionary and extracts keys and values. Note that the format() method converts prices, float values, to strings. A text file format would accept string data types only (Figure 2-27).

```
In [18]:    1  portfolio={"IBM":111.90,"AAPL":155.53,"MSFT":216.39}
            2
            3  obj = open("dummydata.txt", "w", encoding="utf8")
            4  for key, value in portfolio.items():
            5      obj.write("Stock {} Price {}\n".format(key,value))
            6  obj.close()
```

```
● ● ●                    dummydata.txt — Edited
Stock IBM Price 111.9
Stock AAPL Price 155.53
Stock MSFT Price 216.39
```

Figure 2-27. *Writing information from the dictionary in a text file*

Reading Information from a Text File

Reading data from a file is similar to writing a file. All we need to do is leave the function open() in a default reading mode. Some Windows systems would require you to add a little r before the file path. Also, make sure you have the right file path if your file is not in the same directory where the Python script is saved. Otherwise, you would get a FileNotFoundError.

```
obj = open(r"dummydata.txt", "r", encoding="utf8")
obj.read()
```

The method read() parses obj as a string (Figure 2-28). Do not worry about \n signs. Python indicates that these characters are separated by a new line.

```
In [21]:    1  obj = open(r"dummydata.txt", "r", encoding="utf8")
            2  obj.read()

Out[21]:  'Stock IBM Price 111.9\nStock AAPL Price 155.53\nStock MSFT Price 216.39\n'
```

Figure 2-28. *Reading information from a text file*

In fact, we can use \n to split the string into a list. Assign obj.read() to a new variable. There is a string method split(). One thing you have to remember about split() is it is always returning a list data structure. By default, split() would separate strings by an empty space. Conversely, you can pass a keyword or a character to be split by. In our case, we will pass \n as an argument:

```
obj = open(r"dummydata.txt", "r", encoding="utf8")
data = obj.read().split("\n")
```

After split(), the variable data holds the list of strings separated by a comma. A list is a versatile data structure, and we can analyze data going forward (Figure 2-29).

```
In [22]:    1  obj = open(r"dummydata.txt", "r", encoding="utf8")
            2  data = obj.read().split("\n")
            3  data

Out[22]:  ['Stock IBM Price 111.9',
           'Stock AAPL Price 155.53',
           'Stock MSFT Price 216.39',
           '']
```

Figure 2-29. *Parsing information from a text file*

To recapitulate everything we have learned in this chapter, we will do a practical example. Grab any text file you have, or you can follow my steps using the file I had uploaded online. If you decide to use your own file, you can use the open() function as we did in the previous example. Reading a file from a server would require a Python built-in module urllib. Urllib is a package that collects several modules for working with URLs (Uniform Resource Locators). The principle behind urllib is very simple.

It sends a request to a server and fetches the information with the function urlopen(). My text file is located here: `https://bit.ly/text-file`.

It would be a good idea to keep our code clean and neat. My advice is for every job create a new file.

Since urllib is a package, we need to import it first. During the course of this book, we will be using many different packages of libraries. A library is a collection of functions. Simply put, a third-party code. It is very important to import a library at the beginning of the file. You do not want to squeeze a third-party code into the middle of your script. That is why even if you forgot a library at first, get back and import it in the first cell.

```
from urllib.request import urlopen
```

Reading text from a cloud would require the urlopen() function. The information we have received from a server would be stored as an object. The object can be parsed with the method read(). In the case of text coming from an online source, read() will return byte literals with a prefix 'b'. We can use the str() function to be sure it is the regular string (Figure 2-30):

```
data = urlopen("https://bit.ly/text-file")
data = str(data)
```

```
In [1]:   1  from urllib.request import urlopen

In [2]:   1  data = urlopen("https://bit.ly/text-file").read()
          2  data = str(data)
          3  data

Out[2]: "b'\\nGetting started with React\\n\\nIn this chapter, I will explain our choice for a front end, and we will go ove
        r all the pros of using React. We will talk about the difference between React and React Native, and I will show how
        to get started with React and the main modules in React. If you are new to JavaScript and React, I would strongly re
        commend you to go over the next two chapters. In Chapters 3 and 4, I will demonstrate the main components of React t
        hat we will be using in React Native. We will learn all the aspects of React by assembling an intermediate version o
```

Figure 2-30. *Parsing information from a remote text file*

At the moment, our data is represented as a simple string. Our goal is to find ten most frequent words in the text.

Logically, we can use a dictionary data structure. Each word would be a key, and the number of times the word appears in the text would be the value. Sounds like a plan. But before we get to that, we need to convert all words to lowercase. The article "the" with a capital T for Python would be a different string than the same article beginning with a lower t. Also, we need to split the big string by whitespaces into words:

```
data = urlopen("https://bit.ly/text-file")
data = str(data).lower()
data = data.split()
```

After `split()`, the `data` variable holds a list of words. We need a dictionary to accumulate the number of occurrences of each word. I'll initialize a dictionary with the variable d:

```
d = {}
```

We can iterate through the list of words. If a word is in the dictionary, we increase the value by one. Otherwise, we will add a word to d and set the value as 1:

```
for word in data:
    if word in d:
        d[word] = d[word] + 1
    else:
        d[word] = 1
```

In Figure 2-31, you can see the dictionary full of words.

```
In [1]:   1  from urllib.request import urlopen
```

```
In [3]:   1  data = urlopen("https://bit.ly/text-file").read()
          2  data = str(data).lower()
          3  data = data.split()
          4  d = {}
          5  for word in data:
          6      if word in d:
          7          d[word] = d[word] + 1
          8      else:
          9          d[word] = 1
         10  d
```

```
Out[3]:  {"b'\\ngetting": 1,
          'started': 2,
          'with': 14,
          'react\\n\\nin': 1,
          'this': 8,
          'chapter,': 3,
          'i': 9,
          'will': 17,
          'explain': 1,
          'our': 9,
          'choice': 3,
          'for': 14,
          'a': 32,
          'front': 1,
          'end,': 1,
```

Figure 2-31. *The dictionary d holds words as keys and number of times each word appears in the text as values*

All we have to do is to sort these words by values. We cannot sort a dictionary, so we would need to convert it into a list of tuples (Figure 2-32):

```
alist = list(d.items())
```

```
In [1]:   1  from urllib.request import urlopen
```

```
In [4]:   1  data = urlopen("https://bit.ly/text-file").read()
          2  data = str(data).lower()
          3  data = data.split()
          4  d = {}
          5  for word in data:
          6      if word in d:
          7          d[word] = d[word] + 1
          8      else:
          9          d[word] = 1
         10  alist = list(d.items())
         11  alist
```

```
Out[4]:  [("b'\\ngetting", 1),
          ('started', 2),
          ('with', 14),
          ('react\\n\\nin', 1),
          ('this', 8),
          ('chapter,', 3),
          ('i', 9),
          ('will', 17),
```

Figure 2-32. *We have converted the dictionary into a list of tuples*

Before we sort the list of tuples, I would like to explain to you the mechanics of the sort() method. The function help() will reveal all keyword arguments of sort():

```
help(list.sort)
```

There are two arguments, key=None and reverse=False. Reverse simply means how you want to sort the list in ascending or descending order. By default, it is set to False because people prefer to order everything ascendingly. We would need to switch reverse to True because we are interested in the highest values.

The key argument is a little bit trickier. Let me explain what I mean. Suppose we have a plain list of numbers. The method sort() will sort it in ascending order by comparing values:

```
plain_list = [ 9,  5,  7,  4,  8,  3]
plain_list.sort()
[3, 4, 5, 7, 8, 9]
```

To illustrate our case, I'll take a sample of the list and apply the same method sort():

```
my_list = [('will', 17),('explain', 1),('choice', 3),('a', 32)]
my_list.sort()
[('a', 32), ('choice', 3), ('explain', 1), ('will', 17)]
```

You can see that the list is sorted but in alphabetical order. Python knows the order of the alphabet. The method sort() assumes that the first element in a tuple is the important one. By default, it orders all tuples through first elements. We want to order the list by the second element in each tuple. We can accomplish that if we fetch the second element of a tuple and use it as a key in the method sort(). The first step is to get an element:

```
t =('a', 32)
t[1]
```

We would need to perform this operation on every tuple in the list. Sounds like repetition. We need to wrap this statement as a function. I'll name this function get_value:

```
def get_value(t):
    return t[1]
```

The definition of sort() says if a key function is given, it would be applied to all items in the list. The second step would be to use get_value as a key:

```
alist.sort(key=get_value, reverse=True)
```

In Figure 2-33, you can see the list is sorted by words with the highest values. We can slice the list to get the first ten most frequent words in the file.

```
In [1]:   1  from urllib.request import urlopen

In [5]:   1  def get_value(t):
          2      return t[1]
          3
          4  data = urlopen("https://bit.ly/text-file").read()
          5  data = str(data).lower()
          6  data = data.split()
          7  d = {}
          8  for word in data:
          9      if word in d:
         10          d[word] = d[word] + 1
         11      else:
         12          d[word] = 1
         13  alist = list(d.items())
         14  alist.sort(key=get_value, reverse= True)
         15  alist[:10]

Out[5]:  [('and', 38),
          ('the', 37),
          ('a', 32),
          ('to', 27),
          ('of', 25),
          ('react', 22),
          ('is', 20),
          ('will', 17),
          ('in', 15),
          ('with', 14)]
```

Figure 2-33. *Finding ten most frequent words in the text*

Someone might ask, is there a better way to get a key besides defining a function to index an element in a tuple? The answer is yes; lambda would be an elegant solution. We will cover lambda in the next chapter. Later, you could go back to this problem and replace get_value with lambda.

I believe that the first two chapters have built a solid understanding of how Python operates. You can regard these chapters as an introduction to Python programming. We have covered all essential topics from built-in data types and functions to control flow statements.

By now, you should have had built a foundation to address advanced Python topics and approach complex problems.

CHAPTER 3

Data Analysis with Pandas

Modern life challenges require fast-paced solutions. These days, we need to evaluate tons of information in real time. Python is fast, but if you need to go faster, there is Pandas. Pandas is a core Python library for accelerated data manipulation. Originally developed for Wall Street professionals, it quickly became popular among people who crunch numbers, analyze big data, and simply want to switch from spreadsheets to the powerful and more efficient Python programming language. The name Pandas stands for panel data. Panel data is an econometric term for multidimensional data set. Pandas has many useful functions to make a data analysis process more efficient.

Pandas comes with two sophisticated data structures: Series and DataFrame. I like to think of data structures in terms of vehicles. Assuming that a Python list is a simple and reliable car that could take you from point A to point B, the Series would be a fast racecar. A simple car needs regular oil and gas, but a racecar would require premium lube and a special care. In this chapter, we will go over all the main Pandas features, such as filtering, logical operations, and concatenating and merging data sets, and learn how to use them.

© Art Yudin 2021
A. Yudin, *Basic Python for Data Management, Finance, and Marketing*,
https://doi.org/10.1007/978-1-4842-7189-6_3

Series

Before we get to the Series definition and start coding, we would need to import Pandas.

Since Pandas is a third-party library, we would need to import it every time we want to use it at the beginning of a file:

```
import pandas as pd
```

The variable pd is used as a shortcut. pd holds all Pandas functions, and you can see all of them with the help of the tab key on your keyboard. In a new cell, type pd. and press the tab key (Figure 3-1). Do not forget the period after pd. Based on my experience, it might take some time till you see the drop-down menu with all functions, especially on Windows. In **Jupyter**, the tab key works as a completion instrument.

Figure 3-1. *Type pd and press the tab key to see Pandas functions*

A Series is a one-dimensional data structure. We have seen sequential structures before, but this one is different. You can see a formal definition of the Series if you run

```
help(pd.Series)
```

It says "one-dimensional ndarray with axis labels."[1] To understand the definition and appreciate all Series features, we need to create one.

We will start with a list and convert it into a Series to see the differences between two data structures. Define a simple Python list alist with a bunch of numbers:

```
alist = [ 100, 200, 300, 400, 500 ]
```

Using the function pd.Series(), transform the list into a Series:

```
ser = pd.Series(alist)
```

```
In [2]:    1  alist = [ 100, 200, 300, 400, 500 ]

In [3]:    1  ser = pd.Series(alist)
           2  ser
Out[3]:    0    100
           1    200
           2    300
           3    400
           4    500
           dtype: int64
```

Figure 3-2. *Pandas Series*

In Figure 3-2, we can see the Pandas Series, a one-dimensional data structure or simply put a container. On the left side of the Series is the index. An index comes by default. The concept of an index was borrowed from relational databases. In a relational database, each record has a primary key. A primary key is a unique identifier. Using the key, you can fetch a value. A Series uses the same approach. However, in a Series you can get duplicates as a result of concatenating data sets. When we get to concatenation, we will talk about it, and I will explain how to deal with

---

[1] https://pandas.pydata.org/pandas-docs/stable/reference/api/pandas. Series.html

overlapping index values. In the meantime, we can fetch a value by an index:

```
ser[1]
```

The ser[1] operation will get us 200. Using a slicing notation, we can grab a couple of values:

```
ser[1:3]
```

As a result, we get 200 and 300. The stop index is excluded as in the Python slicing notation.

A Series always comes with dtype, a data type identifier of values, on the bottom. Compared to a list, a Series is homogeneous and can hold only the same data type values. The homogeneity of values makes a Series faster than a list. We can perform a simple test to illustrate homogeneity. Replace the first element in the ser Series to a float:

```
ser[0] = 1000.1234
```

The float 1000.1234 was converted to an integer and only then accepted by the Series with dtype: int64 (Figure 3-3). That means all of the values must be the same data type. If it was not possible to convert a value to an integer for some reason, then the Series would convert all values to floats or would raise an error.

```
In [4]:   1  ser[0] = 1000.1234
          2  ser
Out[4]:  0    1000
         1     200
         2     300
         3     400
         4     500
         dtype: int64
```

Figure 3-3. *A Series is always homogeneous*

A Series has two major attributes: index and values. Try ser.index and it will return RangeIndex(start=0, stop=5, step=1), meaning there are five elements. The format of the index reminds us of a function range(). We have used it in the previous chapter. The statement ser.values will reveal that the values are stored as a NumPy array, array([1000, 200, 300, 400, 500]).

NumPy is another core library in Python for scientific calculations. Although the NumPy package is outside of the scope of this book, we will be referring to it. Pandas' data structures build on top of the NumPy array, and they share similar behavior. Thus, we can borrow functions from NumPy and apply them to Pandas objects.

One of the main advantages of a Series is that we can implement operations on the whole structure rather than its items. This behavior is called vectorization. Vectorization is also inherited from NumPy. This behavior makes the Series faster and more efficient than a Python list. For example, if we needed to divide all items in alist by two, then we would have to use a for loop:

```
for item in alist:
    newitem = item / 2
```

However, if all values were stored in a Series, we could apply the mathematical operation to the whole container (Figure 3-4).

```
In [5]:   1 ser / 2

Out[5]:   0    500.0
          1    100.0
          2    150.0
          3    200.0
          4    250.0
          dtype: float64
```

Figure 3-4. *Vectorization applies an operation to the Series*

That is exactly what I meant comparing a Series to a racecar. Any for loop operation would take longer than a vectorized operation. For that reason, you do not want to iterate through a Series with a for loop. First of all, it would make the operation run slower; second, there is no need for it.

Another proof of efficiency would be a vectorized operation example between two Series objects – a simple calculation of a price-to-earnings ratio. The market price of a stock divided by earnings per share would be done faster if we stored all stock prices and earnings in the two Series rather than lists.

Random stock prices held in the Series under the name portfolio

```
portfolio = pd.Series([30,20,45,76,34])
```

would be divided by the same companies' earnings per share, also provided in the Series container:

```
earnings = pd.Series([1.5,3.3,4.5,2.5,2.75])
```

The final result could be saved as a new Series under the variable name pe (Figure 3-5):

```
pe = portfolio / earnings
```

```
In [6]:    1  portfolio = pd.Series([30,20,45,76,34])
           2  earnings = pd.Series([1.5,3.3,4.5,2.5,2.75])
           3  pe = portfolio / earnings
           4  pe

Out[6]: 0     20.000000
        1      6.060606
        2     10.000000
        3     30.400000
        4     12.363636
        dtype: float64
```

Figure 3-5. Division operation between the two Series objects

We can round down the results of the price-to-earnings ratio example to exactly two numbers after the decimal point if we pass the expression in the round() function:

```
pe = round(portfolio / earnings, 2)
```

As I have just mentioned, a Series has two attributes: index and values. That reminds us of keys and values in the dictionary structure. In some sense, a Series is close to the dictionary. The easiest way to create a new Series would be to convert a Python dictionary into a Pandas Series (Figure 3-6).

```
stocks = {"IBM":30, "ORCL":20, "MSFT":45}
portfolio = pd.Series(stocks)
```

```
In [9]:    1  stocks = {"IBM":30, "ORCL":20, "MSFT":45}
           2  portfolio = pd.Series(stocks)
           3  portfolio

Out[9]:    IBM     30
           ORCL    20
           MSFT    45
           dtype: int64
```

Figure 3-6. *Converting a Python dictionary into a Series structure*

The keys from the dictionary are used as the index in the Series (Figure 3-7). You can think of a Pandas Series as a specialization of a Python dictionary.

```
In [10]:    1  portfolio.index
Out[10]:  Index(['IBM', 'ORCL', 'MSFT'], dtype='object')
```

Figure 3-7. *String keys from a dictionary are the indices in the Series*

Using the dictionary notation on the Series, we can append more values to the `portfolio` object. To add an element, we need a new pair, key and value. Try the following code to add more stocks to the `portfolio` Series:

```
portfolio["AAPL"] = 76
portfolio["INTC"] = 34
```

As a result of that operation, the `portfolio` object was appended with two more values (Figure 3-8).

```
In [11]:    1  portfolio["AAPL"] = 76
            2  portfolio["INTC"] = 34
            3  portfolio

Out[11]:  IBM      30
          ORCL     20
          MSFT     45
          AAPL     76
          INTC     34
          dtype: int64
```

Figure 3-8. *Using a dictionary notation, we can add values to a Series*

We have learned that a Series is a one-dimensional data structure in Pandas. Now let's see what we get if we join a few Series together.

DataFrame

A DataFrame is a two-dimensional data structure. You can think of it as a bunch of Series bound together. There are several ways on how you can create a DataFrame, and I will show you all of them as we move along through the book. I want to start with the simplest example of how you can construct a DataFrame from scratch. We will initialize a DataFrame with the Pandas function `pd.DataFrame()` and save it under the `portfolio` variable name.

Constructing a DataFrame

To keep our code clean and neat, place each example into a separate **Jupyter** Notebook. At the beginning of the file in an isolated cell, we need to import Pandas:

```
import pandas as pd
```

In a new cell, define the portfolio variable as a DataFrame with the help of the Pandas DataFrame() function:

```
portfolio  = pd.DataFrame()
```

If you print the portfolio object, you will not see anything because it is empty. We need to populate our container with data. The most straightforward way would be to define a few Series and attach them to the portfolio object. Once again, I am using random numbers for values in all my examples.

```
stock_symbols = pd.Series(["IBM","ORCL","MSFT", "AAPL"])
stock_prices = pd.Series([116.86, 56.91, 216.51, 119.26])
number_shares = pd.Series([50, 100, 50, 100])
```

We need to come up with names for the columns and using the dictionary notation add them with values to the DataFrame:

```
portfolio["Symbol"] = stock_symbols
portfolio["Price"] = stock_prices
portfolio["Qty"] = number_shares
```

In Figure 3-9, you can see the DataFrame we have created from scratch.

```
In [1]:    1  import pandas as pd
```

```
In [2]:    1  portfolio   = pd.DataFrame()
           2  portfolio
```

Out[2]:

—

```
In [3]:    1  stock_symbols = pd.Series(["IBM","ORCL","MSFT", "AAPL"])
           2  stock_prices = pd.Series([116.86, 56.91, 216.51, 119.26])
           3  number_shares = pd.Series([50, 100, 50, 100])
```

```
In [4]:    1  portfolio["Symbol"] = stock_symbols
           2  portfolio["Price"] = stock_prices
           3  portfolio["Qty"] = number_shares
           4  portfolio
```

Out[4]:

	Symbol	Price	Qty
0	IBM	116.86	50
1	ORCL	56.91	100
2	MSFT	216.51	50
3	AAPL	119.26	100

Figure 3-9. *Creating a DataFrame from scratch*

Break the DataFrame down into smaller pieces, and you will see that it is composed of index, columns, and values attributes (Figure 3-10):

```
portfolio.index
portfolio.columns
portfolio.values
```

```
In [5]:    1  portfolio.index
```
```
Out[5]: RangeIndex(start=0, stop=4, step=1)
```

```
In [6]:    1  portfolio.columns
```
```
Out[6]: Index(['Symbol', 'Price', 'Qty'], dtype='object')
```

```
In [7]:    1  portfolio.values
```
```
Out[7]: array([['IBM', 116.86, 50],
               ['ORCL', 56.91, 100],
               ['MSFT', 216.51, 50],
               ['AAPL', 119.26, 100]], dtype=object)
```

Figure 3-10. *The DataFrame has three attributes: index, columns, and values*

We have used the dictionary notation to add columns to the DataFrame. That makes the DataFrame a specialization of the Python dictionary.

Slicing a DataFrame

Using the same approach, we can slice the DataFrame to grab a column:

```
portfolio["Price"]
```

Pass a column name as a string in the square brackets, as we did with a key to fetch a value from the Python dictionary, and it will return just one column (Figure 3-11). The returned column is a Series object.

```
In [8]:    1  portfolio["Price"]
```
```
Out[8]: 0    116.86
        1     56.91
        2    216.51
        3    119.26
        Name: Price, dtype: float64
```

Figure 3-11. *Slicing a column of the DataFrame*

103

The square brackets method using a column as the key allows us to part columns or create new columns. Also, this method would be essential if a column name has empty spaces. If you create a DataFrame from scratch, I would advise you to avoid using spaces in a column name, when using two or more words as a column name. However, sometimes you have to deal with data created by someone else with separated words in a column name. In that case, ["a column name"] would be the only way you could grab a column.

As always, to see all built-in attributes and methods in a DataFrame, run the dir() function on the portfolio object. We can see that Symbol, Price, and Qty are the attributes of our DataFrame. That means we can slice the Price column like this:

```
portfolio.Price
```

Keep in mind that slicing the column method as an attribute (Figure 3-12) will not help you to get multiple columns.

```
In [9]:    1  portfolio.Price

Out[9]:  0      116.86
         1       56.91
         2      216.51
         3      119.26
         Name: Price, dtype: float64
```

Figure 3-12. *Slicing a column of the DataFrame as an attribute*

We would need to pass column names as a list into square brackets to grab a couple of columns (Figure 3-13):

```
portfolio[ ["Symbol","Qty"] ]
```

```
In [10]:    1  portfolio[["Symbol","Qty"]]
Out[10]:
```

	Symbol	Qty
0	IBM	50
1	ORCL	100
2	MSFT	50
3	AAPL	100

Figure 3-13. *Slicing many columns of a DataFrame*

As was mentioned before, the square brackets notation and the name would create a new column. What if we do not have appropriate values for a column yet? That will not be a problem. We can create an empty column using 0 or an empty string as a placeholder for values that would be added later. For example, we would need to have a column for the price paid for each share in our portfolio. We will name it Cost, and since we do not have the actual data yet, use " " as a placeholder:

```
portfolio["Cost"] = " "
```

That statement will create an empty column we could use later (Figure 3-14).

```
In [11]:    1  portfolio["Cost"] = " "

In [12]:    1  portfolio
Out[12]:
```

	Symbol	Price	Qty	Cost
0	IBM	116.86	50	
1	ORCL	56.91	100	
2	MSFT	216.51	50	
3	AAPL	119.26	100	

Figure 3-14. *Using the square brackets notation to create an empty column*

Keep in mind that we could always reassign values under the same column name. All we need is the cost per share data stored as a one-dimensional structure. We have used a Series to add values to the DataFrame before; however, a list or a tuple would do the same job just fine. Most of the time when you are gathering data from different sources, you would use a list as an temporarily structure to hold values. Just make sure the length of the structure would match the number of rows in the DataFrame. Add the values to the portfolio DataFrame through reassignment:

```
portfolio["Cost"] = [115.25, 55.00, 210.30,105.75]
```

Figure 3-15 shows the column Cost with updated values.

```
In [13]:   1  portfolio["Cost"] = [115.25, 55.00, 210.30,105.75]

In [14]:   1  portfolio
Out[14]:
```

	Symbol	Price	Qty	Cost
0	IBM	116.86	50	115.25
1	ORCL	56.91	100	55.00
2	MSFT	216.51	50	210.30
3	AAPL	119.26	100	105.75

Figure 3-15. *Updating values in the column by reassignment*

Earlier in the chapter, we have performed vectorized operations between two Series. Since each column represents a Series, we can do vectorized calculations between columns. The price of a share multiplied by the quantity of shares would get us a dollar amount of the whole position. We can save the results in a new column under the name Amount (Figure 3-16):

```
portfolio["Amount"] = portfolio["Price"] * portfolio["Qty"]
```

```
In [15]:    1  portfolio["Amount"] = portfolio["Price"] * portfolio["Qty"]
```

```
In [16]:    1  portfolio
```

Out[16]:

	Symbol	Price	Qty	Cost	Amount
0	IBM	116.86	50	115.25	5843.0
1	ORCL	56.91	100	55.00	5691.0
2	MSFT	216.51	50	210.30	10825.5
3	AAPL	119.26	100	105.75	11926.0

Figure 3-16. *Vectorized operation to calculate the dollar amount of a position*

Another example of a similar operation would be calculating the profit or loss of each position. This time, we will use a slightly different syntax. We will use column names as attributes of the DataFrame (Figure 3-17). Python follows the math order of operations, and we will use the round brackets to compute the profit or loss per share first, and then the result would be multiplied by the quantity of shares:

```
portfolio["Profit"] = (portfolio.Price-portfolio.
Cost)*portfolio.Qty
```

```
In [17]:    1  portfolio["Profit"] = (portfolio.Price - portfolio.Cost) * portfolio.Qty
```

```
In [18]:    1  portfolio
```

Out[18]:

	Symbol	Price	Qty	Cost	Amount	Profit
0	IBM	116.86	50	115.25	5843.0	80.5
1	ORCL	56.91	100	55.00	5691.0	191.0
2	MSFT	216.51	50	210.30	10825.5	310.5
3	AAPL	119.26	100	105.75	11926.0	1351.0

Figure 3-17. *Calculating the profit or loss, grabbing the columns as attributes of a DataFrame*

A DataFrame comes with the index by default. But we can always reassign the index. Stock symbols are unique, and we can use them as indices. To use a column value as an index, we would need to slice the column and assign it as the index:

```
portfolio.index = portfolio.Symbol
```

In [19]:   `1  portfolio.index = portfolio.Symbol`

In [20]:   `1  portfolio`

Out[20]:

	Symbol	Price	Qty	Cost	Amount	Profit
Symbol						
IBM	IBM	116.86	50	115.25	5843.0	80.5
ORCL	ORCL	56.91	100	55.00	5691.0	191.0
MSFT	MSFT	216.51	50	210.30	10825.5	310.5
AAPL	AAPL	119.26	100	105.75	11926.0	1351.0

Figure 3-18. *Reassigning an index to the values of the Symbol column*

After index reassignment, the portfolio DataFrame has identical values for the index as in the column Symbol. To differentiate an index and a column, Pandas prints the index name on the next line under the columns' names (Figure 3-18).

So far, we have been adding new columns to a DataFrame. With the method drop(), we can remove the unwanted columns. DataFrame methods are more complicated than what we have dealt with in a list or tuple before. I would recommend using the function help() to verify all arguments a method might take:

```
help(portfolio.drop)
```

You have probably noticed that Pandas developers did a good job providing information on functions and methods with relevant examples. The Drop() method takes the following keyword arguments:

```
drop(labels=None, axis=0, index=None, columns=None, level=None,
inplace=False, errors='raise')
```

Parameters vary for a method. However, there are a couple of them that would be common to all Pandas methods. I am talking about axis and inplace.

A DataFrame has two axis – rows and columns (Figure 3-19). The drop() command or any other DataFrame method could be applied either to rows or columns. By default, the axis is set to rows or 0. If we left it as it is and tried to delete the Symbol column from the DataFrame, we would get an error – "Symbol not found in axis". Because the drop() method by default would be looking for the "Symbol" name in the index values. Since we want to get rid of a column, we would need to switch the method drop() axis keyword to "columns". Pandas provides two options, either to set a keyword argument to 1 or literally "columns".

axis=1 or axis='columns'					
Symbol	Price	Qty	Cost	Amount	Profit
Symbol					
IBM	IBM 116.86	50	115.25	5843.0	80.5
ORCL	ORCL 56.91	100	55.00	5691.0	191.0
MSFT	MSFT 216.51	50	210.30	10825.5	310.5
AAPL	AAPL 119.26	100	105.75	11926.0	1351.0

axis=0 or axis='index'

Figure 3-19. *Axis 0 or "index" is referring to rows, and axis 1 or "columns" is referring to columns*

Nonetheless, if our intention was to drop a row, like "IBM", then we should have left the axis as it was or assigned "index" to axis. Keep axis in mind when using a DataFrame method.

Another common parameter in DataFrame methods is inplace. When we are applying a method such as drop() and removing a column from the DataFrame, we are changing the object. The alterations to the object should be saved. Setting inplace = True will save those changes. The argument inplace means that an object is modified in place, within the object itself. So there is no need to assign the expression to a variable to save the changes if inplace is set to True.

There are two options, True or False. In some way, you can think of it as a save button. The method drop() would remove an unwanted column and save the adjustment with inplace = True. Sometimes, by accident people skip the inplace = True step. Would the method drop() still remove a column? The answer is yes, but there might be some issues with the object later. The best practice would be to set the inplace keyword argument to True when you are applying a method and need to preserve the changes.

OK, now we are ready to remove the Symbol column from the DataFrame:

```
portfolio.drop(labels="Symbol", axis=1, inplace=True)
```

Make sure you run the drop() statement in a separate cell, and you run it once (Figure 3-20). A rookie mistake is to rerun the cell and receive the warning message "not found in axis". If you run the drop() command again, it would not be able to find the column. The column is gone, and it is no longer part of the DataFrame.

```
In [21]:   1  portfolio.drop(labels="Symbol", axis=1, inplace=True)
```

```
In [22]:   1  portfolio
```

Out[22]:

Symbol	Price	Qty	Cost	Amount	Profit
IBM	116.86	50	115.25	5843.0	80.5
ORCL	56.91	100	55.00	5691.0	191.0
MSFT	216.51	50	210.30	10825.5	310.5
AAPL	119.26	100	105.75	11926.0	1351.0

Figure 3-20. *The method drop removes the Symbol column*

So far, we have been manipulating DataFrame columns. Rows and values can be sliced as well as columns. There are two methods to retrieve one or more rows – loc and iloc.

Loc stands for location. The loc method requires labels, and iloc takes an index of a row. Noticeably, i means index in the iloc method name. Both loc and iloc will do the same job.

Suppose we need to fetch the row for MSFT out of the portfolio DataFrame. MSFT is a label of an index value. The underlying index value is 2. The index count starts at 0. IBM is 0, ORCL is 1, and MSFT is 2. If we want to use labels, then the loc statement would look like this:

```
portfolio.loc["MSFT"]
```

Consequently, iloc would require an integer for the index and would get you the same result with this statement:

```
portfolio.iloc[2]
```

Compared to other DataFrame methods, loc and iloc use square brackets (Figure 3-21).

```
In [23]:   1  portfolio.loc["MSFT"]
```

```
Out[23]: Price        216.51
         Qty           50.00
         Cost         210.30
         Amount     10825.50
         Profit       310.50
         Name: MSFT, dtype: float64
```

```
In [24]:   1  portfolio.iloc[2]
```

```
Out[24]: Price        216.51
         Qty           50.00
         Cost         210.30
         Amount     10825.50
         Profit       310.50
         Name: MSFT, dtype: float64
```

Figure 3-21. *Methods loc and iloc fetch the MSFT row*

The Python slicing principle could be applied to a DataFrame with loc and iloc methods. The only difference is the method loc with labels would include a stop position. In the iloc method, the stop index is excluded. That is why fetching two rows for ORCL and MSFT would have MSFT as a stop in the loc variant and would require an upper limit for a numeric index value in the iloc expression (Figure 3-22):

```
portfolio.loc["ORCL":"MSFT"]
```

```
portfolio.iloc[1:3]
```

```
In [25]:   1  portfolio.loc["ORCL":"MSFT"]
Out[25]:
```

Symbol	Price	Qty	Cost	Amount	Profit
ORCL	56.91	100	55.0	5691.0	191.0
MSFT	216.51	50	210.3	10825.5	310.5

```
In [26]:   1  portfolio.iloc[1:3]
Out[26]:
```

Symbol	Price	Qty	Cost	Amount	Profit
ORCL	56.91	100	55.0	5691.0	191.0
MSFT	216.51	50	210.3	10825.5	310.5

Figure 3-22. *Slicing rows with loc and iloc methods*

In real life, a DataFrame might have thousands of columns, and you might need to get just a subset of data. Subsetting on a DataFrame would need indices for rows and columns separated by a comma. Rows would always come first. The `iloc` method is similar to the Python slicing notation syntax:

[start : stop : step , start : stop : step]

As in Python, the step is optional and by default is set to 1. As a reminder, the `loc` method takes labels for the index and columns.

We can get the values from `Price` and `Qty` columns for `ORCL` and `MSFT` essentially as

```
portfolio.loc["ORCL":"MSFT", "Price":"Qty"]
```

```
portfolio.iloc[1:3, 0:2]
```

In Figure 3-23, you can see that both methods yield the same result.

Another option would be to slice the columns first and then apply `loc` or `iloc`. For instance, getting values for `MSFT` and `AAPL` out of `Price` and `Profit` columns would be equal to these statements:

```
portfolio[["Price", "Profit"]].loc["MSFT":"AAPL"]
portfolio[["Price", "Profit"]].iloc[2 : ]
```

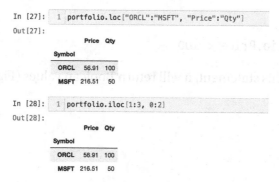

Figure 3-23. *Subsetting with loc and iloc methods*

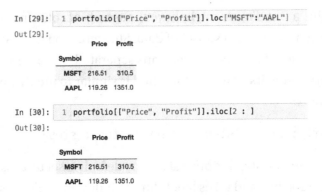

Figure 3-24. *Subsetting on columns with loc and iloc methods*

We are leaving the stop index blank in the iloc method since we want to get all rows after index 2 (Figure 3-24).

Filtering a DataFrame

The filtering process is more efficient in Pandas than what we have done so far with a for loop and if statements. We will start with a simple example. Our goal is to filter the portfolio DataFrame and identify all stocks priced less than $100.00.

The first step would be to grab the column Price either using the dictionary notation portfolio["Price"] or portfolio.Price and define a condition:

```
portfolio.Price < 100
```

If you run this statement, it will return Boolean values (Figure 3-25).

```
In [31]:     1  portfolio.Price < 100
```

```
Out[31]: Symbol
         IBM       False
         ORCL       True
         MSFT      False
         AAPL      False
         Name: Price, dtype: bool
```

Figure 3-25. *Defining a condition for a filter*

The filter is working, but obviously we need more information and the stock itself. One option would be to apply the filter to the whole DataFrame. This option will fetch you the whole row:

```
portfolio[portfolio.Price < 100]
```

Another option would be to apply the condition to a particular column or columns. Specifically, if we want to see how many shares we hold of stocks that are priced less than a hundred, we need to slice the Qty column and apply the filter:

```
portfolio.Qty[portfolio.Price < 100]
```

This would be an example of filtering one column based on another one. As you can see in Figure 3-26, the first statement has retrieved the whole row, and the second filter gets just one value.

```
In [32]:    1  portfolio[portfolio.Price < 100]
```

Out[32]:

	Price	Qty	Cost	Amount	Profit
Symbol					
ORCL	56.91	100	55.0	5691.0	191.0

```
In [33]:    1  portfolio.Qty[portfolio.Price < 100]
```

Out[33]: Symbol
         ORCL   100
         Name: Qty, dtype: int64

Figure 3-26. *Filtering a DataFrame*

There is no need to iterate through values and use if and else statements. Also, we can combine conditions as we did before with conditional operators. In Pandas, &, ampersand, is the equivalent of the and operator in Python. When you use &, both conditions have to be True to return the result. Suppose we need to find all stocks that are priced less than $200, and the number of shares is exactly 50 in the portfolio DataFrame. Then we can couple two conditions as

(portfolio.Price < 200) & (portfolio.Qty == 50)

And apply the filter to the DataFrame:

portfolio[(portfolio.Price < 200) & (portfolio.Qty == 50)]

Please note that each condition must be wrapped in the round brackets. Apparently, only one position in portfolio fully satisfied these two conditions (Figure 3-27).

```
In [34]:    1  portfolio[(portfolio.Price < 200) & (portfolio.Qty == 50)]
Out[34]:
```

Symbol	Price	Qty	Cost	Amount	Profit
IBM	116.86	50	115.25	5843.0	80.5

Figure 3-27. *Filtering a DataFrame based on two conditions*

Another conditional operator in Pandas is |. It is pronounced a toll bar. The equivalent of the or operator in Python, | would filter if either one of the conditions is True. We can filter the DataFrame and filter all positions where the price is greater than $200 or the cost is exactly $55. We need to outline each of the conditions first in parentheses and using | apply them to the portfolio object:

```
portfolio[(portfolio.Price > 200) | (portfolio.Cost == 55)]
```

As we can see in Figure 3-28, two positions fit into our filter – ORCL because its "Cost" value is precisely 55 and MSFT with a price greater than 200.

```
In [35]:    1  portfolio[(portfolio.Price > 200) | (portfolio.Cost == 55)]
Out[35]:
```

Symbol	Price	Qty	Cost	Amount	Profit
ORCL	56.91	100	55.0	5691.0	191.0
MSFT	216.51	50	210.3	10825.5	310.5

Figure 3-28. *Filtering a DataFrame where either one of the conditions is true*

Filtering is very useful, but what if you want to do something to a value based on a condition?

Logic Operations in Pandas

When you need to take actions based on a condition, that is where logical operations come into play. If a condition is True, then do something to the values. There are three different approaches you can use to perform logical operations in Pandas. My favorite is lambda, and I'll explain it first.

Lambda is an anonymous function in Python – in other words, a function with no name that runs like an expression. Beginners find lambda somewhat confusing, but it is not that difficult, believe me – presuming that you grasp the syntax and practice the lambda syntax a couple of times.

I will start with single-expression lambda. Suppose we want to double the number of shares of each stock in our portfolio DataFrame. The easiest and efficient way would be to use portfolio.Qty * 2. However, to explain lambda I would do it differently. An alternative to a vectorized operation would be to go value by value in the column Qty and add each value to itself. That sounds like an iteration through a column. We do not want to use a for loop to iterate over a column because it would slow down the process. The most efficient way to iterate through a Series would be to use the method apply(). The official documentation says that the method apply() takes another function and applies it to all values within a column.[2] To double the number of shares, we would need to compile a function and pass it into the apply() method.

Let's define a simple function that would take the number of shares from each row in the column Qty and add them to themselves:

```
def double(num_shares):
    return num_shares + num_shares
```

---

[2] https://pandas.pydata.org/pandas-docs/stable/reference/api/pandas.DataFrame.apply.html

Now that we have a function, we will apply it to each value within the Series portfolio.Qty:

```
portfolio.Qty.apply(double)
```

Keep in mind that when you use a function as a helper function within some other function, like map(), filter(), or the method apply(), you do not need parentheses at the end. That is why we call the double function inside the apply() method as apply(double). In Figure 3-29, we see that the number of shares for each stock has doubled.

```
In [36]:    1  def double(num_shares):
            2      return num_shares + num_shares
            3
            4  portfolio.Qty.apply(double)
Out[36]:  Symbol
          IBM     100
          ORCL    200
          MSFT    100
          AAPL    200
          Name: Qty, dtype: int64
```

Figure 3-29. *Applying a function double to all values in the Series*

Usually, we define a function because we would want to use it again and again. I doubt that the double function would be needed anymore. Is there a better way? The answer is yes; we can replace a function with lambda.

To write lambda expressions, you need to remember the following setup. Always begin with the lambda keyword. In lambda, there are two parts separated by the colon character. In the first part, you define a variable or variables. Something that goes into a lambda. In the second part, you compose an expression. Something that lambda would return as the result (Figure 3-30).

Figure 3-30. *Lambda syntax*

There is no need to use a return operator because `lambda` always returns the result. Keep in mind that `lambda` has to be used within a function or can be assigned as an expression to a variable name. We can rewrite the `double` function as a `lambda` expression:

```
lambda num_shares : num_shares + num_shares
```

This expression can replace the `double` function in the `apply()` method:

```
portfolio.Qty.apply(lambda num_shares : num_shares + num_shares)
```

If we want to save the result of that operation, we can assign it to a new column name as in Figure 3-31.

```
In [37]:   1 portfolio["New_Qty"] = portfolio.Qty.apply(lambda num_shares : num_shares + num_shares)

In [38]:   1 portfolio

Out[38]:
```

Symbol	Price	Qty	Cost	Amount	Profit	New_Qty
IBM	116.86	50	115.25	5843.0	80.5	100
ORCL	56.91	100	55.00	5691.0	191.0	200
MSFT	216.51	50	210.30	10825.5	310.5	100
AAPL	119.26	100	105.75	11926.0	1351.0	200

Figure 3-31. *Doubling the number of shares and saving the result under a new column name*

Lambda can be used with `if` and `else` statements. The syntax would look like in Figure 3-32.

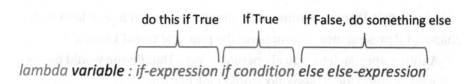

Figure 3-32. *Lambda syntax with if and else conditions*

With lambda returning outcomes based on if and else statements, we can do logical operations on a Series or the whole DataFrame. As an illustration of that, we can provide the recommendations to buy or sell a stock based on the price. Let's say if the stock price is less than $118, we would record Buy in the new column Rating. Otherwise, the record in the Rating column would be Sell. The lambda expression in the apply() method would look like this:

```
lambda stock_price :  "Buy" if stock_price < 118 else "Sell"
```

Again, stock_price is a variable that accurately describes the value. All we have to do is to pass the lambda expression into the apply() method and save the results under the column name Rating:

```
portfolio["Rating"] = portfolio.Price.apply(lambda stock_price :
  "Buy" if stock_price < 118 else "Sell")
```

The Rating column holds outcomes based on if and else statements we have applied to all values in the Price column (Figure 3-33).

```
In [39]:  1  portfolio["Rating"] = portfolio.Price.apply(lambda stock_price : "Buy" if stock_price < 118 else "Sell")

In [40]:  1  portfolio
Out[40]:
```

Symbol	Price	Qty	Cost	Amount	Profit	New_Qty	Rating
IBM	116.86	50	115.25	5843.0	80.5	100	Buy
ORCL	56.91	100	55.00	5691.0	191.0	200	Buy
MSFT	216.51	50	210.30	10825.5	310.5	100	Sell
AAPL	119.26	100	105.75	11926.0	1351.0	200	Sell

Figure 3-33. *Applying lambda with if and else statements*

I know that lambda requires some practice to master it, and later in the chapter, I'll present more examples of the practical use of lambda.

Another approach to logical operations on a DataFrame would be using the method loc. The syntax would look like this:

```
DataFrame.loc[ if condition, new column to save result ] =
result
```

A practical example would be to calculate the profit or loss per share. If values in the Price column are greater than values in the Cost column, then we want to subtract the cost paid from the current price. The results will be stored in a new column. We will name it PL_per_share (Figure 3-34). We can write this logical statement as

```
portfolio.loc[portfolio.Price > portfolio.Cost, "PL_per_share"] =
portfolio.Price - portfolio.Cost
```

```
In [41]:    1  portfolio.loc[portfolio.Price > portfolio.Cost, "PL_per_share"] = portfolio.Price - portfolio.Cost

In [42]:    1  portfolio

Out[42]:
```

Symbol	Price	Qty	Cost	Amount	Profit	New_Qty	Rating	PL_per_share
IBM	116.86	50	115.25	5843.0	80.5	100	Buy	1.61
ORCL	56.91	100	55.00	5691.0	191.0	200	Buy	1.91
MSFT	216.51	50	210.30	10825.5	310.5	100	Sell	6.21
AAPL	119.26	100	105.75	11926.0	1351.0	200	Sell	13.51

Figure 3-34. *Performing a logical operation with the loc method*

There is one more option for outcomes based on if and else conditions – the NumPy function where(). Pandas is built on NumPy, and the NumPy array data structure is the core of a Series and a DataFrame. It means we can borrow functions from the NumPy package and use them in Pandas. Since we have not imported the NumPy library into our file, we would need to scroll up and import NumPy into the first cell right under the Pandas import. Do not forget to rerun the cell:

```
import numpy as np
```

The function where() belongs to NumPy, and we would need to use it as

```
np.where()
```

It would be a good idea to read the description and see all arguments that it takes:

```
help(np.where)
```

Just as the documentation says, where() needs a condition, and then it would provide two outcomes. The first one will be executed if the condition is True and the other one if the condition returns False.

To practice where(), we can run a scenario; if the value in PL_per_share is greater than $5, we need to return True. Otherwise, where() will return False. The results will be stored in the new column under the greater_five name. Following the description of where(), we can compile that logical expression as

```
portfolio["greater_five"] = np.where(portfolio.PL_per_share >5,
True, False)
```

Figure 3-35 shows that where() did a perfect job, and the newly created column greater_five has True values if the profit per share is greater than $5.

```
In [43]:    1  portfolio["graater_five"] = np.where(portfolio.PL_per_share > 5, True, False)

In [44]:    1  portfolio
Out[44]:
```

Symbol	Price	Qty	Cost	Amount	Profit	New_Qty	Rating	PL_per_share	graater_five
IBM	116.86	50	115.25	5843.0	80.5	100	Buy	1.61	False
ORCL	56.91	100	55.00	5691.0	191.0	200	Buy	1.91	False
MSFT	216.51	50	210.30	10825.5	310.5	100	Sell	6.21	True
AAPL	119.26	100	105.75	11926.0	1351.0	200	Sell	13.51	True

Figure 3-35. *Performing a logical operation with the npwhere function*

With the where() function, we can perform more complicated operations than Boolean outcomes.

Using the logic from the previous example, we can increase our position in stock if PL_per_share is less than $5. If the condition is True, then we would multiply the price per share by the value from New_Qty. The result of this operation will update the value in the Amount column. For stocks with the PL_per_share value greater than $5, we will not do anything and leave the amount as it is:

```
portfolio["Amount"] = np.where(portfolio.PL_per_share < 5,
portfolio.Price * portfolio.New_Qty, portfolio.Amount )
```

The Amount column was updated only for IBM and ORCL since the values in the column PL_per_share were 1.61 and 1.91, respectively (Figure 3-35).

Out of these three approaches, my favorites are lambda and the where() function. The method loc would require a separate statement for each if condition. However, you might want to use loc when you have more conditions to test if and else and more if conditions.

I think we have covered enough theory and need to take on a real-life example. We will fetch data from www.sectorspdr.com/sectorspdr/.

Reading Data from a CSV File

Sectorspdr.com provides live data on S&P 500 companies split by industries. Each sector represents an ETF (exchange-traded fund). No worries if you are not into finance. We are not going too much into technicalities here. All we need is a relevant data to read as a DataFrame. We would need to clean the data and analyze it. The reason I have chosen the Sectorspdr.com site is because it serves data as a CSV (Comma- Separated Values) file that can be readed from online without downloading it first.

We will grab a CSV file for XLF – ETF that tracks the S&P Financial Sector Index. You can get data here: `www.sectorspdr.com/sectorspdr/sector/xlf/index`. In case Sectorspdr.com changes something on the site or you would want to follow my example precisely, I've uploaded the data I'll be using here to my server. I have downloaded the CSV file from Sectorspdr.com, and you can find it here: `https://bit.ly/bookcsvxlf`.

In Figure 3-36, you can see two green buttons to download the data in a CSV or Excel format. On the page we have all financial companies included in the XLF fund and their weightings with in the index. We will read this information from the site and analyze it. One option would be to download the data by clicking a green button to your computer and then open it as a DataFrame with the Pandas function `read_csv()`. Pandas can read different formats of data. We will talk more about gathering data in the next chapter. The most popular formats are CSV and xlsx. The main advantage of `read_csv()` and `read_excel()` functions is they return a DataFrame. If you check the description of the `read_csv()` function with `help(pd.read_csv)`, you'll see that you can open a CSV file right from the cloud without downloading the file first. To open it right from a server, we can copy the URL (Uniform Resource Locator) and pass it directly into `pd.read_csv()`.

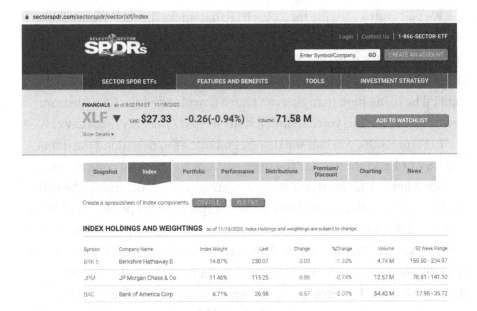

Figure 3-36. *Sectorspdr website with options to download data*

For this exercise, we would need to launch a new **Jupyter** file and import pandas in the first cell:

```
import pandas as pd
```

There are two options how to get the information from the site: the first is to copy the URL from the website by clicking the right button on the mouse and selecting "Copy Link Address". Using the first option, you'll get the most recent data from Sectorspdr.com. The second option would be to use my link of the previously downloaded file to my server. These are two examples of how you can do it:

```
url = "https://www.sectorspdr.com/sectorspdr/IDCO.Client.Spdrs.
Index/Export/ExportCsv?symbol=xlf"

file = pd.read_csv(url, skiprows=1)
```

or

```
url = "https://bit.ly/bookcsvxlf"
file = pd.read_csv(url, skiprows=1)
```

In both instances, you should see the DataFrame like in Figure 3-37.

```
In [1]:   1  import pandas as pd

In [2]:   1  url = "https://www.sectorspdr.com/sectorspdr/IDCO.Client.Spdrs.Index/Export/ExportCsv?symbol=xlf"
          2  file = pd.read_csv(url, skiprows=1)
          3  file.head()

Out[2]:
```

	Symbol	Company Name	Index Weight	Last	Change	%Change	Volume	52 Week Range	Unnamed: 8
0	AFL	AFLAC Inc	0.93%	42.86	-0.14	-0.33%	5.55 M	23.07 - 55.07	NaN
1	AIG	American Intl Group Inc	1.08%	38.55	0.13	+0.34%	6.27 M	16.07 - 56.42	NaN
2	AIZ	Assurant Inc	0.26%	135.62	-2.97	-2.14%	342.50 K	76.27 - 142.61	NaN
3	ALL	Allstate Corp	1.02%	100.07	0.70	+0.70%	2.52 M	64.13 - 125.92	NaN
4	AMP	Ameriprise Financial Inc	0.72%	183.33	-0.90	-0.49%	446.33 K	80.01 - 188.57	NaN

Figure 3-37. *Reading a CSV file from an online location*

The skiprows keyword argument skips the first row in the original
file. Sometimes, files have time stamps or titles that we do not need for
analysis. In the xlf.csv file, the first row was a time stamp, and it was
interfering with the DataFrame format. You can remove skiprows=1 and
rerun the cell to see how the DataFrame would look like without skiprows.

On line 3 in Figure 3-37, I use the method head(). Most of the time, the
data is too big to fit on the screen, and Pandas cannot render the whole
data set. The methods head() and tail() would show the first five rows
or last five rows, respectively. If you want to see more rows, you can pass a
number of rows as an argument into head() or tail(). To examine 20 first
rows, we can

```
file.head(20)
```

Every time I deal with a new data set, I start with the DataFrame
method info():

```
file.info()
```

```
In [3]:    1  file.info()

<class 'pandas.core.frame.DataFrame'>
RangeIndex: 65 entries, 0 to 64
Data columns (total 9 columns):
 #   Column        Non-Null Count  Dtype
---  ------        --------------  -----
 0   Symbol        65 non-null     object
 1   Company Name  65 non-null     object
 2   Index Weight  65 non-null     object
 3   Last          65 non-null     float64
 4   Change        65 non-null     float64
 5   %Change       65 non-null     object
 6   Volume        65 non-null     object
 7   52 Week Range 65 non-null     object
 8   Unnamed: 8    0 non-null      float64
dtypes: float64(3), object(6)
memory usage: 4.7+ KB
```

Figure 3-38. *The method info() provides information on a DataFrame*

The method info() returns all information about the file object (Figure 3-38). First of all, we see that the DataFrame has 65 rows. It takes 4.7 KB of memory. But more importantly, the info() method provides us with the data type of values in each column. Only three columns – Last, Change, and Unnamed: 8 – hold numeric values. All other columns have an object as a data type. An Object dtype means a nonnumeric data type, mostly strings. It would not be possible to use math operations on the "Index Weight" column or "Volume" column because they contain strings. We will need to convert the values to floats if we plan to run any calculations on those columns.

Before we get to data analysis, we need to clean the data set a bit. There is a column "Unnamed: 8" with NaN. NaN stands for not a number and means that there is no value. The column with no values is completely useless to us. We will delete it with a method drop():

```
file.drop( "Unnamed: 8", axis=1, inplace=True)
```

As I warned you earlier, place the drop() statement into a separate cell and run it once only. The column "Unnamed: 8" is gone after we dropped it (Figure 3-39).

```
In [4]:     1  file.drop("Unnamed: 8", axis=1, inplace=True)

In [5]:     1  file.head()
Out[5]:
```

	Symbol	Company Name	Index Weight	Last	Change	%Change	Volume	52 Week Range
0	AFL	AFLAC Inc	0.93%	42.86	-0.14	-0.33%	5.55 M	23.07 - 55.07
1	AIG	American Intl Group Inc	1.08%	38.55	0.13	+0.34%	6.27 M	16.07 - 56.42
2	AIZ	Assurant Inc	0.26%	135.62	-2.97	-2.14%	342.50 K	76.27 - 142.61
3	ALL	Allstate Corp	1.02%	100.07	0.70	+0.70%	2.52 M	64.13 - 125.92
4	AMP	Ameriprise Financial Inc	0.72%	183.33	-0.90	-0.49%	446.33 K	80.01 - 188.57

Figure 3-39. *Deleted Unnamed: 8 column from the DataFrame*

I will show you how to convert a data type of a column to numeric values. Suppose we want to sum up all values in the "Index Weight" column and check if we get 100%. The method info() indicated that the values are strings. Our job is to convert strings to floats. What could be easier you might think for a moment? However, before we get to that part, we would need to get rid of the % sign. Otherwise, we would get an error message because special characters cannot be converted to numeric values. Let's slice the column and run the function dir on it to see what is built into that Series. We will have to use a dictionary notation due to an empty space in the name of the column:

```
dir(file["Index Weight"])
```

If you scroll through all attributes, you will find str, a module that contains string methods. We can see all of them if we include str into the dir() function:

```
dir(file["Index Weight"].str)
```

You should see familiar method names we have seen in a string object in Python. Although the names of methods match Python string methods, all of them were designed for a one-dimensional Series. The implementation of these methods is different from the regular Python string methods. These methods were designed to be applied to a whole Series, not to a string value one by one.

The "Index Weight" column contains numbers with the % sign. We need to remove all % signs. That sounds like an iteration through the column. If we dealt with a list, we would use a for loop and one by one remove % with the string method strip(). With the str.strip() method, there is no need to iterate because it comes from the Series object itself. I want to make it clear strip() and str.strip() will perform the same job, but the first one would do one at a time and the other one through the Series. To remove all % signs before we convert values to a numeric data type, we will do

```
file["Index Weight"].str.strip("%")
```

str.strip() clears % off all values (Figure 3-40).

```
In [6]:    1  file["Index Weight"].str.strip("%")
Out[6]: 0      0.93
        1      1.08
        2      0.26
        3      1.02
        4      0.72
                ...
        60     0.63
        61     0.30
        62     0.32
        63     2.09
        64     0.31
        Name: Index Weight, Length: 65, dtype: object
```

Figure 3-40. *The Series method strstrip removes % signs from all values*

We are halfway there; now we need to convert string values to a numeric data type. There are a couple of options to convert one data type into another. Here, we can apply the Pandas function `pd.to_numeric()` to all values in the Series like this:

`file["Index Weight"].str.strip("%").apply(pd.to_numeric)`

or we can use the Series method `astype()` and pass a `float` data type as an argument:

`file["Index Weight"].str.strip("%").astype(float)`

It is a personal preference how to convert strings to the floats in Pandas; the outcome will be the same. We need to store the results, and I'll assign that statement to a new column name `"IW"`:

`file["IW"] = file["Index Weight"].str.strip("%").astype(float)`

Although visually numbers are the same in the columns `Index Weight` and `IW`, on the latter one we can perform math calculations and filtering (Figure 3-41).

```
In [7]:   1  file["IW"] = file["Index Weight"].str.strip("%").astype(float)

In [8]:   1  file.head()

Out[8]:
```

	Symbol	Company Name	Index Weight	Last	Change	%Change	Volume	52 Week Range	IW
0	AFL	AFLAC Inc	0.93%	42.86	-0.14	-0.33%	5.55 M	23.07 - 55.07	0.93
1	AIG	American Intl Group Inc	1.08%	38.55	0.13	+0.34%	6.27 M	16.07 - 56.42	1.08
2	AIZ	Assurant Inc	0.26%	135.62	-2.97	-2.14%	342.50 K	76.27 - 142.61	0.26
3	ALL	Allstate Corp	1.02%	100.07	0.70	+0.70%	2.52 M	64.13 - 125.92	1.02
4	AMP	Ameriprise Financial Inc	0.72%	183.33	-0.90	-0.49%	446.33 K	80.01 - 188.57	0.72

Figure 3-41. *Converting strings from the Index Weight column to numeric values and saving the result in the IW column*

Table 3-1. *Aggregation methods in Pandas*

Method	Definition
sum()	Compute sum of values
mean()	Compute mean of values
count()	Compute count of rows
std()	Compute standard deviation
var()	Compute variance of values
min()	Compute min of group value
max()	Compute max of group values

The aggregation method max() will get the sum of all values in the column:

```
file.IW.sum()
```

min() and max() methods will get the smallest value from the Series and the largest one:

```
file.IW.min()
file.IW.max()
```

We can fetch the companies with smallest and largest share values in the S&P 500 financial index XLF from the DataFrame by filtering

```
file[file.IW == file.IW.min()]
file[file.IW == file.IW.max()]
```

Apparently, Unum Group has the smallest share, and Berkshire Hathaway is the largest holding in the XLF index (Figure 3-42).

```
In [9]:   1  file[file.IW == file.IW.min()]
```
Out[9]:

	Symbol	Company Name	Index Weight	Last	Change	%Change	Volume	52 Week Range	IW
45	UNM	Unum Group	0.14%	21.4	0.0	0.00%	2.89 M	9.58 - 31.32	0.14

```
In [10]:   1  file[file.IW == file.IW.max()]
```
Out[10]:

	Symbol	Company Name	Index Weight	Last	Change	%Change	Volume	52 Week Range	IW
11	BRK.b	Berkshire Hathaway B	14.87%	230.07	-3.09	-1.33%	4.74 M	159.50 - 234.97	14.87

Figure 3-42. *Filtering companies with smallest and largest shares in the index*

One other method worth noting in the str module is contains(). The contains() method helps to search for substrings within the text. To illustrate, we will do a simple task. The majority of companies in the DataFrame have either Group or Corp words in their company names. Suppose our goal is to compare what would prevail in the XLF index, Group or Corp. To solve this task, we would need to filter the "Company Name" column first:

```
file["Company Name"].str.contains("Group")
```
and

```
file["Company Name"].str.contains("Corp")
```

These statements return True or False. As we did it before, we can apply them to the whole file object and then use the method count():

```
file[file["Company Name"].str.contains("Group")].count()
file[file["Company Name"].str.contains("Corp")].count()
```

The method count() adds up the number of rows in each column with the filtered condition. We can apply that filter not to the whole DataFrame but rather to one column Symbol:

```
file["Symbol"][file["Company Name"].str.contains("Group")].
count()
file["Symbol"][file["Company Name"].str.contains("Corp")].
count()
```

Apparently, financial companies prefer to use the Corp abbreviation in the name than Group as our analysis shows in Figure 3-43.

```
In [11]:    1  file["Symbol"][file["Company Name"].str.contains("Group")].count()
Out[11]: 11

In [12]:    1  file["Symbol"][file["Company Name"].str.contains("Corp")].count()
Out[12]: 16
```

Figure 3-43. *Filtering "Company Name" column by "Group" and "Corp" words*

The method contains() saves a lot of time and iteration. Using the toll bar | sign, we can replace the or operator and search for both Corp and Group instances at the same time:

```
file["Symbol"][file["Company Name"].str.
contains("Group|Corp")].count()
```

This statement will get us 27, the number of companies with Corp and Group words in the Company Name column.

All data sets require some sort of cleaning. The conversion of values to a numeric data type is relatively easy. Nonetheless, there are cases when you would need to compile a function to get the desired format of data.

The column "Value" contains the number of shares that changed hands for each stock in the index. If our goal is to know what the total turnover of all shares was in the index, we would need to convert the values in that column to a numeric type and use the sum method at the end. One obstacle is stopping from using the approach we did before on the "Index Weight" column. Some of the values are in thousands and have K at the end, and others are in millions and contain M. It would not be possible to just strip those letters and add up the numbers. This is a perfect case for lambda. Before we get to the lambda solution, I want to resolve that issue with a function.

We will define a function with a self-explanatory name str_to_num to take a string as an argument and return a number. Within the function, we will have if and else conditions. If the incoming string contains K, we would get rid of the letter, convert it to a numeric value, and multiply by a thousand. Otherwise, we will remove M and multiply it by a million.

```
def str_to_num( value ):
    if "K" in value:
        value = value.strip("K")
        number = float(value)
            number = number * 1000
        else:
        value = value.strip("M")
        number = float(value)
            number = number * 1000000
    return number
```

When I write my code, I always test every step of it. To make sure the function works, I'll invoke it with the first value from the Volume column:

```
str_to_num("5.55 M")
```

The function returns 5550000.0 (Figure 3-44).

```
In [14]:    1  def str_to_num(value):
            2      if "K" in value:
            3          value = value.strip("K")
            4          number = float(value)
            5          number = number * 1000
            6      else:
            7          value = value.strip("M")
            8          number = float(value)
            9          number = number * 1000000
           10      return number

In [15]:    1  str_to_num("5.55 M")
Out[15]:  5550000.0
```

Figure 3-44. *Testing the function str_to_num()*

The conversion of all values in the "Volume" column would require the method apply to loop through all rows and put into use the function str_to_num. The results will be saved in a new column under the "Vol_function" name:

```
file["Vol_function"] = file["Volume"].apply(str_to_num)
```

The same conversion operation could be achieved with lambda. To compare results of the conversion, I'll save the results received from lambda under "Vol_lambda". The lambda expression will have if and else conditions and follow all the steps we made in the str_to_num function.

I specifically broke down all the steps in the str_to_num function in Figure 3-44 so we can implement them in lambda step by step. First, we define value as an argument in lambda and then write the first part of the expression:

```
lambda value : float(value.strip("K"))*1000 if "K" in value
```

The lambda expression is mimicking the function. The order of operations is slightly different because we need to nest the functions. Before we multiply a number with 1000, we need to strip K. Of course, if K is the incoming string.

The second part of lambda's expression is conceptually the same. We do not need to check for M since the else condition means anything else besides K. Whatever is left after we lose M is converted to a float type and multiplied by 1,000,000:

```
else float(value.strip("M"))*1000000
```

The final lambda expression would be passed into the apply() method instead of the str_to_num function like this:

```
file["Vol_lambda"] = file["Volume"].apply(lambda value :
float(value.strip("K"))*1000 if "K" in value else float(value.
strip("M"))*1000000)
```

These two approaches to clean data and convert values to numeric types yield the same results. To prove that, I'll compare the sums of all values in Vol_function and Vol_lambda columns (Figure 3-45).

```
In [16]:  1  file["Vol_function"] = file["Volume"].apply(str_to_num)

In [17]:  1  file["Vol_lambda"] = file["Volume"].apply(lambda value:float(value.strip("K"))*1000 if "K" in value else float(v

In [18]:  1  file["Vol_function"].sum() == file["Vol_lambda"].sum()
Out[18]:  True

In [19]:  1  file.head()
Out[19]:
```

	Symbol	Company Name	Index Weight	Last	Change	%Change	Volume	52 Week Range	IW	Vol_function	Vol_lambda
0	AFL	AFLAC Inc	0.93%	42.86	-0.14	-0.33%	5.55 M	23.07 - 55.07	0.93	5550000.0	5550000.0
1	AIG	American Intl Group Inc	1.08%	38.55	0.13	+0.34%	6.27 M	16.07 - 56.42	1.08	6270000.0	6270000.0
2	AIZ	Assurant Inc	0.26%	135.62	-2.97	-2.14%	342.50 K	76.27 - 142.81	0.26	342500.0	342500.0
3	ALL	Allstate Corp	1.02%	100.07	0.70	+0.70%	2.52 M	64.13 - 125.92	1.02	2520000.0	2520000.0
4	AMP	Ameriprise Financial Inc	0.72%	183.33	-0.90	-0.49%	446.33 K	80.01 - 188.57	0.72	446330.0	446330.0

Figure 3-45. *Two methods to convert the column Volume values to a numeric type*

Which approach to use is up to you. The function would be my choice if I had to do something more sophisticated than if and else conditions. Lambda is a great choice to solve something on the fly. Another example illustrates that.

The "52 Week Range" column provides highest and lowest prices during the year. Suppose we need to get the difference between those numbers. Each value in the column comes as a string. I would split the string into two values and convert them to a numeric type. The results will be saved in two new columns "High" and "Low". Finally, I would get the difference by subtracting "Low" values from "High" values.

Beforehand we need to slice the column:

```
file["52 Week Range"]
```

The Series we have got as a result of slicing contains strings, and we can use one of str methods on it. Each value has a dash between highest and lowest prices. In the previous chapter, we used the split() method to separate strings by empty spaces; now we will use "-" as a separator:

```
file["52 Week Range"].str.split("-")
```

As a result of the operation, all values in the Series represent a Python list with two strings. We need to grab the first and second strings and to convert them into floats. It makes me think of indexing. The index location of the first value is 0, and the second value has an index location of 1. However, indexing would have to be performed on each list in the Series. That could be achieved with the method apply() and lambda():

```
file["Low"] = file["52 Week Range"].str.split("-").apply(
lambda value : float(value[0]))
```

```
file["High"] = file["52 Week Range"].str.split("-").apply(
lambda value : float(value[1]))
```

```
In [20]:  1  file["Low"] = file["52 Week Range"].str.split("-").apply( lambda value : float(value[0]))

In [21]:  1  file["High"] = file["52 Week Range"].str.split("-").apply( lambda value : float(value[1]))

In [22]:  1  file.head()
Out[22]:
```

	Symbol	Company Name	Index Weight	Last	Change	%Change	Volume	52 Week Range	IW	Vol_function	Vol_lambda	Low	High
0	AFL	AFLAC Inc	0.93%	42.86	-0.14	-0.33%	5.55 M	23.07 - 55.07	0.93	5550000.0	5550000.0	23.07	55.07
1	AIG	American Intl Group Inc	1.08%	38.55	0.13	+0.34%	6.27 M	16.07 - 56.42	1.08	6270000.0	6270000.0	16.07	56.42
2	AIZ	Assurant Inc	0.26%	135.62	-2.97	-2.14%	342.50 K	76.27 - 142.61	0.26	342500.0	342500.0	76.27	142.61
3	ALL	Allstate Corp	1.02%	100.07	0.70	+0.70%	2.52 M	64.13 - 125.92	1.02	2520000.0	2520000.0	64.13	125.92
4	AMP	Ameriprise Financial Inc	0.72%	183.33	-0.90	-0.49%	446.33 K	80.01 - 188.57	0.72	446330.0	446330.0	80.01	188.57

Figure 3-46. *Splitting 52 Week Range column values into Low and High columns*

Two columns "Low" and "High" were added to the DataFrame with numeric values (Figure 3-46). Finally, we can calculate the difference and subtract "Low" column values from "High" column values. The result will be saved under the new column name "Diff":

```
file["Diff"] = file["High"] - file["Low"]
```

The preceding examples proved that lambda() is an irreplicable tool in wrangling data. My advice would be to repeat the exercises again to fully comprehend and learn the syntax. Additionally, it would be a good idea to grab another data set and use the apply() method and lambda on a new data.

Combining Data Sets

There are two options on how you can combine data sets. The first one is a simple concatenation of two or more DataFrames together. The second option is merging data sets based on common values.

139

Concatenating Data Sets

We will start with concatenation. As always, we will begin a new exercise in a new file. Do not forget to import Pandas on the top of the file:

```
import pandas as pd
```

We will create two data sets to join. Each data set will contain information about wine. Data set one will have columns "Country" and "Price". This time, we will create a DataFrame out of two lists:

```
country_list = [ "US", "Italy", "France", "Spain"]
price_list = [13.99, 9.99, 12.99, 11.99]
```

These Python lists have to be added to each other with a built-in function `zip()`:

```
data_one = zip(country_list, price_list)
```

The function `zip()` returns an object that we can pass into the `pd.DataFrame()` function. Also, we need to provide column names for the DataFrame:

```
ds_one = pd.DataFrame(data=data_one, columns=["Country","Price"])
```

Data set two will have different columns – "Region" and "Variety":

```
region_list = ["Rioja", "Bordeaux", "Sicilia", "Napa"]
variety_list = ["Red Blend", "Merlot", "Primitivo", "Chardonnay"]
```

The function `zip()` always returns an object, and we will pass the returned object after zipping two Python lists together into the `pd.DataFrame()` function:

```
data_two = zip(region_list, variety_list)

ds_two = pd.DataFrame(data=data_two, columns=["Region",
"Variety"])
```

Now we have two DataFrames to concatenate (Figure 3-47).

In [1]:
```
1  import pandas as pd
```

In [2]:
```
1  country_list = ["US", "Italy", "France", "Spain"]
2  price_list = [13.99, 9.99, 12.99, 11.99]
3  data_one = zip(country_list, price_list)
4  ds_one = pd.DataFrame(data=data_one, columns=["Country","Price"])
5  ds_one
```

Out [2]:

	Country	Price
0	US	13.99
1	Italy	9.99
2	France	12.99
3	Spain	11.99

In [3]:
```
1  region_list = ["Rioja", "Bordeaux", "Sicilia", "Napa"]
2  variety_list = ["Red Blend", "Merlot", "Primitivo", "Chardonnay"]
3  data_two = zip(region_list, variety_list)
4  ds_two = pd.DataFrame(data=data_two, columns=["Region", "Variety"])
5  ds_two
```

Out [3]:

	Region	Variety
0	Rioja	Red Blend
1	Bordeaux	Merlot
2	Sicilia	Primitivo
3	Napa	Chardonnay

Figure 3-47. *Creating two DataFrames from the lists*

Pandas' function concat() joins DataFrames. The function concat() could concatenate more than two objects. If you want to join three or more objects, you would have to pass DataFrames in the form of a Python list. Before we proceed to concatenation, we need to decide how we would attach one to the other one vertically or horizontally. By default, the keyword argument axis in the concat() function is set to 0 or index. That means if we pass our data sets into concat(), it will put one on top of the other one (Figure 3-48):

```
new_ds = pd.concat([ds_one, ds_two])
```

```
In [5]:    1  new_ds = pd.concat([ds_one, ds_two])
           2  new_ds
```

Out[5]:

	Country	Price	Region	Variety
0	US	13.99	NaN	NaN
1	Italy	9.99	NaN	NaN
2	France	12.99	NaN	NaN
3	Spain	11.99	NaN	NaN
0	NaN	NaN	Rioja	Red Blend
1	NaN	NaN	Bordeaux	Merlot
2	NaN	NaN	Sicilia	Primitivo
3	NaN	NaN	Napa	Chardonnay

Figure 3-48. *The function concat() by default concatenates DataFrames vertically*

The new DataFrame object new_ds created as a result of concatenation turned up with NaNs, not a number, and overlapping values in the index. We do not have corresponding values and NaNs in the rows reflect that. I will explain how to deal with missing values later.

Duplicates in the index would be a problem going forward for the new data set. The concat() function comes with the ignore_index keyword, which is by default set to False. If you were sure that the new data set would have overlapping values, you could set ignore_index=True. This option would replace old indices with a brand-new index:

```
pd.concat([ds_one, ds_two],ignore_index=True)
```

I personally prefer another DataFrame method reset_index(). In the previous case, you lose the old index forever. With reset_index(), you have more flexibility and can save the original index with duplicates as a column. Run the help() function on the new_ds object, and you see the keyword argument drop:

```
help(new_ds.reset_index)
```

As you probably noticed by now, I use the help() function every time on every method or function. The Pandas libriary is being updated on a regular basis. Even if you know how to use a method or a function, it would be smart to check if anything has changed, comparing to the previous version. Besides, some methods take so many arguments that it is impossible to remember all of the options. The function help() will save you a lot of time googling.

The argument drop in the reset_index() method is set to the default value False. If we apply reset_index() as it is to a new_ds object, we will get a brand-new index, and the original one would become a column:

```
new_ds.reset_index(inplace=True)
```

The DataFrame new_ds was appended with a column index, and the new index contains unique values only (Figure 3-49). In my opinion, the drop keyword argument in the reset_index() feature gives more flexibility especially if you work with a sensitive data that cannot be obtained again.

```
In [11]:   1  new_ds
Out[11]:
```

	index	Country	Price	Region	Variety
0	0	US	13.99	NaN	NaN
1	1	Italy	9.99	NaN	NaN
2	2	France	12.99	NaN	NaN
3	3	Spain	11.99	NaN	NaN
4	0	NaN	NaN	Rioja	Red Blend
5	1	NaN	NaN	Bordeaux	Merlot
6	2	NaN	NaN	Sicilia	Primitivo
7	3	NaN	NaN	Napa	Chardonnay

Figure 3-49. *Resetting the index on a DataFrame with the drop argument set to False*

If we changed the drop argument to True in the reset_index() method as with ignore_index, we would have lost the original index forever. Now with old index values in the column, we could always go back to them by resetting the index if needed:

```
new_ds.index = new_ds["index"]
```

Do not confuse a DataFrame attribute index with the column "index".

Another way to concatenate ds_one and ds_two DataFrames would be along the columns. We need to switch the axis argument to 1 or "columns":

```
new_ds = pd.concat([ds_one, ds_two],axis=1)
```

This time, the new_ds DataFrame came with four columns and four rows (Figure 3-50).

```
In [7]:   1  new_ds = pd.concat([ds_one, ds_two], axis=1)
          2  new_ds
```

Out[7]:

	Country	Price	Region	Variety
0	US	13.99	Rioja	Red Blend
1	Italy	9.99	Bordeaux	Merlot
2	France	12.99	Sicilia	Primitivo
3	Spain	11.99	Napa	Chardonnay

Figure 3-50. *Concatenating two DataFrames with the axis argument set to columns*

The wine lovers who are reading this book probably noticed the mismatch between countries and wine-growing regions. Keep in mind that the function concat() just joins the data sets. If we need to match data, the best option would be the function merge().

Merging DataFrames

The Pandas function merge() combines DataFrames based on common values in the columns. For starters, we need to have columns with the same values. Let's add a new "Origin" column to ds_two with the following countries:

```
ds_two["Origin"] = ["Spain", "France", "Italy", "US"]
```

Now two DataFrames ds_one and ds_two have the column with the same values. Although in the ds_one DataFrame the column is called "Country" and in ds_two "Origin", we can merge them:

```
merged_ds = pd.merge(ds_one, ds_two,left_on="Country", right_
on="Origin")
```

We have merged two DataFrames by matching values in the "Country" and "Origin" columns (Figure 3-51).

```
In [8]:   1  ds_two["Origin"] = ["Spain", "France", "Italy", "US"]

In [10]:  1  merged_ds = pd.merge(ds_one, ds_two,left_on="Country", right_on="Origin")
          2  merged_ds

Out[10]:
```

	Country	Price	Region	Variety	Origin
0	US	13.99	Napa	Chardonnay	US
1	Italy	9.99	Sicilia	Primitivo	Italy
2	France	12.99	Bordeaux	Merlot	France
3	Spain	11.99	Rioja	Red Blend	Spain

Figure 3-51. *The function merge() matches values in Country and Origin columns*

By default, the function merge() looks for the same column name. If we had the "Country" column in both data sets, then it would merge them by the values of these columns. In that case, we would not need to provide left_on and right_on arguments using the merge() function.

I prefer to use `left_on` and `right_on` keyword arguments in the `merge()` function because you can be more specific. We definitely state that in `ds_one` we want to use the `"Country"` column to match values. The `left_on` argument is referring to the `ds_one` data set because position wise it is on the left in the function `merge()`. Logically, `right_on` is referring to a column in `ds_two` because it is on the right side of data sets' arguments. Also, if we had a couple of columns named the same in data sets, `merge()` would pick the first common column name to match the values. That might not be our plan, so I choose to be specific with columns.

Data sets can be merged by an index. Pandas gives us many options to solve the same with different functions and methods. We can still use the `merge()` function with keyword arguments `left_index` and `right_index` by an index. But there is a method `join()` that is initially merging data sets by matching values in the index. To show the `join()` method in action, we will reset the index in `ds_one` to the `"Country"` column and in `ds_two` to the `"Origin"` column:

```
ds_one.index = ds_one["Country"]
ds_two.index = ds_two["Origin"]
```

At the moment, two DataFrames have an index with the same values, and we can merge them with the help of the method `join()` which by default will match index values:

```
joined_ds = ds_one.join(ds_two)
```

The `joined_ds` DataFrame inherited the index from `ds_one` and matched it with indices of `ds_two` (Figure 3-52).

```
In [10]:    1  ds_one.index = ds_one["Country"]
            2  ds_two.index = ds_two["Origin"]
```

```
In [11]:    1  joined_ds = ds_one.join(ds_two)
            2  joined_ds
```

Out[11]:

	Country	Price	Region	Variety	Origin
Country					
US	US	13.99	Napa	Chardonnay	US
Italy	Italy	9.99	Sicilia	Primitivo	Italy
France	France	12.99	Bordeaux	Merlot	France
Spain	Spain	11.99	Rioja	Red Blend	Spain

Figure 3-52. Merging two DataFrames with the method join() by matching values in an index

Groupby

Groupby is one more essential tool of Pandas I want to discuss before we dive into a sea of practical challenges. The method groupby() is similar to sorting by functionality. If you have used relational databases, you should be familiar with the groupby functionality.

The groupby() method gives an option to regroup a DataFrame based on common values in one or more columns. It sorts values and uses them as new keys. The groupby() method always returns an object. Most of the time, it is used with aggregation methods as count, sum, and mean. It will make more sense if we use groupby in action.

We will take a data set with S&P 500 companies. I'll open the CSV file from an online location, https://bit.ly/booksp500, in a new file.

The S&P 500 index consists of 500 largest companies in the United States from 11 industries. After we read the data from the CSV file located online, the DataFrame we get should look like the one in Figure 3-53.

```
In [1]:    1  import pandas as pd
```

```
In [2]:    1  file = pd.read_csv("http://bit.ly/booksp500")
           2  file.head(10)
```

Out[2]:

	Symbol	Name	Sector
0	MMM	3M Company	Industrials
1	AOS	A.O. Smith Corp	Industrials
2	ABT	Abbott Laboratories	Health Care
3	ABBV	AbbVie Inc.	Health Care
4	ABMD	ABIOMED Inc	Health Care
5	ACN	Accenture plc	Information Technology
6	ATVI	Activision Blizzard	Communication Services
7	ADBE	Adobe Inc.	Information Technology
8	AAP	Advance Auto Parts	Consumer Discretionary
9	AMD	Advanced Micro Devices Inc	Information Technology

Figure 3-53. *DataFrame with S&P 500 companies from a CSV file*

The file DataFrame has three columns. The "Sector" column holds the industry name of a company.

Our goal is to sort all companies in the index by an industry. One option would be to filter by a sector and then count the number of rows. For example, if we wanted to know how many companies from a health-care sector are included in S&P 500, we would do

```
file[file.Sector.str.contains("Health Care")].count()
```

The method groupby() allows us to do the same but for all sectors within the "Sector" column at the same time. The column name is passed as an argument into the groupby() method in square brackets. Square brackets will allow us to pass more than one column into the method. Groupby() splits the DataFrame and reassembles it using values from the "Sector" column as keys or an index:

```
sector_data = file.groupby(["Sector"]).count()
```

Subsequently, the sector_data object has industries as an index. The method count() returned the number of all companies for each index value (Figure 3-54).

In [3]:
```
1  sector_data = file.groupby(["Sector"]).count()
2  sector_data
```

Out[3]:

Sector	Symbol	Name
Communication Services	26	26
Consumer Discretionary	61	61
Consumer Staples	33	33
Energy	26	26
Financials	66	66
Health Care	62	62
Industrials	73	73
Information Technology	71	71
Materials	28	28
Real Estate	31	31
Utilities	28	28

Figure 3-54. *Grouping by values from the Sector column*

As you can see, sector_data is stored as a new DataFrame. That gives us flexibility. We can reset the index, and Sector will be a column. On the other hand, we can plot this data.

Visualization is an important part of data analysis. One of the prominent visualization libraries in Python is Matplotlib. Some of the features of Matplotlib are built-in into a DataFrame. Built-in Matplotlib methods are stored in the plot module. You can see all available options by running the dir() function on the DataFrame:

```
dir(sector_data.plot)
```

The method pie() will help us to plot the number of companies in each S&P 500 sector (Figure 3-55). The column "Name" will be used as the values for a pie chart:

```
sector_data.plot.pie(y="Name", figsize(10,10))
```

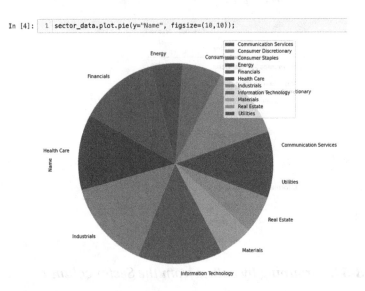

Figure 3-55. *The sector_data plot*

Summary

I think we have armed up with Python and Pandas enough to take on real-life challenges. We know how to initialize a DataFrame and read data from a CSV file. Filtering and lambda logical statements will help us to take some actions on if and else conditions. In the next chapter, we will use the methods we have learned to gather and manipulate data. In addition to Pandas, we will discover more libraries specifically designed to work with different data sources. Our goal is to gather information and analyze it.

CHAPTER 4

Gathering Data with Python

Information is an essential piece of data analysis. It comes from diverse sources in different formats. Some information requires a lot of effort to obtain; other data comes clean and structured. Python is a great tool to gather and manipulate any data in any format.

Programming has automated the tedious manual process of copying and pasting information from online sources to spreadsheets. In this chapter, we will discuss various approaches to gathering data. We will start with web scraping, the process of crawling websites and grabbing information. If information is out there and intended for public use, why not utilize it? Of course, all gathered data should be used solely in legal intentions.

Also, we will work with APIs. All big respected companies provide APIs to their services. Google and Twitter tech giants even have Python libraries to make developers' life easier. Some companies would charge for information; others would give it for free unless you want to make a commercial use out of it.

Numerous libraries to obtain data from online sources are one of the reasons why Python is so popular.

© Art Yudin 2021
A. Yudin, *Basic Python for Data Management, Finance, and Marketing*,
https://doi.org/10.1007/978-1-4842-7189-6_4

Web Scraping

Web scraping is a method of extracting data from websites. The process always starts with a first step – sending a request to a server and receiving the data as a response.

Usually, we use a browser to read the information from the Web. In the computer world, a browser is called a client. A client sends a request for information to a server. You enter a URL (Uniform Resource Locator) address on the top of the browser page, and it sends a message to a server requesting for information. Based on that request, the server would send back a message with data. The data comes as HTML (Hypertext Markup Language). A web browser interprets that information, and we see images and text with styles and colors.

When we scrape websites, Python acts as a client and sends a request to a server. Python does not understand HTML, and received data has to be converted into a string, the data type Python can naturally work with.

There are several Python packages to communicate with a server. In this book, we will use a very popular Requests library. A Requests method sends a request message to a server and handles the response. There is no need to download a Requests package because it is included in Anaconda.

For further examples, you would need a Google Chrome browser. Chrome comes with developer tools. All other browsers would require additional downloads to get developer tools. If you do not have a Chrome browser installed, download it from `www.google.com/chrome/`. Assuming that most of us already have Chrome installed, make sure you have a current version.

Before we get to the scraping part, I would like to explain the nuts and bolts of web scraping on the outdated site: `http://shakespeare.mit.edu/romeo_juliet/romeo_juliet.1.0.html`.

Open the link in a Chrome browser, and you'll see the web page looking like from the 1990s. No images or animation on the site, just plain text. That is exactly what we need to understand the main steps in the web scraping process.

First things first, we need to send a request to the server and fetch the website. This is where Python's Requests library comes in handy.

The Requests library has the method get() to request information from a server. If a request is successful, the server sends the information back with a success code 200. Otherwise, the server would send a message with different error codes like 403 or 404. You have probably seen a 404 error message before when the browser returns "page not found." You do not need to know all the codes to scrape data. Just keep in mind that code 200 means everything is OK. Any other code number would mean that something went wrong.

Getting along with the "Romeo and Juliet" page in a **Jupyter** cell, import the Requests library:

```
import requests
```

Sending a request to the server requires the method get() with the URL you are trying to fetch, like this:

```
page = requests.get("http://shakespeare.mit.edu/romeo_juliet/
romeo_juliet.1.0.html")
```

The method get() returned response 200, meaning that data was received (Figure 4-1).

```
In [1]:   1  import requests

In [2]:   1  page = requests.get("http://shakespeare.mit.edu/romeo_juliet/romeo_juliet.1.0.html")
          2  page

Out[2]:  <Response [200]>
```

Figure 4-1. *Sending a request and receiving a response with the requests.get() method*

The variable page holds a Python object. The returned Python object can be parsed as a string that would form a structure looking similar to an HTML markup. The most popular Python library to work with HTML is BeautifulSoup. The library name was inspired by the title of the poem in the *Alice in Wonderland* novel.

BeautifulSoup recreates all data received from a server as an HTML markup. Make no mistake, it will not be HTML, rather a string object looking like an HTML structure. BeautifulSoup also comes as a part of Anaconda, and all we have to do is import it along with Requests. Get back to the upper cell and import it right after Requests. Do not forget to rerun the cell.

```
from bs4 import BeautifulSoup
```

bs4 is the short name of the package, and BeautifulSoup is the function we will use to generate an object that would look like an HTML structure. Pass the content from a server as page.content into the function and parse it as HTML:

```
data = BeautifulSoup(page.content, "html.parser")
```

Print data and you will see an object that looks like HTML code (Figure 4-2).

```
In [1]:   1  import requests
          2  from bs4 import BeautifulSoup

In [2]:   1  page = requests.get("http://shakespeare.mit.edu/romeo_juliet/romeo_juliet.1.0.html")
          2  data = BeautifulSoup(page.content, "html.parser")
          3  data

Out[2]:   <!DOCTYPE HTML PUBLIC "-//W3C//DTD HTML 4.0 Transitional//EN"
          "http://www.w3.org/TR/REC-html40/loose.dtd">

          <html>
          <head>
          <title>PROLOGUE
          </title>
          <meta content="text/html; charset=utf-8" http-equiv="Content-Type"/>
          <link href="/shake.css" media="screen" rel="stylesheet" type="text/css"/>
          </head>
          <body bgcolor="#ffffff" text="#000000">
          <table bgcolor="#CCF6F6" width="100%">
          <tr><td align="center" class="play">Romeo and Juliet
          <tr><td align="center" class="nav">
          <a href="/Shakespeare">Shakespeare homepage</a>
            | <a href="/Shakespeare/romeo_juliet/">Romeo and Juliet</a>
            | Act 1, Prologue
          <br/>
          <a href="romeo_juliet.1.1.html">Next scene</a>
          </td></tr></td></tr></table>
          <h3>PROLOGUE</h3>
          <blockquote>
          <a name="1">Two hous Screenshot th alike in dignity,</a><br/>
```

Figure 4-2. *BeautifulSoup parsed data from a server as an HTML markup*

You do not need to be proficient in HTML to scrape the Web. Yet I'll give you a crash course. Every element rendered on a web page has to be wrapped in <> tags. In Figure 4-2 closer to the bottom, you can find <h3>PROLOGUE</h3>. h means heading and 3 is a font size. Flip back to the web browser, and you see the bold PROLOGUE header. Navigate to PROLOGUE with the mouse and highlight it. Then click the right button. I hope you use a Chrome browser as we agreed. In the context menu, you should see the Inspect option. Click Inspect and it will reveal how the web page looks under the hood, an HTML markup (Figure 4-3).

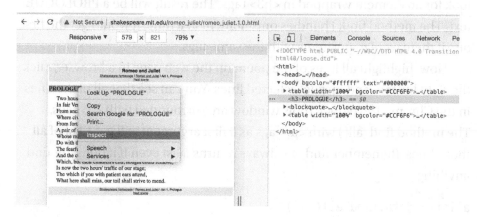

Figure 4-3. *Inspecting the HTML code of a web page in Chrome Developer Tools*

You can see that in Figures 4-2 and 4-3, <h3>PROLOGUE</h3> looks the same. That is because BeautifulSoup totally reconstructed the HTML markup structure of the web page. Each <> tag is an attribute of the BeautifulSoup object we saved with the data variable. That means we can grab elements from the page object by tags. Try to run data.h3 in a **Jupyter** cell, and you'll see a PROLOGUE text.

There are two major functions in BeautifulSoup to fetch elements out of the HTML structure – find() and find_all(). The difference is simple; find() looks for one element, and find_all() will fetch all items that fit the criteria. Run help on `find()` and `find_all()` to see all available arguments they accept:

```
help(data.find)
help(data.find_all)
```

Methods `find()` and `find_all()` take an HTML tag as an argument to find an element on a page. Other element attributes such as a class or a color could be used to precisely reference the item on a web page.

For example, run the statement data.find("h3"). The method find() will look for an element wrapped in <h3> tags. The result will be a PROLOGUE text. The method find() handles one element at a time; it would get the first one if there were many items with the same tags.

Now, highlight all lines of the poem on the web page in a browser, click the right button, and inspect selected lines. You can see that all of the lines in the Chrome Developer Tools window are surrounded with <a> tags. The method find_all() with <a> tags as a first argument will get a list of all those lines. Remember find_all always returns a list even if it does not find anything.

```
alist = data.find_all("a")
```

In Figure 4-4, you can see that we have fetched all the lines wrapped in <a> tags.

```
In [3]:   1  alist = data.find_all("a")
          2  alist
```

```
Out[3]:  [<a href="/Shakespeare">Shakespeare homepage</a>,
          <a href="/Shakespeare/romeo_juliet/">Romeo and Juliet</a>,
          <a href="romeo_juliet.1.1.html">Next scene</a>,
          <a name="1">Two households, both alike in dignity,</a>,
          <a name="2">In fair Verona, where we lay our scene,</a>,
          <a name="3">From ancient grudge break to new mutiny,</a>,
          <a name="4">Where civil blood makes civil hands unclean.</a>,
          <a name="5">From forth the fatal loins of these two foes</a>,
          <a name="6">A pair of star-cross'd lovers take their life;</a>,
          <a name="7">Whose misadventured piteous overthrows</a>,
          <a name="8">Do with their death bury their parents' strife.</a>,
          <a name="9">The fearful passage of their death-mark'd love,</a>,
          <a name="10">And the continuance of their parents' rage,</a>,
          <a name="11">Which, but their children's end, nought could remove,</a>,
          <a name="12">Is now the two hours' traffic of our stage;</a>,
          <a name="13">The which if you with patient ears attend,</a>,
          <a name="14">What here shall miss, our toil shall strive to mend.</a>,
          <a href="/Shakespeare">Shakespeare homepage</a>,
          <a href="/Shakespeare/romeo_juliet/">Romeo and Juliet</a>,
          <a href="romeo_juliet.1.1.html">Next scene</a>]
```

Figure 4-4.   *Text elements with HTML <a> tags*

The fetched lines in the list have <a> tags and href (Hypertext REFerence). We need to remove tags and other attributes off the text. In the BeautifulSoup library, there is a method get_text() to extract strings out of <> tags. We would need to apply it to each item in alist to get clean text.

```
for item in alist:
    print(item.get_text())
```

What if we need to grab a particular line from the web page? For instance, "From forth the fatal loins of these two foes" text from the whole poem. The first step would be to highlight the text and inspect it in HTML code (Figure 4-5).

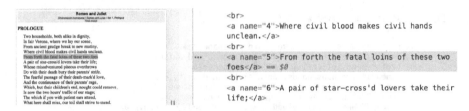

Figure 4-5. *Locating and inspecting a line from the text in Chrome*

The second step would be to investigate the element in Chrome Developer Tools, right side in Figure 4-5, and find the hooks we can use to fetch the text. The text `"From forth the fatal loins of these two foes"` is surrounded by `<a>` tags and has an attribute `name=5`. Again, we do not need to know what `name=5` means.[1] This is some attribute used for something by a developer who built the website. All we care is a combination that would be unique to the text we want to get. If we used just a tag in `find()`, then it would get us the first element wrapped in the `<a>` tags. Fortunately, `name=5` is unique to the line of the text we need. Using the `find()` method, we will pass the `<a>` tag as a first argument, because `"From forth the fatal loins of these two foes"` begins with it, and as a second argument, we will pass `name=5`. Attributes should be passed in the form of a dictionary like this:

```
element = data.find("a", {"name":5} )
```

```
In [4]:    1  element = data.find("a", {"name":5} )
           2  element.get_text()
```

Out[4]: 'From forth the fatal loins of these two foes'

Figure 4-6. *Getting the line of the text by using the find() method and HTML attributes*

---

[1] If you are curious what all these HTML tags mean, you'll find all of them here: `https://eastmanreference.com/complete-list-of-html-tags`

We have fetched the text and have cleaned it with the get_text() method (Figure 4-6).

As you have seen, the whole web scraping process in a nutshell consists of the following steps:

1. Get the data from a server with the Requests method get().

2. Pass the received data into the BeautifulSoup() function; it parses data as an object looking like an HTML web structure.

3. In a browser, inspect the element you need to grab.

4. Using find() or find_all(), fetch the text with hooks like tags and attributes.

Now that we have learned the essential steps of web scraping, we can take on a popular website investing.com. Investing.com provides important news that every trader needs to know before the trading day starts. The URL to the news page is www.investing.com/news/.

If you open that page in a browser, you can see news titles and short teasers. Click a title and it will take you to the full article. We will start collecting titles and hrefs (Hypertext REFerence) so we could access the full article later. Href is just a URL that leads somewhere. They are also called web links.

First things first, we need to fetch the website. Start with imports:

```
import requests
from bs4 import BeautifulSoup
```

Bear in mind that most of the websites do not want to provide information to the bots. The requests.get() method sends a message to a server, and the message kind of saying "Hi, I am Python", and the website does not want to respondse to Python bot. To go around it, we'll make our request for information look like it comes from a web browser. That is quite simple; all we have to do is to provide different headers in a message to a server:

```
headers={'User-agent' : 'Mozilla/5.0'}
```

Headers are passed into the requests.get() method as a keyword argument right after the URL. Mozilla/5.0 is a common browser token. When a server receives the message with a token in the header, it would accept it as a regular browser call for information. You can try to run the following statement with and without headers:

```
page = requests.get("https://www.investing.com/news/",
headers={'User-agent':'Mozilla/5.0'})
```

With headers, the requests.get() method returns response 200 (Figure 4-7).

```
In [1]:   1  import requests
          2  from bs4 import BeautifulSoup

In [2]:   1  page = requests.get("https://www.investing.com/news/", headers={'User-agent':'Mozilla/5.0'})
          2  page
Out[2]:  <Response [200]>
```

Figure 4-7. *Successful response from a server with the requests library*

The successful response can be parsed as a BeautifulSoup object:

```
data = BeautifulSoup(page.content, "html.parser")
```

Print data and see what's in there. A bit messy at first, there is a lot of JavaScript functions, but <!DOCTYPE HTML> clearly states that we deal with HTML (Figure 4-8). Keep in mind investing.com is a more sophisticated website than the one we have dealt before.

```
In [1]:    1  import requests
           2  from bs4 import BeautifulSoup

In [2]:    1  page = requests.get("https://www.investing.com/news/", headers={'User-agent':'Mozilla/5.0'})
           2  data = BeautifulSoup(page.content, "html.parser")

In [3]:    1  data

Out[3]:    <!DOCTYPE HTML>

           <html class="com" dir="ltr" geo="US" lang="en" xml:lang="en" xmlns="http://www.w3.org/1999/xhtml" xmlns:schema="http
           ://schema.org/">
           <head>
```

Figure 4-8. *Data received from a server parsed with the BeautifulSoup() function*

Flip back to the www.investing.com/news/ page in a browser. Choose any title you like, navigate the mouse on it, and click the right button. I have chosen "Oil Inventories Rose by 4M Barrels Last Week: API".

Click Inspect and it will reveal how the web page looks under the hood (Figure 4-9).

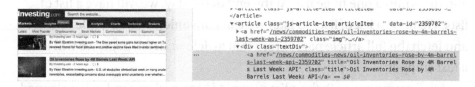

Figure 4-9. *Inspecting a title with Chrome Developer Tools*

Take a closer look at the highlighted HTML code, and you can see exactly the same title you have clicked. In my case, in Figure 4-9 it is "Oil Inventories Rose by 4M Barrels Last Week: API". This text is wrapped into <a></a> tags. An <a> tag means a web link, and right after it, we see the class="title" attribute. That looks like a unique combination. Our goal is to grab all titles and collect hrefs, which are also included into <a> tags. find_all() would be the right choice for collecting all titles on the web page. As a first argument, we will pass the <a> tag, and the second argument will be class="title". Also, we will need to include href=True to collect hrefs:

```
titles = data.find_all("a", class="title", href=True)
```

We have received all titles from the web page with hrefs (Figure 4-10).

```
In [3]:   1  titles = data.find_all("a", {"class":"title"}, href=True)
          2  titles
Out[3]:  [<a class="title" href="/news/stock-market-news/dow-futures-soar-330-pts-vaccines-hope-extends-rally-2359198" title=
          "Dow Futures Soar 330 Pts; Vaccines Hope Extends Rally">Dow Futures Soar 330 Pts; Vaccines Hope Extends Rally</a>,
           <a class="title" href="/news/stock-market-news/dow-climbs-on-renewed-stimulus-hopes-vaccine-news-2359581" title="Do
          w Climbs on Renewed Stimulus Hopes, Vaccine News">Dow Climbs on Renewed Stimulus Hopes, Vaccine News</a>,
           <a class="title" href="/news/commodities-news/oil-inventories-rose-by-4m-barrels-last-week-api-2359702" title="Oil
          Inventories Rose by 4M Barrels Last Week: API">Oil Inventories Rose by 4M Barrels Last Week: API</a>,
           <a class="title" href="/analysis/1-stock-to-buy-1-stock-to-dump-when-markets-open-docusign-nikola-200546174" title=
          "1 Stock To Buy, 1 To Dump When Markets Open: DocuSign, Nikola">1 Stock To Buy, 1 To Dump When Markets Open: DocuSig
          n, Nikola <span class="middle videoIconNew"> </span> </a>,
           <a class="title" href="/analysis/3-stocks-to-watch-in-the-coming-week-amazon-zoom-video-crowdstrike-200546166" titl
          e="3 Stocks To Watch In The Coming Week: Amazon, Zoom Video, CrowdStrike">3 Stocks To Watch In The Coming Week: Amaz
          on, Zoom Video, CrowdStrike</a>,
           <a class="title" href="/analysis/zoom-video-earnings-preview-explosive-growth-should-justify-600-stock-jump-2005462
          30" title="Zoom Video Earnings Preview: Explosive Growth Should Justify 600% Stock Jump">Zoom Video Earnings Preview
          : Explosive Growth Should Justify 600% Stock Jump</a>,
```

Figure 4-10. *The list of titles received with the find_all() method*

The variable titles holds a list, and we can go through item by item to get a clean text and extract href. Each title and corresponding href should be packed together as another list. Then we can place all lists with titles and hrefs into a one huge list. At the end of the day, we will have a list of lists. We need a list of lists so later we can conveniently grab a title and href and fetch the full article page. From that article or detail page, we will take a text snippet.

I will create a new Python list clean_titles and append to it a cleaned title and href packaged as a separate list under a variable small_list, like this:

```
clean_titles = [ ]

for item in titles:
    small_list = [item.get_text(), item["href"]]
        clean_titles.append(small_list)
```

The clean_titles list holds a bunch of small lists with a title and a URL to the full article (Figure 4-11).

```
In [4]:    1  clean_titles = []
           2
           3  for item in titles:
           4      small_list = [item.get_text(), item["href"]]
           5      clean_titles.append(small_list)
           6  clean_titles

Out[4]:  [['Dow Futures Soar 330 Pts; Vaccines Hope Extends Rally',
            '/news/stock-market-news/dow-futures-soar-330-pts-vaccines-hope-extends-rally-2359198'],
           ['Dow Climbs on Renewed Stimulus Hopes, Vaccine News',
            '/news/stock-market-news/dow-climbs-on-renewed-stimulus-hopes-vaccine-news-2359581'],
           ['Jobs, Mnuchin, Retail Results: 3 Things to Watch',
            '/news/stock-market-news/jobs-mnuchin-retail-results-3-things-to-watch-2359669'],
           ['1 Stock To Buy, 1 To Dump When Markets Open: DocuSign, Nikola \xa0 ',
            '/analysis/1-stock-to-buy-1-stock-to-dump-when-markets-open-docusign-nikola-200546174'],
           ['3 Stocks To Watch In The Coming Week: Amazon, Zoom Video, CrowdStrike',
            '/analysis/3-stocks-to-watch-in-the-coming-week-amazon-zoom-video-crowdstrike-200546166'],
           ['Zoom Video Earnings Preview: Explosive Growth Should Justify 600% Stock Jump',
            '/analysis/zoom-video-earnings-preview-explosive-growth-should-justify-600-stock-jump-200546230'],
           ['Asian stocks rise after vaccine optimism drives Wall Street to record highs',
            '/news/economy/asian-stocks-rise-after-vaccine-optimism-drives-wall-street-to-record-highs-2359797'],
           ['Oil Inventories Rose by 4M Barrels Last Week: API',
            '/news/commodities-news/oil-inventories-rose-by-4m-barrels-last-week-api-2359702'],
```

Figure 4-11. *List of lists with titles and hrefs*

Before we hit the URL for each title, we need to understand the HTML structure of a full article web page. Let's investigate further; in the browser, click any title and it should take you to a full article or, as web developers call it, a detail view.

On the full article page (Figure 4-12), I am clicking the first paragraph with the right mouse button and choosing the inspect option.

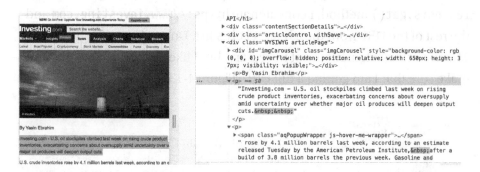

Figure 4-12. *Inspecting a full article web page in Chrome Developer Tools*

On the right part of my screen (Figure 4-12), I see that the whole article is enclosed with <p> tags, paragraphs. If we want to get the full article, we would need to use the find_all() method and use a <p> tag as an argument.

To get a paragraph of each article, we will create a small web crawler. We already have URLs for all articles, and we will have to hit page by page to grab a text snippet from each object. As we fetch a web page, we will parse the data with the BeautifulSoup() function and apply the find_all() method.

Using a for loop, we will iterate through the clean_titles list and fetch each URL with requests.get() pretty much like we did before:

```
for item in clean_titles:
    url = item[1]
    page = requests.get("https://www.investing.com{}".
    format(url), headers={'User-agent':'Mozilla/5.0'})
    print("now fetching", "https://www.investing.com{}".
    format(url))
```

Each item in clean_titles represents a list, and we need to extract the second element, URL, by indexing it item[1]. To fetch the article, we need to recreate a full URL beginning with https://www.investing.com. In the requests.get() method, I concatenate https://www.investing.com and the rest of the URL from the clean_titles list. Do not forget the headers. The last print statement is not necessary, but I like to see how it works and make sure that I am getting a full URL (Figure 4-13).

```
In [5]:    1  for item in clean_titles:
           2      url = item[1]
           3      page = requests.get("https://www.investing.com{}".format(url), headers={'User-agent':'Mozilla/5.0'})
           4      print("now fetching", "https://www.investing.com{}".format(url))

now fetching https://www.investing.com/news/stock-market-news/dow-futures-soar-330-pts-vaccines-hope-extends-rally-2
359198
now fetching https://www.investing.com/news/stock-market-news/jobs-mnuchin-retail-results-3-things-to-watch-2359669
now fetching https://www.investing.com/news/stock-market-news/dow-climbs-on-renewed-stimulus-hopes-vaccine-news-2359
581
now fetching https://www.investing.com/analysis/1-stock-to-buy-1-to-dump-when-markets-open-docusign-nikola-200546174
now fetching https://www.investing.com/analysis/3-stocks-to-watch-in-the-coming-week-amazon-zoom-video-crowdstrike-2
00546166
now fetching https://www.investing.com/analysis/zoom-video-earnings-preview-explosive-growth-should-justify-600-stoc
k-jump-200546230
now fetching https://www.investing.com/news/economy/asian-stocks-rise-after-vaccine-optimism-drives-wall-street-to-r
ecord-highs-2359797
now fetching https://www.investing.com/news/commodities-news/oil-prices-drop-on-us-stock-build-delay-in-opec-meeting
-2359828
now fetching https://www.investing.com/news/stock-market-news/salesforcecom-earnings-revenue-beat-in-q3-2359674
now fetching https://www.investing.com/news/stock-market-news/singapore-becomes-first-country-to-approve-sale-of-lab
grown-meat-2359882
```

Figure 4-13. *Calling a URL for each article*

In the scope of the `for` loop, we would need to use the `BeautifulSoup()` function on every page object. We will save the HTML structure of each article page under the variable name `article`. The last step is to apply `find_all()` with a `<p>` tag to the article object. The `find_all()` method returns a list, and we will save it under the `list_article` name.

Here, I would like to stop for a minute and introduce a concept that would save us some time going forward – list comprehension.

List Comprehensions

A list comprehension is a Python syntax that makes your code run faster. This is especially important when you deal with a huge amount of data. I prefer to use a list comprehension in gathering information when you have to scrape thousands of web pages.

Before we get to the list comprehension syntax, I would like you to do a simple exercise. Suppose we have a `alist` full of numbers. We want to filter it and find all 5s. Then we would need to save all 5s in a new list. Let's name it `blist`. The solution would be

```
alist = [1,2,3,5,5,5,6,7,5,5]
blist = []

for number in alist:
    if number == 5:
        blist.append(number)
```

We iterate through the list in search of 5. If we find 5, we add it to blist with a list method `append()`. The method `append()` is implemented in Python as a module, and it takes some time to call it every time we get 5. To make this code run faster, we can skip the `append()` method and rewrite the solution as a list comprehension. The same searching for 5s example would look like this:

```
blist = [ number for number in alist if number == 5 ]
```

The whole statement is wrapped in square brackets, and the result is returned as a list. That is why we no longer need the append() method. The outcome of a list comprehension statement is always a list type, and in our case it is saved as blist. A list comprehension would be roughly twice faster than using an append() method, and you could feel that on a list with more than 10,000 elements.

The syntax of a simple list comprehension consists of three parts: the for loop, filter, and expression. The filter is optional:

```
[ expression for loop filter ]
```

If you compare the first solution with the one done as the list comprehension, you will see that they are pretty much the same. The one in square brackets starts with an expression. In our case, the expression is a number itself, because we just want to keep a value if it is equal to 5. In some other cases, you might want to do something else, maybe multiply the number by 10 if the value is equal to 5. Then we use the same for loop, where the number variable is defined. The filter is an if statement. Sometimes you need it, sometimes not. In case an if statement is needed, you place it right after the for loop.

Let's consider another example; suppose we need to take all numbers in the alist container and multiply them by 10. In that case, we do not need a filter, and the list comprehension would look like this:

```
blist = [ number * 10 for number in alist ]
```

You need to remember that a list comprehension always returns a list data structure. You save that list by assigning a list comprehension statement to a variable.

Let's get back to our scraping example armed with a list comprehension syntax. Our final goal is to write a title and article snippet into a text file. To smooth the process, we will strip off <p> tags from all items in the list_article using a list comprehension [p.get_text() for p in list_article]. The result of this list comprehension would be a list of strings. To concatenate all strings, from the list, we will use a string method join(). I have noticed that the first <p> tags on each full article contain "No results matched your search". Since we grabbed all <p> tags, we have that message as a first item in list_article. We do not need it, and we will slice it off starting with the second element in list_article[1:].

We will do the whole cleaning and concatenation operation at the same time as

```
clean_article = " ".join([p.get_text() for p in list_
article[1:]).
```

clean_article will be a full article. At the end of the for loop, we will append each article as a string to mega_list:

```
mega_list = [ ]
for item in clean_titles:
    url = item[1]
    page = requests.get("https://www.investing.com{}".
    format(url), headers={'User-agent':'Mozilla/5.0'})
    print("now fetching", "https://www.investing.com{}".
    format(url))
      article = BeautifulSoup(page.content, "html.parser")
    list_article = article.find_all("p")
    clean_article = " ".join([p.get_text() for p in list_
    article])
    mega_list.append(clean_article)
```

In Figure 4-14, you can see the code in action and a small part of mega_list in Figure 4-15.

```
In [6]:    1  mega_list = [ ]
           2
           3  for item in clean_titles:
           4      url = item[1]
           5      page = requests.get("https://www.investing.com{}".format(url), headers={'User-agent':'Mozilla/5.0'})
           6      print("now fetching", "https://www.investing.com{}".format(url))
           7      article = BeautifulSoup(page.content, "html.parser")
           8      list_article = article.find_all("p")
           9      clean_article = " ".join([p.get_text() for p in list_article[1:]])
          10      mega_list.append(clean_article)
```

```
now fetching https://www.investing.com/news/stock-market-news/dow-futures-soar-330-pts-vaccines-hope-extends-rally-2
359198
now fetching https://www.investing.com/news/stock-market-news/jobs-mnuchin-retail-results-3-things-to-watch-2359669
now fetching https://www.investing.com/news/economy/powell--mnuchin-show-bitcoin-ath-stocks-at-new-highs--whats-up-i
n-markets-2359174
```

Figure 4-14. *Gathering articles from investing.com*

```
In [7]:    1  mega_list
```

```
Out[7]: ["By Peter Nurse\xa0\xa0\xa0 Investing.com – U.S. stocks are seen opening higher Tuesday, continuing November's reco
         rd-breaking gains, helped by the expected prompt delivery of Covid-19 vaccines and signs of a global economic recove
         ry.\xa0\xa0 At 7:05 AM ET (1205 GMT), the Dow Futures contract rose 330 points, or 1.1%, S&P 500 Futures traded 36 p
         oints, or 1%, higher, and Nasdaq 100 Futures climbed 91 points, or 0.8%.\xa0 The Dow Jones Industrial Average ended
         November almost 12% higher on the month, its best individual month since January 1987. The S&P 500 and Nasdaq Compos
         ite both gained around 11%. Earlier Tuesday, American pharmaceutical giant  Pfizer  (NYSE:PFE), and German partner B
         ioNtech, announced that they have applied to European authorities for authorization to rollout their Covid-19 vaccin
         e. This follows similar moves in the U.S. and the U.K. This adds to Monday's positive news from  Moderna  (NASDAQ:MR
         NA), with the biotech firm stating it was applying for U.S. and European emergency authorization for its vaccine can
         didate after full results from a late-stage study showed it was effective, with no serious safety concerns. The outl
         ook for the global economy is improving as vaccines emerge, the Organisation for Economic Cooperation and Developmen
         t said in its latest report, raising its view on growth this year to a contraction of 4.2%, from a drop of 4.5% at i
```

Figure 4-15. *Parsing and cleaning information for each article*

The final part is to create a report in a text format. We will use the function zip() to combine clean_titles and mega_list lists:

```
final_list = list(zip(clean_titles, mega_list))
```

Before we write the data into a text file, we will format it a bit and print just to make sure everything looks OK.

We can create a string template under a variable name TEMP:

```
TEMP = """

Title: {}

Snippet: {}

URL: {}

"""
```

This template will format nicely a title of an article; a short snippet, no longer than 300 letters from an article; and a URL in case we want to read the full article.

We will pass all this information into TEMP from the `final_list` container:

```
for item in final_list:
    title, url = item[0]
    url="https://www.investing.com{}".format(url)
    snippet = item[1][:300]
    print(TEMP.format( title, snippet, url))
```

The `final_list` list contains tuples with two lists. We are assigning two variable names to the first list from a tuple:

```
title, url = item[0]
```

To have a fully clickable URL, we will add `www.investing.com`:

```
url = https://www.investing.com{}.format(url)
```

Then slice the first 300 characters out of the second list. You can change the number based on how much of a snippet you want to see:

```
snippet = item[1][:300]
```

Finally, pass the variable into TEMP via the `format()` method (Figure 4-16).

```
In [8]:   1  final_list = list(zip(clean_titles, mega_list))
```

```
In [9]:   1  TEMP = """
          2
          3  Title: {}
          4
          5  Snippet: {}
          6
          7  URL: {}
          8
          9  """
         10
         11  for i in final_list:
         12      title, url = i[0]
         13      url = "https://www.investing.com{}".format(url)
         14      snippet = i[1][:300]
         15      print(TEMP.format(title,snippet,url))
```

Title: Dow Futures Soar 330 Pts; Vaccines Hope Extends Rally

Snippet: By Peter Nurse   Investing.com - U.S. stocks are seen opening higher Tuesday, continuing November's reco
rd-breaking gains, helped by the expected prompt delivery of Covid-19 vaccines and signs of a global economic reco
very.   At 7:05 AM ET (1205 GMT), the Dow Futures contract rose 330 points, or 1.

URL: https://www.investing.com/news/stock-market-news/dow-futures-soar-330-pts-vaccines-hope-extends-rally-2359198

Title: Jobs, Mnuchin, Retail Results: 3 Things to Watch

Snippet: By Christiana Sciaudone Investing.com -- Markets made a quick come back after a soft Monday as stimulus i
s back on our tongues and vaccines appear to be on the horizon. Europe's inching toward approving Pfizer (NYSE:P
FE) and Moderna (NASDAQ:MRNA) vaccines, which is good news as U.S. infections r

URL: https://www.investing.com/news/stock-market-news/jobs-mnuchin-retail-results-3-things-to-watch-2359669

Figure 4-16. *Formatting the text into a readable format with a template*

If it looks nice, we can write TEMP into a text file. For this task, we will initialize a new report object with the function open():

```
report = open("report.txt", "w")
```

Finally, we will pass TEMP.format(title, snippet, url) into the write() method:

```
for item in final_list:
    title, url = item[0]
    snippet = item[1][:300]
    print(TEMP.format( title, snippet, url))
    report.write(TEMP.format(title,snippet,url))
```

The final report.txt file should look like in Figure 4-17.

```
1
2
3  Title: Dow Futures Soar 330 Pts; Vaccines Hope Extends Rally
4
5  Snippet: By Peter Nurse    Investing.com - U.S. stocks are seen opening higher Tuesday, continuing November's record-breaking
   gains, helped by the expected prompt delivery of Covid-19 vaccines and signs of a global economic recovery.    At 7:05 AM ET
   (1205 GMT), the Dow Futures contract rose 330 points, or 1.
6
7  URL: https://www.investing.com/news/stock-market-news/dow-futures-soar-330-pts-vaccines-hope-extends-rally-2359198
8
9
10
11 Title: Jobs, Mnuchin, Retail Results: 3 Things to Watch
12
13 Snippet: By Christiana Sciaudone Investing.com -- Markets made a quick come back after a soft Monday as stimulus is back on our
   tongues and vaccines appear to be on the horizon. Europe's inching toward approving  Pfizer  (NYSE:PFE) and  Moderna
   (NASDAQ:MRNA) vaccines, which is good news as U.S. infections r
14
15 URL: https://www.investing.com/news/stock-market-news/jobs-mnuchin-retail-results-3-things-to-watch-2359669
16
17
18
19 Title: Powell & Mnuchin Show, Bitcoin ATH, Stocks at New Highs - What's up in Markets
20
21 Snippet: By Geoffrey Smith  Investing.com -- Congress hears testimony from Fed Chair Powell and Treasury chief Mnuchin for the
   first time since their spat over the Fed's crisis lending facilities. Zoom fails to match sky-high expectations but stocks are
   set to open at new highs anyway. Bitcoin hits an all-ti
22
23 URL: https://www.investing.com/news/economy/powell--mnuchin-show-bitcoin-ath-stocks-at-new-highs--whats-up-in-markets-2359174
24
25
```

Figure 4-17. *The final output of the web scraping operation is stored in a text file*

As you can see, the process of web scraping itself is not that complicated. I would say it is more time-consuming. You need to spend some time looking for the right tags and attributes to pull out an element.

Also, data cleaning takes some time. Keep in mind that websites get maintained, and developers rename attributes or change the website layout. If the developers of that site change a few things, the code will not be working, and we will have to start the whole process from scratch.

Web Scraping with Selenium

Modern websites heavily rely on JavaScript libraries that update information without reloading a web page. I do not want to get into web development because it is outside of the scope of the book. Simply put, some elements on a web page are generated on the user side, and the BeautifulSoup cannot pick them up. In those cases, we need to simulate a web browser experience with Selenium. Initially, Selenium was developed for web application testing purposes but quickly became a popular tool for automation and gathering data. Selenium features allow to simulate mouse and keyboard actions. You can write a script to flip over several pages with mouse clicks and entering information in online forms on web pages.

Unfortunately, Selenium does not come with Anaconda, and you need to install it separately. Selenium is a third-party library, and to install it, we need a package manager like PIP or Conda.

A Python package manager or PIP is a simple and reliable built-in aid to find and install Python libraries. Although PIP is a standard feature in the latest Python version, sometimes you need to launch it.

On Mac, you would need to search for a **Terminal** either in the search prompt or **Other** apps in **Launchpad**. Please do not use the **Terminal** window running Anaconda's Kernel. Make sure in the **Terminal** you open a brand-new window through a menu: **Terminal ➤ Shell ➤ New Window**.

In that new empty Terminal window, run the `pip --version` command to check the PIP version on your machine:

```
pip -- version
```

If for some reason it would get you an error message `"pip command not found"`, launch PIP with the following code:

```
sudo easy_install pip
```

The Sudo command will prompt you to enter a password for admin installation rights on the computer and will launch PIP. If `sudo easy_install pip` would not work, then open python.org/downloads and install Python from the official Python downloads page. Then repeat the `sudo easy_install pip` command again.

Windows users click the search prompt located in the left-bottom corner and type the name **CMD, command prompt**. The **CMD** abbreviation should get a command prompt window. To see whether you have PIP working or would require the PIP installation, run the

```
pip -- version
```

command in a command prompt. If you get a response with a version number, then you have PIP on your computer; otherwise, you would need to download the PIP module.

In the case that you get the "pip command not found" message, go to the official Python page (www.python.org/downloads) and download the latest version of Python. As you start the installation process, on the first screen mark the "Add Python 3.9 to PATH" option on the bottom (Figure 4-18). After the installation process finished, close and reopen the **CMD** prompt.

Figure 4-18. *Installation of Python and adding it to PATH on Windows*

Try the *pip -- version* command one more time. If the problem persists, download the get-pip.py[2] file. Usually, I would recommend saving the get-pip.py file to the Downloads folder. To install PIP from the get-pip.

---

[2]https://bootstrap.pypa.io/get-pip.py

py file, you would need to open a new **CMD** window and navigate to the Downloads directory with a **CMD** command cd, change directory:

```
cd Downloads
```

After you get into the Downloads directory, execute the get-pip.py file:

```
python get-pip.py
```

Now the *pip -- version* command should work, and you can install Python libraries with the pip install <package> statement. In some rare cases that the PIP command still raises an error message, refer to the official Python documentation at https://packaging.python.org/tutorials/installing-packages/.

Assuming PIP is in place, we are ready to install Python packages. To add third-party libraries to Anaconda, I would recommend opening a **Terminal** or **command prompt** directly from Anaconda Navigator.

Step 1. On the left-side menu in Anaconda Navigator, click **Environments** and navigate to **Base (root)**.

Step 2. Right next to **Base (root)** should be a **play** button.

Click that **play** button, and you will see a menu with **Open Terminal** as the first option.

Step 3. Launch a Terminal window by clicking **Open Terminal**. Right after that, a new Terminal window should pop up.

Step 4. In the **Terminal** window, run a PIP command to install Selenium or any other library:

```
pip install selenium
```

Besides installing Selenium itself, we would need to download a Chrome driver. Selenium can be used with any web browser. Due to its popularity and built-in developer tools, in this example we will be using a Chrome browser. Before downloading a driver, check what browser version you have installed on your machine. You can find this information in the

About Google Chrome section in the Chrome settings. We are interested in the first two digits of a long version number. Currently, I have the 87 Google Chrome version running on my Mac.

With this information in mind, find and download a driver for your operational system from `https://chromedriver.chromium.org/downloads`.

I would definitely recommend updating a Chrome browser if you can't find your Chrome browser version in the Current Releases section of the `https://chromedriver.chromium.org/downloads` page. A driver comes compressed as a zip file. Unzip it and save ChromeDriver to the same directory where your **Jupyter** Notebook or Python file is. Make sure you know where ChromeDriver is saved because you would need to provide the full relative PATH to it.

Introduction to Selenium

I would like to start the Selenium introduction with an amazon.com scraping example. We will open any product page on amazon.com and gather information about that product. Open a new **Jupyter** Notebook, and after importing Selenium, get it connected to ChromeDriver:

```
from selenium.webdriver import Chrome
```

I'll create a variable `driver_path` and assign the relative PATH to the ChromeDriver. `Chapter4` is a folder where I keep the **Jupyter** file alone with ChromeDriver, and `programwithus` is my home directory. Please note that the little `r` before the quotes might be required for some Windows users. It would be optional for Mac users. Also, Windows users would need to include the full file name with the extension .exe, like `chromedriver.exe`.

For Mac users

```
driver_path = "/Users/programwithus/Chapter4/chromedriver"
```

For Windows users

```
driver_path = r"/Users/programwithus/Chapter4/chromedriver.exe"
```

In the same cell, pass `driver_path` into the `Chrome()` function we have imported earlier from Selenium:

```
page = Chrome(executable_path=driver_path)
```

Run the cell, and the `Chrome()` function should launch a browser window with a note on top, "Chrome is being controlled by automated test software". Now the `page` variable holds an instance of the browser managed by Python code. In case you get a `FileNotFoundError` with a message `"chromedriver executable needs to be in PATH"`, check the `driver_path` and make sure it leads to the ChromeDriver file correctly.

If a browser window popped up, you are ready to scrape data. The scraping process itself will be similar to what we did earlier with BeautifulSoup. First, we need to fetch the website. The `page` variable will hold the Python Selenium object. Then find the hooks for HTML elements in the Selenium object. Only this time the Selenium `Chrome()` function will replace the `requests.get()` method and the `BeautifulSoup()` function.

Navigate to amazon.com and choose any product you like. I have chosen the Ring Video Doorbell. You can see it here: `www.amazon.com/dp/B08N5NQ869`.

You can choose any product on amazon.com for this example. Usually, the Amazon URL is much longer than `www.amazon.com/dp/B08N5NQ869`. Amazon and other big companies collect a lot of marketing information about their customers – information such as the region, browser, and timezone the request is coming from – and add it to a URL after the ? sign. These additional parameters after the ? sign are not important for us and can be removed. In short, any product sold on Amazon would have an ASIN number, a unique identifier. The ASIN number is the part of a product URL that comes after `/dp/`.

As a matter of fact, any URL usually contains some kind of unique identifier either as a numeric ID or a slug. A slug is a distinctive part of a URL referring to a particular piece of information. For example, the www. cnn.com/style/article/new-years-eve-ball-design-history/index. html URL has a new-years-eve-ball-design-history slug that is unique and leads to the "A brief history of the Times Square New Year's Eve ball drop" article on cnn.com. So, if you are trying to fetch a web page, spend a couple of minutes understanding a URL pattern of the website you want to grab information from.

On Amazon, all products are stored in a database under ASIN and can be accessed by www.amazon.com/bp/ plus ASIN. Anything else in the Amazon URL is optional parameters.

Sending a request to the Amazon server for the www.amazon.com/dp/ B08N5NQ869 URL would require the Selenium method get():

```
page.get("https://www.amazon.com/dp/B08N5NQ869")
```

The method get() will launch a browser window and return an instance of the Ring Video Doorbell web page (Figure 4-19).

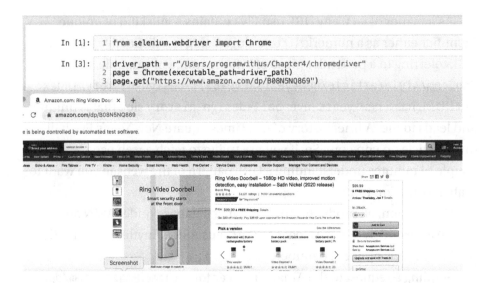

```
In [1]:    1  from selenium.webdriver import Chrome

In [3]:    1  driver_path = r"/Users/programwithus/Chapter4/chromedriver"
           2  page = Chrome(executable_path=driver_path)
           3  page.get("https://www.amazon.com/dp/B08N5NQ869")
```

Figure 4-19. *Selenium has taken a control over a Chrome browser and opened a product page*

Suppose we want to gather the product name and the price from the page. The routine to find HTML hooks will be the same as we did before. Navigate to the product name, click the right button on a mouse, and inspect the element in Chrome Developer Tools.

As you can see in Figure 4-20, the product name in Chrome Developer Tools fully matches the title on a page.

Figure 4-20. *Examining a web page element with Chrome Developer Tools*

If for some reason you cannot see the title highlighted in your browser, click the text inspect one more time.

We need to choose an HTML tag to grab the element by. As in the previous example, we can get an HTML element by the class. However, I think that the `"a-size-large"` class (Figure 4-20) might be used somewhere else on that page. The Id attribute would be a better choice because id is unique. `"productTitle"` id cannot be used again in HTML code on the same page. To fetch the title by id, we would need to use the Selenium method `find_element_by_id()`. You can find all available the Selenium locating elements methods either by going to the documentation[3] or running the `dir()` function on the object stored under the page variable:

```
dir(page)
```

The `find_element_by_id()` method is easy to use. All you have to do is to pass the element's id attribute. Selenium locating elements methods return objects, and converting them to strings requires a `text` method.

---

[3] `https://selenium-python.readthedocs.io/locating-elements.html`

In the same cell, create the variable `title` to hold a product name, and using the `find_element_by_id()` method, fetch the information:

```
title = page.find_element_by_id("productTitle")
title = title.text
print(title)
```

The same process can be used to grab the price of a product. If we point on the price and inspect it, we will see that Amazon uses "priceblock_ourprice" `id` for a $99.99 value. Take into account that if you are expecting a different product page on Amazon, there might be another `id` attribute for a price. Based on my research, they also use `"priceblock_dealerprice"`.

In the same cell, I'll get the price for the product. This time, I'll chain a text method to `page.find_element_by_id()`:

```
price = page.find_element_by_id("priceblock_ourprice").text
print(title, price)
```

By now, you probably have two or three Chrome browsers opened. The method `close()` after we get the looked-for information will shut down a browser.

In Figure 4-21, you can see the name and price for a product we fetched.

```
In [1]:   1  from selenium.webdriver import Chrome

In [4]:   1  driver_path = r"/Users/programwithus/Chapter4/chromedriver"
          2  page = Chrome(executable_path=driver_path)
          3  page.get("https://www.amazon.com/dp/B08N5NQ869")
          4  title = page.find_element_by_id("productTitle")
          5  title = title.text
          6  price = page.find_element_by_id("priceblock_ourprice").text
          7  print(title, price)
          8  page.close()

Ring Video Doorbell — 1080p HD video, improved motion detection, easy installation — Sat
in Nickel (2020 release) $99.99
```

Figure 4-21. *Fetching the name and price of a product from amazon.com*

Selenium is a truly automation solution. Besides grabbing data from HTML, you can fill web forms and imitate mouse clicks. Let's consider an example of gathering information on all Ring Video Doorbells available on Amazon. Our first step would be to find all ASIN numbers in the category.

On the top of the Amazon page, there is a search prompt. We can program Selenium to insert a name of a product we are interested in and submit the search. In order to do that, we would need to use the Selenium module Keys. The Keys module implements all major keyboard functions.

Import the Keys module right under the Selenium Chrome function in the upper cell and rerun the cell:

```
from selenium.webdriver import Chrome
from selenium.webdriver.common.keys import Keys
```

In the next cell, comment out for now title and price statements and replace the product URL we have been using with the www.amazon.com Amazon landing page, like in Figure 4-22.

```
In [1]:   1  from selenium.webdriver import Chrome
          2  from selenium.webdriver.common.keys import Keys

In [2]:   1  chromedriver = r"/Users/programwithus/Chapter4/chromedriver"
          2  page = Chrome(executable_path=chromedriver)
          3  page.get("https://www.amazon.com")
          4  # title = page.find_element_by_id("productTitle")
          5  # title = title.text
          6  # price = page.find_element_by_id("priceblock_ourprice").text
          7  # print(title, price)
          8  page.close()
```

Figure 4-22. *Preparing a Selenium setup to enter values in the input prompt on web pages*

Before we will fill in a search prompt with a desired product name, we will need to locate the input in HTML code. Open www.amazon.com in a web browser, navigate the mouse on the text box, and click with a right button to inspect the element. Locate the text box attribute we could use to grab the element in HTML. I think id="twotabsearchtextbox" would be perfect to capture a text box (Figure 4-23).

Figure 4-23. *Inspecting web page elements in Chrome Developer Tools*

After we have managed to locate the input box in HTML, using the method send_keys() we can pass any text into that box:

```
prompt = page.find_element_by_id("twotabsearchtextbox")
prompt.send_keys("ring video doorbell")
```

Try the code and make sure it fills out the search prompt.

If everything works correctly, we can click the submit button of the form with an ENTER key:

```
prompt.send_keys(Keys.ENTER)
```

Keys.ENTER will mimic the return button action on a keyboard, and the search action will be triggered.

In Figure 4-24, you can see that we have managed to enter a name of the product into the input box and received all available products in that category. The Ring Video Doorbells are listed on a different web page.

Figure 4-24. *Running a Selenium script to find products by a category name*

A new web page means the whole inspection routine starts again. To gather information on all available Ring Video Doorbells, we need to collect all ASIN product numbers from the page, so later we could pull them one by one. Highlight an item on the page and try to figure out how to grab the ASIN number. Apparently, each item is wrapped into `<div>` tags, a generic HTML container, with a `data-asin` attribute (Figure 4-25). The `data-asin` attribute holds the ASIN number for a product within the `<div>` container. You might ask if we necessarily need to use a `data-asin` attribute or there is another way to capture an element. Probably there is another way to pull out a desired element. I encourage you to experiment. The `data-asin` attribute is unique to this particular example. In other cases, on different web pages, there will be other attributes or HTML tags. Also, in the future Amazon developers might replace the `data-asin` attribute with something else. That is why inspection is an essential part of the web scraping process. Web scraping is all about investigating and finding HTML hooks that would help you to grab elements. It took me a couple minutes to realize that in our case `data-asin` would work to get ASIN from the page.

Figure 4-25. *Inspecting a div container with a product information in Chrome Developer Tools*

Capturing the `data-asin` attribute directly is not an easy task. The solution would be to get the whole `<div>` container of each product on the page and then extract the value of the `data-asin` attribute. The task is getting more complicated; the `<div>` container we need to fetch has no unique `id` (Figure 4-24), and we will need to use another Selenium method. Run the `dir()` function on the `page` object, and there in the list of all methods, you should see the `find_elements_by_class_name()` method. With the `find_elements_by_class_name()` help, we could get a hold of all `<div>` containers with the class `"s-result-item"` (Figure 4-25) for all products on the page:

```
asin_numbers = page.find_elements_by_class_name("s-result-
item")
```

The find_elements_by_class_name() method returns a list of Selenium elements stored under the asin_numbers variable. You could either convert them to strings by applying a text method:

```
rings = [item.text for item in asin_numbers]
```

or extract data-asin attributes, like this:

```
asin_list = [item.get_attribute('data-asin') for item in asin_
numbers]
print(asin_list)
```

After we used get_attribute('data-asin'), we have all ASIN numbers from that page stored in asin_list (Figure 4-26). Containers with no data-asin attribute returned empty strings ' '. That is OK; we will deal with empty values later.

```
In [1]:    1  from selenium.webdriver import Chrome
           2  from selenium.webdriver.common.keys import Keys

In [2]:    1  chromedriver = r"/Users/programwithus/Chapter4/chromedriver"
           2  page = Chrome(executable_path=chromedriver)
           3  page.get("https://www.amazon.com")
           4  prompt = page.find_element_by_id("twotabsearchtextbox")
           5  prompt.send_keys("ring video doorbell")
           6  prompt.send_keys(Keys.ENTER)
           7  asin_numbers = page.find_elements_by_class_name("s-result-item")
           8  rings = [item.text for item in asin_numbers]
           9  asin_list = [item.get_attribute('data-asin') for item in asin_numbers]
          10  print(asin_list)
          11
          12  # title = page.find_element_by_id("productTitle")
          13  # title = title.text
          14  # price = page.find_element_by_id("priceblock_ourprice").text
          15  # print(title, price)
          16  # page.close()
```

```
['B08N5NQ69J', 'B0849J7W5X', 'B07GG3XXNX', '', '', 'B07GTHT6QP', 'B085VHPH8P', 'B01DM6BD
A4', 'B0842BYVSY', 'B085DVTYHN', 'B07NZ28XZP', 'B086F24DK9', 'B072QLXK2T', 'B07N9WW7CG',
'B08PL9YFBY', 'B08F1DYRBM', 'B07X134Z5Y', 'B082XG5LR8', 'B01N9EX0YR', 'B00TZA09D0', 'B07
WHMQNPC', 'B083Y92DG4', 'B085DVTYHN', 'B07ZJS3L5Y', '', '', '']
```

Figure 4-26. *Fetching ASIN numbers for all products on the web page*

After we collected ASIN numbers for Ring Video Doorbells, we can fetch the details on each one of them and store information into a CSV file.

Python comes with a CSV module for working with CSV files. We will use it to write gathered information into a CSV file. Since CSV is a built-in module, there is no need to download and install it. But we still need to import it in the upper cell:

```
import csv
```

To get details on each Ring Video Doorbell in our list, we will need to fetch a product page and grab the title and price from each page. Also, we will collect the description details from each product page.

We have managed to get the title and price of a product before. Now we need to inspect the bullet points on www.amazon.com/dp/B08N5NQ869 to grab the product details. It looks like all bullet points located in the `<div>` container with `id="feature-bullets"`. Using the familiar Selenium method `find_element_by_id()`, we will grab them.

It is time to piece all statements together. We will assemble a small crawler that will gather information on products from finding them on Amazon to saving data. I'll go step by step and then post the whole solution.

We have left off on a list full of ASIN numbers. We will iterate through the list and append each ASIN number to the www.amazon.com/dp/ URL to fetch an Amazon product page. In real life while web scraping for information, many things could go wrong. The Wi-Fi might be out, or Amazon discontinued to support a product. In addition, some elements might return no values, like empty strings we have in the `asin_list`. Any of these issues might break our code down. That will interrupt the whole process, and because of one or two bad URLs or pages, we will not get others. That is very disappointing when you are trying to hit thousands of pages, and one small thing cease the running code. To avoid that and keep executing the code even if we get the obstacles along the way, we would wrap each statement into `try` and `except` blocks.

Exception handling is a great way to avoid stopping after Python code returns an error message. Let me explain exception handling on our Amazon example:

```
for number in asin_list:
    try:
        page.get("https://www.amazon.com/dp/{}".format(number))
        print("fetching {}".format(number))
    except:
        print("could not get the page for {}".format(number))
```

In the code, we loop through all collected ASIN numbers within asin_list and pass each unique number into the string method format() to append it to the Amazon URL. The Selenium page.get() method will try to pull each product page from the server. If an Amazon server returns a valid response, the variable page would save it, and we could parse elements out of the Selenium object. However, if the URL was broken or server was not responding for some reason, instead of getting an error message and stopping, the code would jump to except block and print "Could not get the page for some ASIN".

If a statement in the try block fails, the except block will prevent an error. After all statements in the except block are executed, Python will continue its normal course within the for loop. In the preceding example, it will try to fetch the next web page in asin_list.

Try and except blocks are a very popular way to avoid crashing the code. Very often, they are used to capture error messages, so later you can take a close look at what went wrong. Sometimes, professional developers would place a function in an except block to send them a message with an exception to quickly address an issue.

Also, within the for loop, we will define an empty list. We would need it to store all scraped information for a product. In case we hit a page with missing data for title and price, we would define them as None:

```
for number in asin_list:
    data = []
    title = None
    price = None
    try:
        page.get("https://www.amazon.com/dp/{}".format(number))
        print("fetching {}".format(number))
    except:
        print("could not get the page for {}".format(number))
```

Next, we will try to get a product title; if there is no id=" productTitle" on a page, the except block would print "productTitle is not there".

```
try:
    title = page.find_element_by_id("productTitle").text
except:
    print("productTitle is not there")
```

As I have mentioned before, the price element is a little bit tricky. Amazon uses different id attributes for the price element. I have located id=" priceblock_ourprice" and id=" priceblock_dealprice". In case the product is sold out and the product page says "Currently unavailable", there will be no price element at all. That is the case where price would be set to None.

```
try:
    price = page.find_element_by_id("priceblock_ourprice").text
except:
    print("priceblock_ourprice is not there")
```

```
try:
    price = page.find_element_by_id("priceblock_dealprice").text
except:
    print("priceblock_dealprice is not there")
```

The results for the product title and price should be added to the data list:

```
data.extend([title,price])
```

The product description from the bullet points would be grabbed by id= "feature-bullets" and saved into bullets_list by a new line. bullets_list values would extend the same data list:

```
try:
    bullets = page.find_element_by_id("feature-bullets").text
    bullets_list = bullets.split("\n")
    data.extend(bullets_list)
except:
    print("feature-bullets id is not there")
```

At the end, we will write a data list into a CSV file. Go back up, and using the function open(), define a file object. A CSV module comes with a write() method that would insert a data list as a row into the amazon-results file:

```
csv_file = open("amazon-results.csv", 'w')
writer = csv.writer(csv_file)
```

Since some of the pages produced no results before we write data into the file, check if the first element is not None. If the data list contains information, then we would add it as a row to the amazon-results.CSV file. The following if block should be placed into the scope of the for loop:

```
if data[0] != None:
        writer.writerow(data)
```

Finally, outside of the `for` loop, we need to save the file object and close the browser window:

```
csv_file.close()
page.close()
```

At the end of the day, the code will generate the amazon-results.CSV file saved in the same directory where the current **Jupyter** Notebook is. Each product would be written in a separate row and details separated by a comma. In Figure 4-27, you can see the amazon-results.CSV opened in Excel.

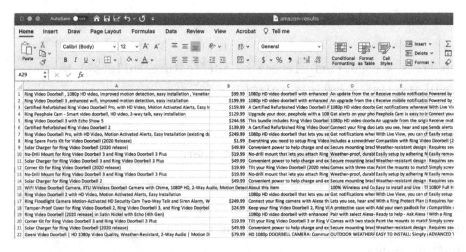

Figure 4-27. *Saving the results in an Excel file*

As I promised here, you can see the full solution for the Amazon example done with Selenium:

```
#importing packages
from selenium.webdriver import Chrome
from selenium.webdriver.common.keys import Keys
import csv
```

```
#initiating a csv file
csv_file = open("amazon-results.csv", 'w')
writer = csv.writer(csv_file)

#ChromeDriver PATH
chromedriver = r"/Users/programwithus/Chapter4/chromedriver"
page = Chrome(executable_path=chromedriver)

#openning amazon.com and gathering ASIN numbers for Ring
doorbells
page.get("https://www.amazon.com")
prompt = page.find_element_by_id("twotabsearchtextbox")
prompt.send_keys("ring video doorbell")
prompt.send_keys(Keys.ENTER)
asin_numbers = page.find_elements_by_class_name("s-result-item")
rings = [item.text for item in asin_numbers]
asin_list = [item.get_attribute('data-asin') for item in asin_
numbers]

#fetching details for each product and writing it into amazon-
results.csv
for number in asin_list:
    data = []
    title = None
    price = None
    try:
        page.get("https://www.amazon.com/dp/{}".format(number))
        print("fetching {}".format(number))
    except:
        print("could not get the page for {}".format(number))
    try:
        title = page.find_element_by_id("productTitle").text
```

```
    except:
        print("productTitle is not there")
    try:
        price = page.find_element_by_id("priceblock_ourprice").
text
    except:
        print("priceblock_ourprice is not there")
    try:
        price = page.find_element_by_id("priceblock_
        dealprice").text
    except:
        print("priceblock_dealprice is not there")
    data.extend([title,price])
    try:
        bullets = page.find_element_by_id("feature-bullets").
text
        bullets_list = bullets.split("\n")
        data.extend(bullets_list)
    except:
        print("feature-bullets id is not there")
    if data[0] != None:
        writer.writerow(data)

#saving file and closing browser
csv_file.close()
page.close()
```

Working with APIs

So far, we have been working with HTML web pages. I have mentioned at the beginning of the chapter a relationship between a client/browser and a server. A browser receives HTML and presents it as images and styled text.

We are humans and want to see information presented in a nice colorful way. There are other clients that do not need to see images and colors. I am talking about devices. A device sending a request to a server also would be a client. For example, these days you can get a fridge that would place an order with a grocery store for delivery if you run out of milk. Another example would be a smartphone exchanging Facebook messages or a car receiving weather updates from a server. These devices need data in a simple format with no styles and colors. The data format they consume is JSON (JavaScript Object Notation) that comes as a string. Servers may send data as HTML or JSON based on a requesting client.

Usually, JSON comes from an API (Application Programming Interface), an interface specifically designed to communicate with computer applications or devices.

If your work is to analyze financial data, then you can subscribe for the Bloomberg API. On the other hand, if you are in a digital marketing and need to receive information from Google Analytics, you would use the Google Analytics Reporting API. As a matter of fact, Google even has a Python library to help developers get connected to their APIs and access all Google applications. We will work with them later in the book.

All APIs are designed differently, and most of the time companies have developer documentation explaining how to use them and how to get authenticated. Some of the APIs are free; others require a subscription.

Here, we will take a look at a very popular source of financial data, Alpha Vantage. In the following example, I'll explain to you the main principles of working with APIs.

All API providers require some sort of authentication, and Alpha Vantage is no excuse of the rule. Compared to other API services, it is very easy to get an API Key at `www.alphavantage.co/support/#api-key`. You need to answer two simple questions and provide your email address. Make sure you get your own API Key because the one I use here will expire. After a successful registration, you should see the message:

Welcome to Alpha Vantage! Your API key is: ZIIROPRQCMEREHR8.
Please record this API key at a safe place for future data
access.

The API Key acts as a user id and a password at the same time. The API
Key's job is to authenticate a person or device requesting the information.
Also, if it is a paid service, make sure that the account is current.

Getting acquainted with any API should begin with the developer
documentation of the API provider. We are new to Alpha Vantage
services, and it would be smart to start with www.alphavantage.co/
documentation/.

Alpha Vantage provides several APIs to get stock prices, companies'
fundamental data, forex, cryptocurrencies, and technical indicators. We'll
use the TIME_SERIES_DAILY_ADJUSTED API to fetch historic daily prices for
stocks.

The demo URL looks like this:

```
https://www.alphavantage.co/query?function=TIME_SERIES_DAILY_AD
JUSTED&symbol=IBM&apikey=demo
```

Open the reference in a browser, and you will see JSON data that
contains open, high, low, and close values for IBM stock. If you take a
closer look, you'll see that JSON reminds a Python dictionary data type.

The demo URL gives us a good understanding of how to use it. An
IBM value in the API endpoint could be replaced with any other symbol
of a stock we want to get historic prices. In the apikey=demo argument, the
demo should be changed to an API Key you have obtained.

Using a time series API, we will get historic prices for AAPL and store
them as a DataFrame. In a new **Jupyter** file, import two libraries we would
need for this example, Requests and Pandas:

```
import requests
import pandas as pd
```

We need to define the API Key as a string, a URL for the API, and a stock we want to get:

```
API_Key = "ZIIROPRQCMEREHR8"
url = "https://www.alphavantage.co/query?function=TIME_SERIES_
DAILY_ADJUSTED&symbol={}&apikey={}"

stock = "AAPL"
```

In the URL, I have replaced the IBM symbol and demo with {}; later, we will insert our own values into them with the format() method.

For starters, we need to send a request to a server with the requests. get() method. We will pass "AAPL" with the stock variable and API_Key we have defined. The Python string method format() makes the code cleaner, and it would be easy to replace "AAPL" with any other symbol down the road:

```
data = requests.get(url.format(stock, API_Key))
```

Run the code and data will return response 200, meaning that everything is OK, and we got the information from the API. As I have mentioned before, the Python library Requests supports different data types, and since the API serves JSON, we would use the method json() to extract the values. You can just chain json() to requests.get():

```
data = requests.get(url.format(stock, API_Key)).json()
```

Finally, the data we have received from the Alpha Vantage API looks like in Figure 4-28.

```
In [1]:    1  import requests
           2  import pandas as pd
```

```
In [2]:    1  API_Key = "ZIIROPRQCMEREHR8"
           2
           3  url = "https://www.alphavantage.co/query?function=TIME_SERIES_DAILY_ADJUSTED&symbol={}&apikey={}"
           4  stock = "AAPL"
           5
           6  data = requests.get(url.format(stock, API_Key)).json()
           7  data
```

```
Out[2]:  {'Meta Data': {'1. Information': 'Daily Time Series with Splits and Dividend Events',
           '2. Symbol': 'AAPL',
           '3. Last Refreshed': '2021-01-08',
           '4. Output Size': 'Compact',
           '5. Time Zone': 'US/Eastern'},
          'Time Series (Daily)': {'2021-01-08': {'1. open': '132.43',
           '2. high': '132.63',
           '3. low': '130.23',
           '4. close': '132.05',
           '5. adjusted close': '132.05',
           '6. volume': '105158245',
           '7. dividend amount': '0.0000',
           '8. split coefficient': '1.0'},
          '2021-01-07': {'1. open': '128.36',
           '2. high': '131.63',
           '3. low': '127.86',
           '4. close': '130.92',
```

Figure 4-28. *Receiving data from an API*

The JSON syntax is similar to a Python dictionary. Every time I am dealing with a new source data, I use the type() function. Pass data into type(), and you'll see that Python took it as a dictionary.

We have received a lot of information from the API, and it is difficult to visually identify the keys in the dictionary. The Python dictionary method keys() will help us to get all the keys:

```
data.keys()
```

The method keys() has returned dict_keys(['Meta Data', 'Time Series (Daily)']). We are not interested in 'Meta Data' and will take a closer look at 'Time Series (Daily)'. data is a dictionary, and we can get the values by a key 'Time Series (Daily)'. Time Series is another dictionary, so we will use the keys() method again:

```
data['Time Series (Daily)'].keys()
```

Apparently, data['Time Series (Daily)'] contains all information as dictionaries too. The method keys() has returned dates that were used as a key. Each inner dictionary contains more keys with daily values for "AAPL". To get them, you can apply the same method keys() to any date:

```
data['Time Series (Daily)']['2021-01-08'].keys()
```

Every day has the same set of keys to hold values:

```
dict_keys(['1. open', '2. high', '3. low', '4. close', '5.
adjusted close', '6. volume', '7. dividend amount', '8. split
coefficient'])
```

If I needed to get a closing price for AAPL stock for '2021-01-08', I would fetch it like this (Figure 4-29):

```
data['Time Series (Daily)']['2021-01-08']['4. close']
```

```
In [3]:  1  data.keys()
Out[3]:  dict_keys(['Meta Data', 'Time Series (Daily)'])

In [4]:  1  data['Time Series (Daily)'].keys()
Out[4]:  dict_keys(['2021-01-08', '2021-01-07', '2021-01-06', '2021-01-05', '2021-01-04', '2020-12-31', '2020-12-30', '2020-1
         2-29', '2020-12-28', '2020-12-24', '2020-12-23', '2020-12-22', '2020-12-21', '2020-12-18', '2020-12-17', '2020-12-16
         ', '2020-12-15', '2020-12-14', '2020-12-11', '2020-12-10', '2020-12-09', '2020-12-08', '2020-12-07', '2020-12-04', '
         2020-12-03', '2020-12-02', '2020-12-01', '2020-11-30', '2020-11-27', '2020-11-25', '2020-11-24', '2020-11-23', '2020
         -11-20', '2020-11-19', '2020-11-18', '2020-11-16', '2020-11-13', '2020-11-12', '2020-11-11', '2020-11-
         10', '2020-11-09', '2020-11-06', '2020-11-05', '2020-11-04', '2020-11-03', '2020-11-02', '2020-10-30', '2020-10-29',
         '2020-10-28', '2020-10-27', '2020-10-26', '2020-10-23', '2020-10-22', '2020-10-21', '2020-10-20', '2020-10-19', '202
         0-10-16', '2020-10-15', '2020-10-14', '2020-10-13', '2020-10-12', '2020-10-09', '2020-10-08', '2020-10-07', '2020-10
         -06', '2020-10-05', '2020-10-02', '2020-10-01', '2020-09-30', '2020-09-29', '2020-09-28', '2020-09-25', '2020-09-24'
         , '2020-09-23', '2020-09-22', '2020-09-21', '2020-09-18', '2020-09-17', '2020-09-16', '2020-09-15', '2020-09-14', '2
         020-09-11', '2020-09-10', '2020-09-09', '2020-09-08', '2020-09-04', '2020-09-03', '2020-09-02', '2020-09-01', '2020-
         08-31', '2020-08-28', '2020-08-27', '2020-08-26', '2020-08-25', '2020-08-24', '2020-08-21', '2020-08-20', '2020-08-1
         9', '2020-08-18'])

In [5]:  1  data['Time Series (Daily)']['2021-01-08'].keys()
Out[5]:  dict_keys(['1. open', '2. high', '3. low', '4. close', '5. adjusted close', '6. volume', '7. dividend amount', '8. s
         plit coefficient'])

In [6]:  1  data['Time Series (Daily)']['2021-01-08']['4. close']
Out[6]:  '132.05'
```

Figure 4-29. *Accessing values from the received data converted to a Python dictionary*

If you need to get all close prices from the Alpha Vantage Time Series API, then you can iterate through a dictionary. In this example, I'll use dict_of_prices as an intermediate variable just to make the code cleaner and clearer (Figure 4-30):

```
dict_of_prices = data['Time Series (Daily)']

for key in dict_of_prices:
    print(key, dict_of_prices[key]['4. close'])
```

```
In [7]:    1  dict_of_prices = data['Time Series (Daily)']
           2
           3  for key in dict_of_prices:
           4      print(key, dict_of_prices[key]['4. close'])

         2021-01-08 132.05
         2021-01-07 130.92
         2021-01-06 126.6
         2021-01-05 131.01
         2021-01-04 129.41
```

Figure 4-30. *Iterating through the dict_of_prices dictionary object*

I went through all these steps to illustrate how to get any value from an API. Assuming that we want to convert the received data into a DataFrame, then we can take dict_of_prices or data['Time Series (Daily)'] and pass it directly into the Pandas function DataFrame:

```
df = pd.DataFrame(dict_of_prices)
```

When a dictionary is passed into the DataFrame function, it might use wrong values for columns. In our case, the pd.DataFrame function used dates for columns, which is not a desired outcome. To pivot a two-dimensional data structure, we will apply a T attribute to the transpose index and columns of the DataFrame:

```
df = pd.DataFrame(dict_of_prices).T
```

The attribute T is an accessor for the transpose() method, and you can use them interchangeably. With the T attribute at the end, df should look like in Figure 4-31.

```
In [8]:   1  df = pd.DataFrame(dict_of_prices).T
          2  df
```

Out[8]:

	1. open	2. high	3. low	4. close	5. adjusted close	6. volume	7. dividend amount	8. split coefficient
2021-01-12	128.5	129.69	126.86	128.8	128.8	90440255	0.0000	1.0
2021-01-11	129.19	130.17	128.5	128.98	128.98	100620880	0.0000	1.0
2021-01-08	132.43	132.63	130.23	132.05	132.05	105158245	0.0000	1.0
2021-01-07	128.36	131.63	127.86	130.92	130.92	109578157	0.0000	1.0
2021-01-06	127.72	131.0499	126.382	126.6	126.6	155087970	0.0000	1.0

Figure 4-31. *Transposing a DataFrame with a built-in method T*

Take into consideration that JSON served by APIs is a string, and all values in df are stored not as numeric data types. Meaning we cannot use them for math calculations. You do not need to remember that; instead, run the method info() on a DataFrame to check the values' data types:

```
df.info()
```

To work with these values, we would need to convert them to numeric data. Going column by column would be tedious. We will use an applymap() method. The concept of applymap() is similar to an apply() method; it iterates through values. The difference is that applymap() would be used on all values in a DataFrame. applymap() has no inplace argument, and we would need to save the value conversion with the same variable df:

```
df = df.applymap(pd.to_numeric)
```

Run df.info() again, and you will see that all values were converted to either float or integer data types. The last thing we could do is to convert index values to datetime objects:

```
df.index = pd.to_datetime(df.index)
```

The datetime objects in the index will help us to manipulate data, for example, plot the last 120 days of closing prices from the DataFrame (Figure 4-32):

```
df.loc['2020-09-01':'2021-01-12':-1]['4. close'].plot.line()
```

The method loc slices data from '2020-09-01' to '2021-01-12'. We use the –1 step since the original DataFrame begins with the '2021-01-12' index, and we need to go in reverse. To plot closing prices, we grab the '4. close' column and plot it as a line (Figure 4-32).

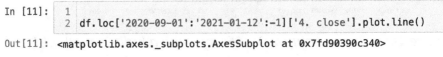

Out[11]:   <matplotlib.axes._subplots.AxesSubplot at 0x7fd90390c340>

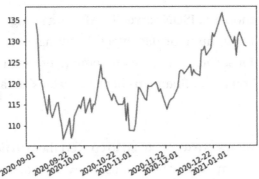

Figure 4-32. *Plotting data from a DataFrame*

Pandas-Datareader

Popular APIs have wrappers like Pandas-Datareader. A wrapper is a small program usually designed to make the process of working with data seamless. Pandas-Datareader unifies the mechanism of accessing information from Yahoo Finance, Google, NASDAQ, Federal Reserve Economic Data, and many others. The full list of data providers can be found in the Pandas-Datareader documentation.[4] As the name implies, Pandas-Datareader works with Pandas and returns received information in the form of a DataFrame.

---

[4]https://pydata.github.io/pandas-datareader/readers/index.html

Initially designed as a part of Pandas to receive remote financial and economic data, Pandas-Datareader was a spin-off and now is a stand-alone Python package. We need to install it separately in Anaconda Navigator ➤ Environments ➤ Terminal using a `pip` command:

```
pip install pandas-datareader
```

Most of Pandas-Datareader data sources can be accessed via the `DataReader()` function. To see `DataReader()` in action, open a new **Jupyter** Notebook and import Pandas and Pandas-Datareader:

```
import pandas as pd
import pandas_datareader.data as web
```

For starters, we will get historic prices for IBM stock from Yahoo Finance. Yahoo Finance requires no registration, and all we need is to pass a stock symbol, source of data, and time range:

```
stock_price = web.DataReader('IBM', 'yahoo', '2020-01-01',
'2021-01-15')
```

Dates for start and end days shall be passed into the function either as strings or datetime objects. The first argument `'IBM'` can be replaced with any other valid stock symbol. `DataReader()` returns prices in a DataFrame format, and you can apply Pandas functions and methods to the `stock_price` object:

```
stock_price.head()
```

`DataReader()` connects to the Yahoo service, and it may take time to get a response (Figure 4-33).

```
In [1]:    1  import pandas as pd
           2  import pandas_datareader.data as web

In [2]:    1  stock_price = web.DataReader('IBM', 'yahoo', '2020-01-01','2021-01-15')
           2  stock_price.head()
```

Out[2]:

Date	High	Low	Open	Close	Volume	Adj Close
2020-01-02	135.919998	134.770004	135.000000	135.419998	3148600.0	128.671951
2020-01-03	134.860001	133.559998	133.570007	134.339996	2373700.0	127.645760
2020-01-06	134.240005	133.199997	133.419998	134.100006	2425500.0	127.417740
2020-01-07	134.960007	133.399994	133.690002	134.190002	3090800.0	127.503242
2020-01-08	135.860001	133.919998	134.509995	135.309998	4346000.0	128.567429

Figure 4-33. *Receiving data from Yahoo Finance with the DataReader() function*

The Investors Exchange (IEX) is another popular data source that would work with DataReader(). The Investors Exchange provides tons of data for individual and professional accounts on a paid basis. Here, we will use a free account to illustrate how to use an API Key in a DataReader() function and get access to IEX. You can register and claim your API Key on the IEX cloud platform at https://iexcloud.io. Upon registering, you'll get access to API tokens. Define an API_Key as a string and pass it as the last argument in DataReader():

```
API_Key = 'pk_1386c11694f7887a90694cd588149'
```

```
msft_prices = web.DataReader('MSFT', 'iex', '2020-01-01',
'2021-01-15', api_key=API_Key)
```

The API Key I use here is just an example and not a valid token.

'iex' is a data source argument you have to use for connection to the Investors Exchange. The prices we have received are stored as DataFrame under the variable msft_prices (Figure 4-34).

```
In [3]:    1  API_Key = 'pk_1386c11694f7887a90694cd588149'
           2
           3  msft_prices = web.DataReader('MSFT', 'iex', '2020-01-01','2021-01-15', api_key=API_Key)
           4  msft_prices.iloc[0:2]
```

Out[3]:

date	open	high	low	close	volume
2020-01-02	158.78	160.730	158.33	160.62	22634546
2020-01-03	158.32	159.945	158.06	158.62	21121681

Figure 4-34. *Receiving data from the Investors Exchange with the DataReader() function*

Besides the stock market prices, Pandas-Datareader provides access to economic indicators from FRED (Federal Reserve Bank of St. Louis). Let's take a look at two most important indicators: Gross Domestic Product (GDP) and Total Nonfarm Payrolls.

FRED provides GDP numbers starting from 1947, and we can get them with the same DataReader() function. All we have to do is to pass the symbol 'A191RL1Q225SBEA' and change the source to 'fred'. The symbols for economic indices can be found on the FRED website at https://fred. stlouisfed.org. Usually, the symbol comes right after the indicator title (Figure 4-35).

```
gdp = web.DataReader('A191RL1Q225SBEA', 'fred', '1947-04-01',
'2021-01-15')
```

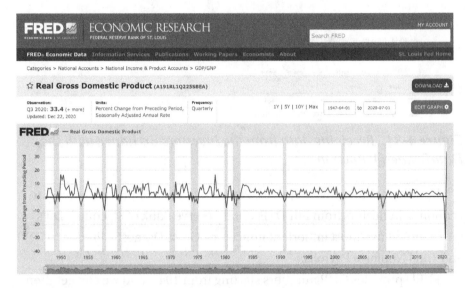

Figure 4-35. *Real Gross Domestic Product information on* `https://fred.stlouisfed.org`

We can plot the data with the method `plot.line()` and add a title as an argument (Figure 4-36).

```
In [4]:   1  gdp = web.DataReader('A191RL1Q225SBEA', 'fred', '1947-04-01', '2021-01-15')
          2  gdp.plot.line(title='GDP');
```

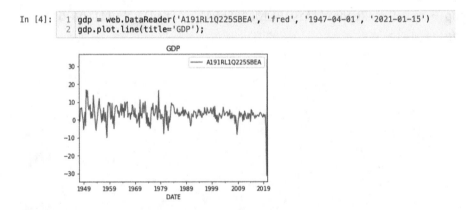

Figure 4-36. *Plotting Gross Domestic Product received from the FRED source with the DataReader() function*

Similar to GDP, we can plot Total Nonfarm Payrolls. The symbol for Total Nonfarm Payrolls is PAYEMS. We will fetch the maximum available information with the start date '1939-01-01' up to December 2020:

```
nonfarm = web.DataReader('PAYEMS', 'fred', '1939-04-01',
'2020-12-01')
nonfarm.plot.line(title='Total Nonfarm Payrolls');
```

In Figure 4-37, you can see the plot of historic employment data we received from FRED using the DataReader() function.

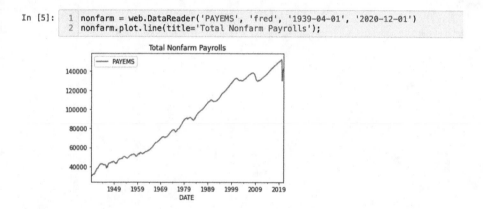

Figure 4-37. *Plotting Total Nonfarm Payrolls received from the FRED source with the DataReader() function*

In this chapter, we have covered the main principles of working with APIs. In the next chapter, we will continue using APIs to gather and analyze information. In particular, we will work with the Google Data Python Library to get access to popular Google apps.

CHAPTER 5

Data Visualization

Visualization is an essential piece of data analysis. It is not enough to gather, manipulate, and analyze data. You need to present your findings. Numbers should tell a story. A story with no images would be a dull one. We, humans, consume information with our eyes, and as they say, "a picture is worth a thousand words." A brighter picture will keep your attention longer.

Being the most popular programming language for data science and machine learning, Python has numerous visualization solutions. In this chapter, we will learn how to use the most prominent Python library for visualization – Matplotlib. All other Python visualization libraries either are built on top of Matplotlib or share the same principles in plotting data.

Matplotlib

We have briefly used Matplotlib via Pandas in previous chapters; now it is time to take a closer look at the popular visualization package.

The Matplotlib library is the first major Python library for plotting data. It would not be a stretch to say that Matplotlib is the mostly used visualization Python solution in the world. Matplotlib allows to graph data as different types of plots. Lines, bar charts, scatter, and histogram are the main types of plots you can easily do with Matplotlib. Beyond that, many Matplotlib extensions exist to help you visualize astronomical, geographical, or scientific data.

© Art Yudin 2021
A. Yudin, *Basic Python for Data Management, Finance, and Marketing*,
https://doi.org/10.1007/978-1-4842-7189-6_5

Line Plot

Matplotlib is a part of Anaconda. All you need is to import it into a file to start using it. In a new **Jupyter** file, import the Matplotlib module pyplot:

```
import matplotlib.pyplot as plt
```

Matplotlib is a big library, and rather than importing it all, we are selecting the main module pyplot. plt, as you have probably guessed, is a convention shorthand.

I want to start the introduction to Matplotlib with a simple line example. Create two Python lists with a few numbers:

```
x = [ 2, 5, 7 ]
y = [ 2, 7, 3 ]
```

The choice for x and y variables is not random. To draw a line, we need to connect points. Each point has two numbers or coordinates x and y to map it. In our example, there will be three points. We can graph them with the Matplotlib function plot():

```
plt.grid(True)
plt.plot(x,y, marker="o");
```

I have added the function plt.grid(True) to illustrate that the position of each point is unique to values on x and y axes derived from x and y lists (Figure 5-1).

```
In [1]:     1  import matplotlib. pyplot as plt

In [2]:     1  x = [ 2, 5, 7 ]
            2  y = [ 2, 7, 3 ]
            3
            4  plt.grid(True)
            5  plt.plot(x,y, marker="o");
```

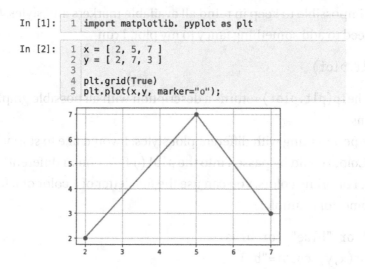

Figure 5-1. *Plot of a line*

Also, I have placed an optional keyword argument marker="o" to accent that the function plt.plot() connects the dots based on values we have provided. Remove marker="o" and you will see a simple line:

```
plt.plot(x,y)
```

The semicolon I have right after the plt.plot() function is a little trick to hide the memory address of a line object. If you rerun the plt.plot(x,y) expression without a semicolon at the end, you will see [<matplotlib.lines.Line2D at 0x7f97da40b9a0>] printed right above the graph.

The function plt.plot() is easy to use. All you have to do is to pass any two iterables like a list or a tuple or a Pandas Series or a NumPy array as x and y coordinates, and it would draw a line.

The Matplotlib function plt.plot() allows you to use different styles and any possible color. There are so many variations that the function plot simply states that it takes *args and **kwargs. *args and **kwargs mean that a function can take multiple arguments and keyword arguments.

It is impossible to keep in mind all available markers and styles. Every time I need to add something fancy to my plot, I run

```
help(plt.plot)
```

The `help(plt.plot)` returns a description with all possible graph variations.

In experimenting with different plot styles, I would like to start with colors. Colors could be passed into the `plot()` function in different formats. For prime colors, you can use the first letter of a color or a full color name, for example:

```
Use "b" or "blue" for blue
plt.plot(x,y, color="b")
plt.plot(x,y, color="blue")

use "r" or "red" for red
plt.plot(x,y, color="r")
plt.plot(x,y, color="red")

use "g" or "green" for green
plt.plot(x,y, color="g")
plt.plot(x,y, color="green")
```

If you find it boring to use preset colors, you might use HEX or RGB formats. I would recommend visiting `https://htmlcolorcodes.com` for a color palette. On that website, you can pick any color with HEX or RGB code. For example, my favorite light coral color could be used like this:

```
plt.plot(x, y, color="#F08080");
```

or even with the name of the color:

```
plt.plot(x, y, color="LightCoral");
```

Any graph requires a legend and a title. Matplotlib has special functions `plt.legend()` and `plt.title()` to add annotations to a plot.

Needless to say, all available Matplotlib functions could be seen with the dir(plt) command.

The plt.legend() function reflects the data displayed in the plot. It is very easy to use. All you have to do is to add a keyword argument label to your plot, and the function plt.legend() will render it:

```
plt.plot(x, y, color="#F08080", label="Line");
plt.legend()
```

The plot annotation could be rendered in any place of a graph. Add the argument loc, stands for location, and assign any position from the "Location string" list. The "Location string" list can be found in the function description help(plt.legend).

I'll place label="Line" referred to in plt.plot() to the lower center of the graph (Figure 5-2):

```
plt.plot(x, y, color="#F08080", label="Line")
plt.legend(loc="lower center");
```

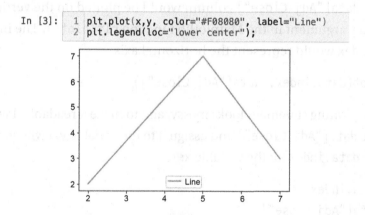

Figure 5-2. *The function legend() adds an annotation to a graph*

Along with the legend, we can attach any name to a plot with the function plt.title(). The graph label should be passed as a string in the plt.title() function. The plt.title() function allows to specify a position, color, and font size of a label. Using the argument loc, a label can be placed in one of three positions: left, right, and default center. To set a label custom color as in the plt.plot() function plot, we can either use prime colors or HEX and RGB codes. A label text size should be passed in points with the keyword fontsize.

As a case in point, I'll plot a stock price. For this task, we would need to get historic stock prices. Scroll back to the first cell in a file and import Pandas-Datareader:

```
import pandas_datareader as pdr
```

Fetch historic prices for Apple or any other stock from the "yahoo" source within any date range:

```
data = pdr.DataReader("AAPL","yahoo", "2020-01-01","2021-02-12")
```

The data["Adj Close"] column would be plotted on the vertical axis as a y argument in the Matplotlib function plt.plot(). The index data.index would represent the horizontal axis:

```
plt.plot(data.index, data["Adj Close"])
```

This plotting statement looks messy, and to make it readable, I will slice the data["Adj Close"] and assign it to the variable y. I will do the same to data.index for the variable x:

```
x = data.index
y = data["Adj Close"]

plt.plot(x, y)
```

We added two more lines of code, but it is worth it. Now it is readable and clear to other people who might use our code. Also, it would be easier to plug in any other values we might want to plot.

Put in a label into the plt.plot() function and render it on the lower right with the plt.legend() method:

```
plt.plot(x, y, color="#196F3D" label="AAPL")
plt.legend(loc="lower right")
```

Attach a title positioned on the left in the same color as the stock price line with a font size of 22:

```
plt.title("Apple Inc. Stock Price", loc="left",
color="#196F3D", fontsize=22)
```

Run the code, and you'll see a nice plot with a custom title and a legend label. One thing is bothering me, overlapping horizontal axis values.

Matplotlib provides xticks() and yticks() functions to set custom labels for horizontal and vertical axes. In the current example, it would be difficult to match custom labels to data.index values, and besides we might change the date range in the future; thus, to make dates readable, we will pivot them a bit. The xticks() and yticks() functions come with an argument rotation that changes an angle of text. We can set half of a right angle for x labels with the numeric value 45:

```
xticks(rotation=45)
```

Finally, the plot should look like in Figure 5-3. Experiment with colors and label styles.

```
In [1]:    1  import matplotlib. pyplot as plt
           2  import pandas_datareader as pdr
```

```
In [2]:    1  data = pdr.DataReader("AAPL","yahoo", "2020-01-01","2021-02-12")
           2  x = data.index
           3  y = data["Adj Close"]
           4  plt.plot(x, y, color="#196F3D", label="APPL")
           5  plt.legend(loc="lower right")
           6  plt.xticks(rotation=45)
           7  plt.title("Apple Inc. Stock Price",loc="left",color="#196F3D", fontsize=22);
```

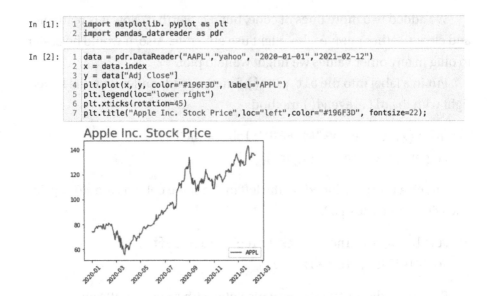

Figure 5-3. *Plot of a stock price with a title and a legend*

There are several additional styling options we can apply to our graph. The Matplotlib function `grid()` adds the grid lines of any style and color:

```
plt.grid(color="brown", linestyle=":")
```

As many Matplotlib functions, `grid()` is highly customizable. You can provide colors and line styles. The graph size can be set with the `figure()` method. In Matplotlib, the term figure refers to a plotted data. That is why the dimensions of a graph should be used with a keyword `figsize`. The width and height should be passed as either a list or a tuple and dimensions specified in inches:

```
plt.figure(figsize=(12,8))
```

One of my students asked me if it would be possible to use corporate colors in the plots since it was a requirement at her company. The answer is yes. You already have seen that we can set any color for a line or grid. Moreover, there is the `style` package in Matplotlib. You can define any style variations by calling the plt.style.use() method. I am not going into details how to compose styles; that is outside of the scope of the book. If for some reason you need to set a particular style sheet, you can find the information on how to do it here: https://matplotlib.org/stable/api/style_api.html.

For the rest of us who just want to have stylish graphs, I would recommend using one of the preset style sheets. All available options are listed here: https://matplotlib.org/stable/gallery/style_sheets/style_sheets_reference.html.

For example, a very popular "seaborn" style can be applied to a plot like this:

```
plt.style.use("seaborn")
```

Python code runs in sequence, and functions plt.style.use() and figure() should be defined before plot() on the top (Figure 5-4).

```
In [1]:   1  import matplotlib. pyplot as plt
          2  import pandas_datareader as pdr
```

```
In [3]:   1  data = pdr.DataReader("AAPL","yahoo", "2020-01-01","2021-02-12")
          2  x = data.index
          3  y = data["Adj Close"]
          4  plt.figure(figsize=(12,8))
          5  plt.style.use("seaborn")
          6  plt.plot(x, y, color="#196F3D", label="APPL")
          7  plt.legend(loc="lower right")
          8  plt.xticks(rotation=45)
          9  plt.title("Apple Inc. Stock Price",loc="left",color="#196F3D", fontsize=22);
         10  plt.grid(color="brown", linestyle=":")
```

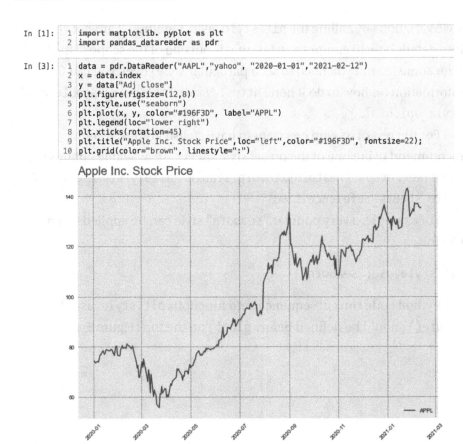

Figure 5-4. *Applying style.use() and figure() functions to a plot*

Histogram Plot

A histogram is another popular type of graph. Compared to the plot()
function, the hist() method requires one set of data. It is often used to
illustrate the distribution of the data.

Using Apple stock historic prices, we can calculate the daily returns for
the stock and plot them as a histogram:

```
stock_return = data['Adj Close'].pct_change(1)*100
```

The Pandas method pct_change() returns the percentage change between the current and the prior date. The first value in the `stock_return` Series is NaN, and we need to throw it out to plot a histogram:

```
stock_return.dropna(inplace=True)
```

After the method `dropna()` removes all NaNs, the Series can be passed into the `hist()` function as an x argument:

```
plt.hist(stock_return)
```

The data passed into the `hist()` function is split in the number of equal-width bins. Using the second argument `bins`, you can change the range and, if the number of observations allow, get more precise results by increasing the number of bins:

```
plt.hist(stock_return, bins=100)
```

As in the previous example, we will add a title to the histogram plot:

```
plt.title('Distribution of APPL Daily Return')
```

Along with the title text, Matplotlib provides options to label horizontal and vertical axes. As the name of the `xlabel()` and `ylabel()` functions suggests, they can be used to name axes:

```
plt.xlabel('Daily Percentage Return')
plt.ylabel('Frequency')
```

With the added title and axis labels, the histogram graph would look like in Figure 5-5.

```
In [4]:    1  stock_return = data['Adj Close'].pct_change()
           2  stock_return.dropna()
           3
           4  plt.hist(stock_return, bins=100)
           5  plt.title('Distribution of AAPL Daily Returns')
           6  plt.xlabel('Daily Percentage Returns')
           7  plt.ylabel('Frequency');
```

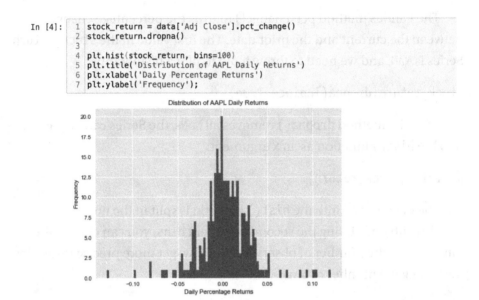

Figure 5-5. *The function hist() plots the daily returns of a stock*

The histogram plot can be saved as a separate file in png, jpeg, pdf, or svg formats.

The Matplotlib function savefig() will generate a brand-new file with a plot. All you need is to provide a unique file name as a string argument:

```
plt.savefig("AAPL return.png")
```

or you can save it as a PDF file:

```
plt.savefig("AAPL return.pdf")
```

Keep in mind that the savefig() function should be the last Matplotlib command after you run all the statements for the graph you are plotting.

Scatter Plot

The Python library Matplotlib can use three different backends. I would call them here formats. The one we have used so far is a default one called "inline". The "Inline" format generates static images and stores them in a **Jupyter** Notebook. The main advantage of the "inline" format is that you can have as many static graphs per **Jupyter** file as you want.

In the event that you want to use interactivity in plots, you would need to switch to "notebook" mode. You can have only one interactive image per **Jupyter** file. That is why I would recommend composing the next example in a separate new file. Interactive mode requires a magic Python function before you import Matplotlib:

```
%matplotlib notebook
import matplotlib.pyplot as plt
```

I did not exaggerate when I called a function magical. A magic function is an official Python term for functions prefixed with the % sign.[1]

A scatter plot is one of the essentials in data analysis, and we will use the scatter() function to map the US population in 2019. The Matplotlib function scatter() not only plots data but also allows to adjust the size and color of dots based on values. We will grab the Excel file with an estimate of the resident population for the United States in 2019[2] and plot the data as a scatter graph. The file is located here: https://bit.ly/bookScatterExample.

---

[1] https://ipython.readthedocs.io/en/stable/interactive/tutorial.html#magics-explained

[2] The original version of the file can be downloaded from www.census.gov/data/datasets/time-series/demo/popest/2010s-state-total.html using API www2.census.gov/programs-surveys/popest/tables/2010-2019/state/totals/nst-est2019-01.xlsx

In addition to the plotting library, we will need Pandas; import it along Matplotlib like this:

```
%matplotlib notebook
import matplotlib.pyplot as plt
import pandas as pd
```

The Excel file with data is online, and we can read it with the Pandas read_excel() function.[3] The first row is a header, and we can skip it with the keyword argument skiprows=1:

```
data = pd.read_excel("https://bit.ly/bookScatterExample",
skiprows=1)
```

As always, we would need to clean the data a bit and grab only columns that contain information:

```
data = data[["State", "Population"]]
```

We will convert population numbers into millions for readability:

```
data["Population_Mill"] = data["Population"]/1000000
```

The data range is too wide, and to plot a neat scatter, we can filter the data and get states with a population from two to eight million:

```
filtered_data =  data[(data["Population_Mill"] > 2.0)
&(data["Population_Mill"]< 8.0)]
```

---

[3] If for any reason https://bit.ly/bookScatterExample is not available, you can always get the file from https://book.nyc3.digitaloceanspaces.com/ Estimates_Population_US_2019.xlsx

The scatter() function is similar to the plot() method. It takes x and y values as coordinates. In order to make the code readable, I'll slice the filtered_data DataFrame and assign filtered_data["State"] to x and filtered_data["Population_Mill"] to y variables:

```
x = filtered_data["State"]
y =  filtered_data["Population_Mill"]
```

Now we can pass x and y objects into scatter() and rotate the state names on horizontal axes:

```
plt.scatter(x, y)
plt.xticks(rotation=90)
```

The %matplotlib notebook has generated us an interactive graph (Figure 5-6). The menu under the plot allows us to zoom in and move data around. The little diskette works as a save button.

```
In [1]:    1  %matplotlib notebook
           2  import matplotlib.pyplot as plt
           3  import pandas as pd
```

```
In [2]:    1  data = pd.read_excel("https://bit.ly/bookScatterExample", skiprows=1)
```

```
In [3]:    1  data = data[["State", "Population"]]
           2  data["Population_Mill"] = data["Population"]/1000000
           3  filtered_data =  data[(data["Population_Mill"] > 2.0) &(data["Population_Mill"]< 8.0)]
```

```
In [4]:    1  x = filtered_data["State"]
           2  y = filtered_data["Population_Mill"]
           3  plt.scatter(x,y)
           4  plt.xticks(rotation=90);
```

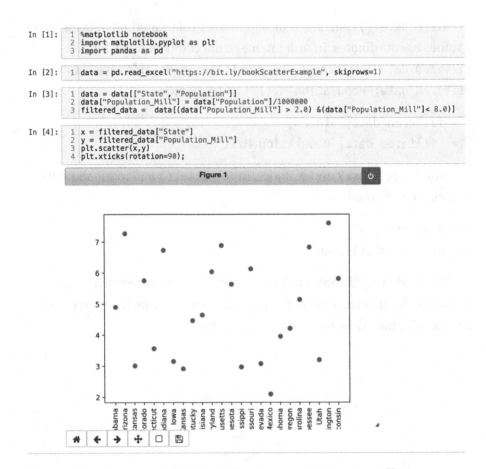

Figure 5-6. *Scatter plot of the US state population in millions*

I have mentioned before the Matplotlib function scatter() lets us control the size and color of the dots with keyword arguments s and c. We can make the scatter plot more presentable by assigning filtered_ data["Population_Mill"] data as the size and color. I'll magnify the data dots by raising the values into a power of four:

```
size = filtered_data["Population_Mill"]**4
color = filtered_data["Population_Mill"]
plt.scatter(x, y, s=size, c=color)
```

Some dots are overlapping others, and to make them transparent, we will add another Matplotlib styling attribute `alpha`. The value under 1 makes the plot more transparent:

```
plt.scatter(x, y, s=size, c=color, alpha=0.5)
```

As all Matplotlib plotting functions, `scatter()` allows to provide colormaps either custom or the one you can choose from the documentation. (You can find all colormaps listed here: `https://matplotlib.org/stable/tutorials/colors/colormaps.html`.) From the list, I have picked the "plasma" colormap and will pass it into the `scatter()` function with the attribute `cmap="plasma"`. The scatter plot will be more informative if we add a colorbar scale (Figure 5-7):

```
plt.scatter(x, y, s=size, c=color, alpha=0.5, cmap="plasma")
plt.colorbar()
```

```
In [11]:    1  x = filtered_data["State"]
            2  y = filtered_data["Population_Mill"]
            3  size = filtered_data["Population_Mill"]**4
            4  color = filtered_data["Population_Mill"]
            5  plt.scatter(x,y, s=size, c=color, alpha=0.5, cmap="plasma")
            6  plt.xticks(rotation=90);
            7  plt.colorbar();
```

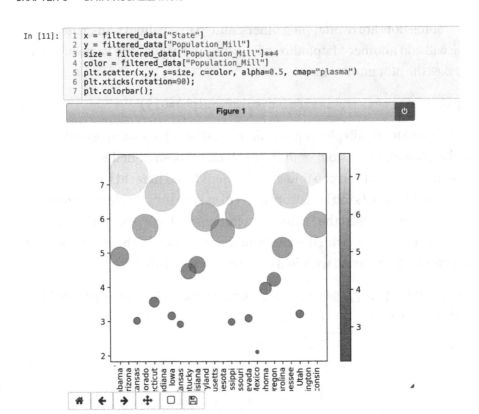

Figure 5-7. *Scatter plot with a colorbar scale*

We defiantly should add a title and vertical axis label. I think the plotted data will look better if we increase the figure size to 10 by 8. We need to define figsize in the function figure() before using scatter(), so insert the statement plt.figure(figsize=(10,8)) into the code:

```
plt.figure(figsize=(10,8))
plt.scatter(x,y, s=size, c=color, alpha=0.5, cmap="plasma")
plt.xticks(rotation=90)
plt.colorbar()
plt.title("The States with population estimates between 2 and 8 million, 2019")
plt.ylabel("Population in millions")
```

You have probably noticed that I always move down a semicolon character to the last line of code. Again, that hides a plot object reference in Python memory.

This time, I do not want to add grid lines to the plot, but rather annotate each value date with a state name.

The Matplotlib function annotate() can place a text label anywhere on a graph based on x and y coordinates. Try placing the label "Here" on the "Indiana" dot:

```
plt.annotate("Here", ("Indiana", 6.4))
```

The x and y coordinates should be passed in the form of a tuple as ("Indiana", 6.4). "Indiana" represents the x value on horizontal axes and 6.4 is the population on y axes.

Rerun the **Jupyter** Notebook cell, and you'll see the "Here" text attached to the orange dot representing the Indiana state. Obviously, we do not want to manually add a text annotation to all values. We can iterate through all x values and get the coordinates by an index. The task would require the Python built-in function enumerate(). The enumerate() function will provide an index to all values in filtered_data["State"] stored under the x variable. With the help of a for loop, we will go through the enumerated object and pass the index and name of each state to the annotate() function. The x and y variables hold the Pandas Series objects, and we need to use the method .iloc[] to map the index to the values:

```
for index, label in enumerate(x):
    plt.annotate(label, (x.iloc[index], y.iloc[index]) )
```

After that, all dots would be assigned text labels from the x object (Figure 5-8).

In [4]:
```
1  x = filtered_data["State"]
2  y = filtered_data["Population_Mill"]
3  size = filtered_data["Population_Mill"]**4
4  color = filtered_data["Population_Mill"]
5  plt.figure(figsize=(10,8))
6  plt.scatter(x,y, s=size, c=color, alpha=0.5, cmap="plasma")
7  plt.xticks(rotation=90)
8  plt.colorbar()
9  plt.title("The States with population estimates between 2 and 8 million, 2019")
10 plt.ylabel("Population in millions");
11 for index, label in enumerate(x):
12     plt.annotate(label, (x.iloc[index], y.iloc[index]) )
```

Figure 1

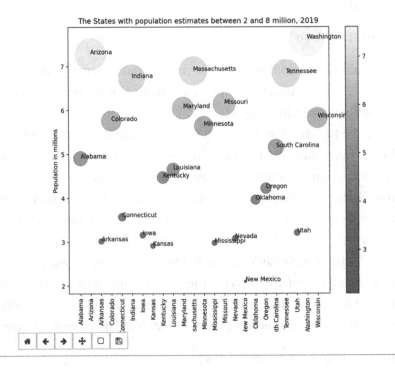

Figure 5-8. *Annotating values in the scatter plot*

The interactive scatter graph we have created allows users to magnify data with the zoom option in the menu (Figure 5-8) and move it around with a left mouse click. The home button in the menu resets everything to default dimensions. "Notebook" mode we have set in the upper cell will not let you to generate another plot in the file because of the recursive nature of the interactive mode. The default "inline" and interactive "notebook" formats are the main modes for **Jupyter**.

Aside from **Jupyter**, Matplotlib might use your computer operational system as a backend engine. You can try it by using the magic function: %matplotlib with no arguments

```
%matplotlib
import matplotlib.pyplot as plt
```

In this case, Matplotlib will generate an interactive plot similar to "notebook" mode in a separate Python shell. One thing to remember when you toggle between the Matplotlib modes is that they cannot be used together at the same time, and you need to reboot the Kernel if you replace one with another one within a **Jupyter** file.

Pie Plot

We will generate a pie chart in an interactive shell. Import Matplotlib using the %matplotlib format:

```
%matplotlib
import matplotlib.pyplot as plt
```

in a new **Jupyter** file, and it will return

```
Using matplotlib backend: MacOSX
```

or Windows, depending on the operational system your computer is running on. Using matplotlib backend means that Matplotlib is connected to your operational system and will use it to generate images.

Continuing the previous example, we will plot the resident population for the US geographic areas as a pie plot. According to the US Census Bureau, 38.26% of all population in the United States reside in the South, 23.87% in the West, 20.82% in the Midwest, and 17.06% in the Northeast.

We need to define values and labels for the pie plot:

```
population = [38.26, 23.87, 20.82, 17.06]
areas = ["South", "West", "Midwest", "Northeast"]
```

The Matplotlib pie() function will generate a simple pie chart. To see all available arguments to customize the pie diagram, run help(plt.pie). Pass population into pie() as x values and areas as labels:

```
plt.pie(x=population, labels=areas)
```

The Matplotlib backend engine should generate a pop-up window with a simple pie chart (Figure 5-9).

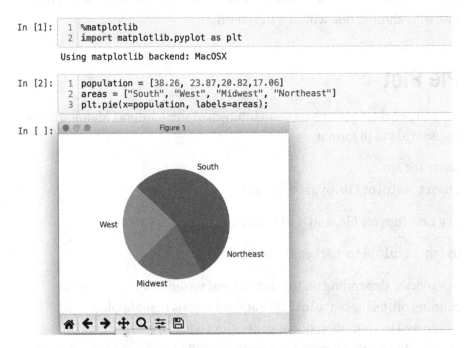

Figure 5-9. Population data plotted as a pie chart

The function pie() as well as other Matplotlib functions accepts custom colors. For this example, I decided to pick a bright color palette on https://htmlcolorcodes.com:

```
palette = ["#00FFFF"," #FF00FF"," #00FF00"," #800080"]
```

```
plt.pie(x=population, labels=areas, colors=palette)
```

Sometimes, you want to emphasize a wedge of a pie diagram to make a point. This can be done with the pie() function argument explode. Explode accepts an iterable such as a list or a tuple with floats for the position of each wedge to the center.

For instance, the explode=[0, 0.1, 0, 0] argument will push the second wedge from the center by 0.1. In our case, I'll display the "West" wedge 0.2 from the center of the pie plot:

```
standout =[0, 0.2, 0, 0]
```

```
plt.pie(x=population, explode=standout, labels=areas,
colors=palette)
```

Another style argument in the pie() function is shadow. If you want to add a 3D look to the pie plot, switch the shadow argument to True:

```
plt.pie(x=population, explode=standout, labels=areas,
shadow=True, colors=palette)
```

Along with labels, you might want to display the actual values of each region in the plot. The autopct argument will display the values. We need to assign the format of a value as a string. The format of a string should be done in a Python formatting style you can find at https://pyformat.info. In particular, the expression '%.2f' would show two numbers after the decimal point, and '%.2f%%' would place a % character after the value:

```
plt.pie(x=population, explode=standout, labels=areas,
autopct='%.2f%%', shadow=True, colors=palette)
```

With additional styling attributes, we have generated a very stylish pie plot (Figure 5-10). If something went wrong during the process of generating the plot, rebooting the Kernel should help.

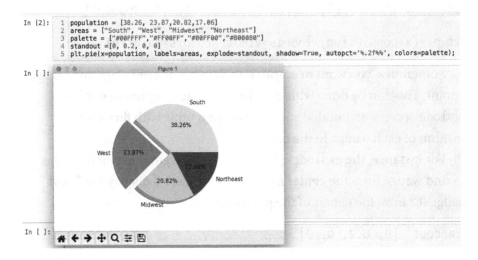

```
In [2]:   1  population = [38.26, 23.87,20.82,17.06]
          2  areas = ["South", "West", "Midwest", "Northeast"]
          3  palette = ["#00FFFF","#FF00FF","#00FF00","#800080"]
          4  standout =[0, 0.2, 0, 0]
          5  plt.pie(x=population, labels=areas, explode=standout, shadow=True, autopct='%.2f%%', colors=palette);
```

Figure 5-10. *A pie plot with styling attributes*

Of course, you can add a title to the pie plot as we did it in the previous cases.

Matplotlib is a very useful tool to get a sense of data. It is easy to use. We have covered all main functions to visualize and style diagrams. We have learned how to build basic graphs, but with Matplotlib and numerous additions and plugins, you can do so much more. For sophisticated styles and plots, I would recommend visiting the Matplotlib documentation gallery page: https://matplotlib.org/stable/gallery/index.html.

CHAPTER 6

Essential Financial Tasks Done with Python

In the previous chapters, we have covered all the nuts and bolts of Python. We have used some financial examples to illustrate in finance. In this chapter, we will dive more in everyday finance tasks. My goal here is to show you a practical use of Python and to get you started so you could write your own code. Also, you should regard this book as your first step in Python learning and continue your education by reading the Pandas and other libraries' documentation, follow professional blogs, and master Python by practicing. There will never be a magical function or a preset solution to solve all real-life challenges. So use the examples in the chapter to build a base for your own projects.

NumPy Financial

I would like to begin this chapter with elementary financial functions every student learns in the first year of business college. The future value of money, internal rate of return, present value, and net present value of future cash flows are the pillars of financial analysis. Knowing Python basics, you can write the formulas and calculate these measures from scratch, yet to save us some time and effort, there is a Numpy-Financial package. Numpy-Financial does all the necessary work for you, providing clean results with no bugs.

© Art Yudin 2021
A. Yudin, *Basic Python for Data Management, Finance, and Marketing*,
https://doi.org/10.1007/978-1-4842-7189-6_6

To get started with Numpy-Financial, you need to install it in the **Terminal**. As a reminder, you can find the Terminal in Anaconda Navigator **Environments** by clicking the **base (root)** menu. Make sure that you are installing the package into a new Terminal shell and not interfering with the working Kernel.

```
pip install numpy-financial
```

After you see the message that Numpy-Financial was successfully installed, the Terminal can be closed, and you can import the package in a new **Jupyter** Notebook:

```
import numpy_financial as npf
```

I do not want to spend a lot of time explaining the financial metrics in detail and their importance in financial analysis, but rather concentrate on their implementation in the Numpy-Financial functionality.

Numpy-Financial is a small library that has only ten essential functions (Table 6-1).

Table 6-1. *Numpy-Financial functions*

Function	Description
fv(rate, nper, pmt, pv[,when])	Compute the future value
ipmt(rate, per, nper, pv[,fv,when])	Compute the interest portion of a payment
irr(values)	Return the internal rate of return (IRR)
mirr(values,finance_rate,reinvest_rate)	Modified internal rate of return

(continued)

Table 6-1. (*continued*)

Function	Description
nper(rate, pmt, pv[,fv,when])	Compute the number of periodic payments
npv(rate, values)	Return the NPV (Net Present Value) of a cash flow series
pmt(rate, nper, pv[,fv,when])	Compute the payment against loan principal plus interest
ppmt(rate, per, nper, pv[,fv,when])	Compute the payment against loan principal
pv(rate, nper, pmt[,fv,when])	Compute the present value
rate(nper, pmt, pv, fv[,when, guess,tol,...])	Compute the rate of interest per period

As you have seen it is not necessary to memorize all functions and their arguments. All you have to do is to run dir(npf) to see objects' available methods and help() to learn a particular function arguments.

Future Value fv()

The value of money is the first thing you learn in Finance 101. Let's take a look at a classic problem. Suppose you have a choice to get $3000.00 today earning 3% annually or agree to be paid $3300.00 three years from now. We will solve the problem with the pv() function. The given statements will be saved under variable names deposit, annual_interest, and years:

```
deposit = 3000
annual_interest = 0.03
years = 3
```

```
future_value = npf.fv(annual_interest, years, 0, -deposit)
print("Future value of ${:.2f} is ${:.2f}".format(deposit,
future_value))
```

I use a minus sign before deposit as an argument because we can regard that as an investment. If you do not use a minus sign, then the result will come out as a negative number.

As a result of the calculation, we see that $3300.00 would be a better deal than earning 3% annually on the deposit of $3000.00 (Figure 6-1).

```
In [1]:    1  import numpy_financial as npf

In [4]:    1  deposit = 3000
           2  annual_interest = 0.03
           3  years = 3
           4
           5  future_value = npf.fv(annual_interest, years, 0, -deposit)
           6  print("Future value of ${:.2f} is ${:.2f}".format(deposit, future_value))

Future value of $3000.00 is $3278.18
```

Figure 6-1. *Future value calculation with the fv() function*

Present Value pv()

The opposite of the future value of money formula is the present value of money. An amount of money today is worth more than the same amount in the future. But how much more exactly? Numpy-Financial will help us to answer that question with the function pv().

Continuing with the preceding example, we can assume that you have a choice to receive $3300 in three years, or you can claim them now. We will leave an interest rate at 3% annually.

The pv() function takes the interest rate, number of periods, and future value as arguments. The interest rate could be passed as an annual or monthly value. The number of periods would depend on the annual or monthly interest. We will define future_value as $3300; annual_rate and years values stay the same:

```
future_value = 3300
annual_rate = 0.03
years = 3

present_value = npf.pv(annual_rate, years,0,-future_value)
print("Present value of ${:.2f} is ${:.2f}".format(future_
value, present_value))
```

The present value of $3300.00 is $3019.97 according to the result we have returned by the pv() formula (Figure 6-2).

```
In [3]:   1  future_value = 3300
          2  annual_rate = 0.03
          3  years = 3
          4
          5  present_value = npf.pv(annual_rate, years, 0, -future_value)
          6  print("Present value of ${:.2f} is ${:.2f}".format(future_value, present_value))

Present value of $3300.00 is $3019.97
```

Figure 6-2. *Calculating the present value of money with the pv() function*

Net Present Value npv()

Numpy-Financial can help to determine priority between investment projects based on profitability using the Net Present Value of future cash inflows discounted at the cost of capital rate. The function npv() returns the Net Present Value of a cash flow series. It is easy to use; all we need is a cost of capital or opportunity cost of capital and future expected cash flows. Expected cash flows should be passed as an array. According to the documentation, investments have to be negative floats and inflows should be passed as positive numbers.

Suppose there is a company planning to expand and choosing between two investment opportunities. One choice is to expand production and invest $100,000 in new facilities and equipment. The production expansion will bring $25,000 of annual income in the next five years.

Another investment alternative is to buy securities yielding 5% annually. We assume that the risks are equal for simplicity of the example.

Based on the assumptions, we will calculate NPV (Net Present Value) of the expansion project. We will define investment as a negative value and cash_flows as a Python list holding future cash flows:

```
discount_rate = 0.05

investment = -100000

cash_flows = [investment, 25000, 25000, 25000, 25000, 25000]

net_present_value = npf.npv (discount_rate, cash_flows)

print("Net Present Value of the project is ${:.2f}
".format(net_present_value))
```

The Net Present Value of the project is $8236.92 (Figure 6-3).

```
In [4]:    1  discount_rate = 0.05
           2  investment = -100000
           3  cash_flows = [investment, 25000,25000,25000,25000,25000]
           4
           5  net_present_value = npf.npv(discount_rate, cash_flows)
           6  print("Net Present Value of the project is ${:.2f} ".format(net_present_value))

Net Present Value of the project is $8236.92
```

Figure 6-3. *Calculating the Net Present Value of a project*

Using the same npv() function, we can compare two projects. Also, we can run scenarios for a range of discounted interest rates and see how project profitability would be affected by changing interest rates.

The second project we want to compare to would have the same initial investment of $100,000 and gradually increasing inflows of $5000, $10,000, $40,000, $40,000, and $40,000 in the next five years, respectively.

The discounted rates can be presented as a range of floats stored in a Python list:

```
cash_flows_project_one = [-100000,
25000,25000,25000,25000,25000]
cash_flows_project_two = [-100000,
5000,10000,40000,40000,40000]
discount_rates = [0.0,0.05,0.10,0.20,0.25]
```

The first initial investment number in cash_flows_project_one and cash_flows_project_two is negative because we invested that amount, and it represents a cash outflow.

We need to initialize two empty lists to store the outcomes of scenario analysis:

```
npv_project_one =[]
npv_project_two =[]
```

Finally, to calculate NPV for projected cash flows, we would need to dynamically pass each rate from the discount_rates list. A for loop will iterate through the list of discount_rates and will send a value by value into the npv() function. The outcomes will be temporarily stored under variables npv_one and npv_two and appended to npv_project_one and npv_project_two lists:

```
for rate in discount_rates:
    npv_one = npf.npv(rate, cash_flows_project_one)
    npv_project_one.append(npf.npv(rate, cash_flows_projetct_one))
    npv_two = npf.npv(rate, cash_flows_project_two)
    npv_project_two.append(npv_two)
```

Now that we have run scenarios for different discount rates and saved the NPV results, we can plot them.

Besides the Matplotlib library, we would need the Shapely package to find an intersection of two plotted lines representing the NPV values.

Open a Terminal or a command prompt and download and install Shapely:

```
pip install shapely
```

Shapely is a Python library to analyze geometric objects.[1] Of course, we could have found the intersection coordinates without the help of Shapely, but it would require many lines of code. The Shapely method intersection() would do a better job more precisely.

After you have installed Shapely, import it and Matplotlib on top of the **Jupyter** Notebook:

```
import numpy_financial as npf
import matplotlib.pyplot as plt
from shapely.geometry import LineString
```

I want my graph to have perfectly scaled axes, and I'll set x and y axes' limits as 0.0 and 0.25:

```
plt.xlim(0.0, 0.25)
```

The Matplotlib method xlim() sets the x limits of the current axis based on the start and end points. We can hardcode them as 0.0 and 0.25 discount rates or make them change based on the values in the discount_rates list. That means assigning the start point as the first value from the list discount_rates[0] and the end point as the last value from the same list discount_rates[-1]:

```
plt.xlim(discount_rates[0], discount_rates[-1])
```

---

[1] https://pypi.org/project/Shapely/

Y axes will be scaled using the Matplotlib method ylim(), and we will pass the start and end points as the last value from the NPV results stored in the npv_project_two list:

```
plt.ylim(npv_project_two[-1],npv_project_two[0])
```

After that, we can plot the NPV results using discount rates as the x axis:

```
plt.plot(discount_rates, npv_project_one, label="Project One")
plt.plot(discount_rates, npv_project_two, label="Project Two")
```

The NPV values will be plotted as two lines when you run the cell. The intersection point of two lines or, as it is called in finance, the crossover rate can be precisely calculated and marked on the plot.

The Shapely function LineString will convert the x and y coordinates into a straight geometrical object:

```
line1 = LineString(list(zip(discount_rates, npv_project_one)))
line2 = LineString(list(zip(discount_rates, npv_project_two)))
```

The values from discount_rates, npv_project_one, and npv_project_two we have used as x and y coordinates in the plot have to be combined with the help of the Python built-in function zip(). The function zip() will package them as a list of tuples and pass into the LineString() function.

Let me step back and say a couple of words about the function zip(). Very often, we need to map values that came from different sources. For example, the names of cities and population. Both come as lists where population values are in millions:

```
cities = ["New York", "Chicago", "Huston"]
population = [8.3, 2.7, 2.3]
```

The function `zip()` will match the `population` value to a city in the `cities` list:

```
zip(cities, population)
```

The function `zip()` as many other functions in Python returns an object:

```
<zip at 0x7fe2366e4700>
```

To unpack the `zip` object, we need either to iterate through it with a for loop and get pairs one by one or to wrap the `zip` object as a list:

```
list(zip(cities, population))
```

Now we can see pairs stored as tuples in the list:

```
[('New York', 8.3), ('Chicago', 2.7), ('Huston', 2.3)]
```

Getting back to our NPV example, the result of the `LineString` operation is stored under the `line1` and `line2` variables. The method intersection will get us coordinates of that crossing point:

```
point = line1.intersection(line2)
```

The object `point` now has x and y coordinates that can be plotted on the graph as `point.x` and `point.y` attributes. The `point.x` and `point.y` give the exact dollar amount and interest rate at the intersection on NPV values of two evaluated projects.

We can mark the intersection on a graph as a red dot with dashed lines dropping on x and y axes:

```
plt.plot(point.x, point.y, marker="o", color="red")
```

As you can see, to plot a dot, we use the same `plot()` function we have practiced in the previous chapter. The difference is the style. Now we use a marker. There are many preset markers in the function `plot()`. You can find the one you like with `help(plt.plot)`.

Matplotlib functions `hline()` and `vline()` will plot horizontal and vertical lines based on x and y coordinates:

```
plt.hlines(y=point.y, xmin=0.0, xmax=point.x, color='red',
linestyles='dotted', label=str(round(point.x*100,3)))

plt.vlines(x=point.x, ymin=-40000, ymax=point.y, color='red',
linestyles='dotted',label=str(round(point.y,2)))
```

The Matplotlib functions `hline()` and `vline()` are similar to other plotting methods we have been working before. The straight lines go from the origin of the point that is defined as xmax=point.x and ymax=point.y. X and y limits are identified as 0.0 on x and –40000 on y axes.

The final touch is grids and labels:

```
plt.grid()
plt.legend()
plt.title("NPV profile")
plt.xlabel("Discount Rate")
plt.ylabel("NPV (Net Present Value)")
```

The full solution and the graph are shown in Figures 6-4 and 6-5.

```
1  cash_flows_project_one = [-100000, 25000,25000,25000,25000,25000]
2  cash_flows_project_two = [-100000, 5000,10000,40000,40000,40000]
3  discount_rates = [0.0,0.05,0.10,0.20,0.25]
4  npv_project_one =[]
5  npv_project_two =[]
6
7
8  for rate in discount_rates:
9      npv_one = npf.npv(rate, cash_flows_project_one)
10     npv_project_one.append(npf.npv(rate, cash_flows_project_one))
11     npv_two = npf.npv(rate, cash_flows_project_two)
12     npv_project_two.append(npv_two)
13
14
15 plt.xlim(discount_rates[0],discount_rates[-1])
16 plt.ylim(npv_project_two[-1],npv_project_two[0])
17 plt.plot(discount_rates, npv_project_one, label="Project One")
18 plt.plot(discount_rates, npv_project_two, label="Project Two")
19
20 line1 = LineString(list(zip(discount_rates, npv_project_one)))
21 line2 = LineString(list(zip(discount_rates, npv_project_two)))
22
23 point = line1.intersection(line2)
24
25
26 plt.hlines(y=point.y, xmin=0.0, xmax=point.x, color='red', linestyles='dotted', label=str(round(point.x*100,3)))
27 plt.vlines(x=point.x, ymin=-40000, ymax=point.y, color='red', linestyles='dotted',label=str(round(point.y,2)))
28 plt.plot(point.x, point.y, marker="o", color="red")
29
30 plt.grid()
31 plt.legend()
32 plt.title("NPV profile")
33 plt.xlabel("Discount Rate")
34 plt.ylabel("NPV (Net Present Value)")
```

Figure 6-4. Calculating and plotting NPV of two projects

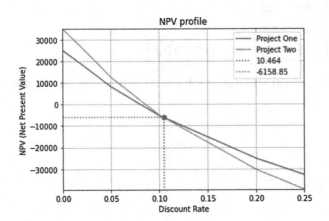

Figure 6-5. Plot of the crossover rate of NPV of two projects

Value at Risk (VAR)

Financial regulation became tougher over the past years, and these days compliance managers have to use modern tools to generate tons of reports working with huge data sets. This is where Python comes to the rescue.

Value at risk is a very popular statistical measure to evaluate the level of financial risk for an investment. In VAR (value at risk), the risk is defined as the maximum loss at a specified time.

Here, we will take a look at how to calculate the parametric VAR model based on a normal distribution and volatility.

Suppose we have a portfolio of common stocks. In our portfolio, we hold positions in the following stocks: Microsoft, Apple, and IBM. For simplicity of the example, let's say we hold 100 shares of each company.

To make future assumptions, we would need to get historic prices for the stock in the portfolio. I hope you have already installed the Pandas-Datareader library; if not, in Chapter 4 we have discussed the installation and the purpose of the package in detail.

Import NumPy, Pandas, Matplotlib, and Pandas-Datareader on the top of a new **Jupyter** Notebook:

```
import numpy as np
import pandas as pd
import matplotlib.pyplot as plt
import pandas_datareader.data as web
```

To fetch historic prices, we need to place the stock symbols into a Python list. The variable name portfolio would perfectly reflect the list purpose:

```
portfolio =  [ "MSFT","AAPL","IBM"]
```

We will need a DataFrame to store the historic prices for our stocks, so we initialize one under the variable name prices:

```
prices = pd.DataFrame()
```

Using Pandas-Datareader, get historic prices from Yahoo for each stock by its symbol. You can specify any period range as a string format:

```
for stock in portfolio:
    prices[stock] = web.DataReader(stock, 'yahoo', '2017-01-01',
    '2021-03-20')["Adj Close"]
```

Keep in mind that Pandas-Datareader returns a DataFrame containing columns for open, high, low, close, volume, and adjusted close prices. The adjusted close price, which reflects a stock price after splits and dividends, is what we need. We grab it from each DataFrame by column name ["Adj Close"]. Using the dictionary notation, we add the ["Adj Close"] column to the DataFrame we have defined before. The variable stock holding a value from the portfolio list will set the symbol for each company as a column name in prices while we iterate through the list.

At the end of the day, we should have the prices DataFrame filled with historic prices. You can check them with msft_prices.head().

The method head() will reveal the first five rows of the DataFrame with historic prices (Figure 6-6).

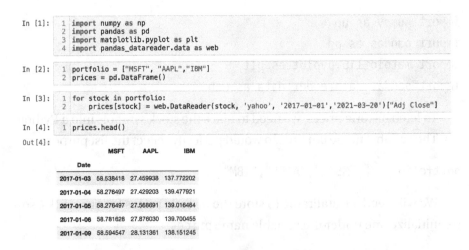

Figure 6-6. *Retrieving historic prices for the portfolio of stocks*

We can visualize the historic prices by plotting them. It would be difficult to plot and compare stocks with different values, like AAPL at 27.45 and IBM at 137.77. We would need to normalize the prices using 100 as a base on the first date of data. `prices.iloc[0]` will get us the prices on the first date in the DataFrame:

```
first_date  = prices.iloc[0]

normalized_prices = prices/first_date * 100
```

The plotting part is easy; we have done it before in Chapter 5:

```
[line1,line2,line3] = plt.plot(prices.index , normalized_
prices, label=["MSFT","AAPL","IBM"])
plt.legend(loc="lower right")
plt.xticks(rotation=45)
plt.title("Portfolio of stocks");
plt.grid()
plt.legend([line1,line2,line3],["MSFT","AAPL","IBM"],
loc="upper left");
```

I use the DataFrame `index` as the x axis since it contains dates. `normalized_prices` is my y axis. The `[line1,line2,line3]` list is used purely for labels to differentiate what line is what stock.

The historic performance of three stocks can be seen in Figure 6-7.

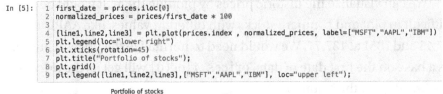

```
In [5]:  1  first_date   = prices.iloc[0]
         2  normalized_prices = prices/first_date * 100
         3
         4  [line1,line2,line3] = plt.plot(prices.index , normalized_prices, label=["MSFT","AAPL","IBM"])
         5  plt.legend(loc="lower right")
         6  plt.xticks(rotation=45)
         7  plt.title("Portfolio of stocks");
         8  plt.grid()
         9  plt.legend([line1,line2,line3],["MSFT","AAPL","IBM"], loc="upper left");
```

Figure 6-7. *Normalized historic prices*

The VAR calculation begins with historic stock returns. There are two methods how you can do that. The first one is using the Pandas method shift() that shifts a row by a specific number:

stocks_return = prices/prices.shift(1)-1

Or to be more precise, you can calculate logarithmic returns with the NumPy function log():

stocks_return = np.log(prices/prices.shift(1))

The second option is to use the method pct_change(). Pct_change() also accepts an argument for a number of periods. In our case, it is one day or one row:

return = prices.pct_change(1)

No matter what approach you use, `stocks_return` and `return` should have the same results. The first value in both cases is NaN (not a value), and we will eliminate it with the `dropna()` method:

```
return.dropna(inplace=True)
```

In case you forgot, `inplace` is an argument that saves changes within the object.

Visualization of returns will help us better comprehend the numbers. The Matplotlib function `hist()` will present the picture in the form of histograms.

We can plot all three stocks on the same graph. The keyword argument will make them transparent:

```
plt.hist(return["MSFT"], alpha=0.5,  bins=100)
plt.hist(return["AAPL"], alpha=0.5,  bins=100)
plt.hist(return["IBM"], alpha=0.5,  bins=100);
```

Or if the graph is too busy to understand anything, you can plot each stock return individually (Figure 6-8). I have mentioned before that the Pandas DataFrame supports Matplotlib, and you can apply the method `hist()` directly to `return`:

```
return.hist()
```

```
In [7]:  1  plt.hist(returns["MSFT"], alpha=0.5,  bins=100)
         2  plt.hist(returns["AAPL"], alpha=0.5,  bins=100)
         3  plt.hist(returns["IBM"], alpha=0.5,  bins=100);
```

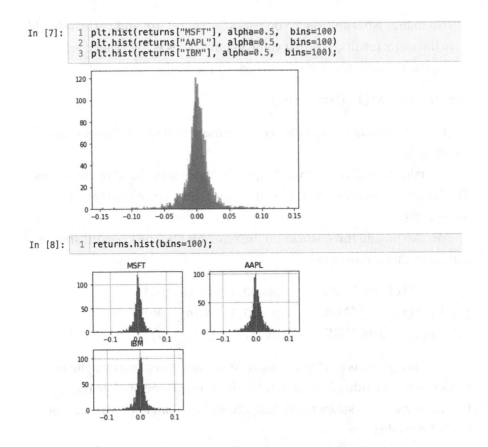

```
In [8]:  1  returns.hist(bins=100);
```

Figure 6-8. *Plotting historic stock returns*

The Pandas Series has a method describe(). The method describe() could be applied only to a Series or columns in a DataFrame holding numeric values:

```
return.describe()
```

Figure 6-9 displays statistical measures of the stock returns the method describe() computed.

```
In [9]:    1  returns.describe()
Out[9]:
```

	MSFT	AAPL	IBM
count	1059.000000	1059.000000	1059.000000
mean	0.001458	0.001594	0.000086
std	0.018093	0.020033	0.017200
min	-0.147390	-0.128647	-0.128507
25%	-0.005818	-0.006481	-0.006447
50%	0.001451	0.001141	0.000489
75%	0.009880	0.010875	0.007114
max	0.142169	0.119808	0.113011

Figure 6-9. *The method describe() returns statistical measures*

After we have applied the describe method to the historic returns, we can see where a mean of the data set is and how big is a spread of std (standard deviation). Min and max values indicate the boundaries of the data set. Besides, we can see 25%, 50%, and 75% percentiles.

The describe() method is a very useful tool to get statistical measures of any set of numeric values on the fly.

For our VAR calculation, we will need the mean and standard deviation of the portfolio. We can grab the mean value from the describe() method:

```
return.describe().loc["mean"]
```

or use the special mean() method:

```
mean_return = return.mean()
```

The standard deviation of a portfolio or volatility would require a covariance between each pair of stocks. In Pandas, we can create a covariance matrix on the returns with the function cov():

```
covar = return.cov()
```

Figure 6-10 displays a covariance matrix of the portfolio we will use to get the volatility of the portfolio.

```
In [10]:    1  mean_returns = returns.mean()
```

```
In [11]:    1  covar = returns.cov()
            2  covar
```

Out[11]:

	MSFT	AAPL	IBM
MSFT	0.000327	0.000269	0.000168
AAPL	0.000269	0.000401	0.000159
IBM	0.000168	0.000159	0.000296

Figure 6-10. *Covariance matrix*

Additionally, we would need the percentage of each stock within the portfolio. For the simplicity of this example, we assume that we have invested 50% of the total dollar value of the portfolio into Microsoft, 25% in Apple, and 25% in IBM. This assumption has to be saved in the NumPy array:

```
weights = np.array([0.5,0.25,0.25])
```

The NumPy array can be regarded as a vector. Also, the NumPy array is used as a core in the Series and DataFrame. That means we can derive the dot product or single numerical value out of the vector.

The variable mean_return holds the mean of historic returns of three stocks, and we would need to normalize them again in portfolio stock percentages with the method dot():

```
portfolio_mean = mean_return.dot(weights)
```

The standard deviation is the square root of the variance, and we can get it with the NumPy sqrt() method:

```
volatility = np.sqrt(weights.T.dot(covar).dot(weights))
```

The capital T is a transpose method; it changes the relative position of a vector or a matrix. If you run dir() on an array, Series, or DataFrame, it always would be the first one in the list.

Additionally, the mean and standard deviation have to be calculated for the total value of the portfolio. Here, we will assume that the total value of the portfolio is $1,000,000:

```
portfolio_value = 1000000
investment_mean = (1 + portfolio_mean) * portfolio_value
investment_volatility = portfolio_value * volatility
```

After we have all the necessary values at hand, we can calculate the inverse of the normal cumulative distribution. For that, we would need ppf(), percent point function, from the SciPy (science Python) package. SciPy is included in Anaconda, and all we need is to import it at the beginning of the file:

```
import scipy.stats as scs
```

The ppf() method uses default values for the mean, 0, and standard deviation, 1, which are standard for a normal bell distribution. We will overwrite them with investment_mean and investment_volatility. A risk manager will need to pass the confidence level into ppf(); usually, it is 95%:

```
confidence = 95
```

```
normsinv = scs.norm.ppf((1-95/100), investment_mean,investment_
volatility)
```

The final step is to subtract the inverse of the normal cumulative distribution from the portfolio value:

```
var = portfolio_value - normsinv
```

You can round down the result to two figures after the decimal point:

```
np.round(var,2)
```

The final result is 25088.94 (Figure 6-11). After all these calculations, we can say with 95% degree of certainty that a portfolio with MSFT, AAPL, and IBM shares currently valued at $1,000,000 may lose $25,088.94 in one day.

```
In [12]:    1  weights = np.array([0.5,0.25,0.25])
```

```
In [13]:    1  portfolio_mean = mean_returns.dot(weights)
            2  portfolio_mean
```

```
Out[13]:  0.0011490780317016758
```

```
In [14]:    1  volatility = np.sqrt(weights.T.dot(covar).dot(weights))
            2  volatility
```

```
Out[14]:  0.0159515837852558
```

```
In [15]:    1  portfolio_value = 1000000
            2  investment_mean = (1 + portfolio_mean) * portfolio_value
            3  investment_volatility = portfolio_value * volatility
```

```
In [16]:    1  confidence = 95
            2  normsinv = scs.norm.ppf((1-95/100), investment_mean,investment_volatility)
            3  var = portfolio_value - normsinv
            4  np.round(var,2)
```

```
Out[16]:  25088.94
```

Figure 6-11. *The value at risk calculation*

If you need to project what VAR will be over five days, you can multiply one day VAR by a square root of the number of days.

We will place the var * np.sqrt(day) expression into the for loop within a range of days. Initialize an empty list to store the results. We will plot them:

```
var_results = []

number_of_days = 5
days_list = list(range(1, number_of_days+1))

for day in days_list:
    result = var * np.sqrt(day)
    var_results.append(result)
```

We need to add 1 to number_of_days since in the function range, the stop point is exclusive.

Conclusively, we will plot var_results:

```
plt.plot(days_list, var_results)
plt.title("Value at Risk")
plt.ylabel("Portfolio loss")
plt.xticks(days_list,["1st day","2nd day","3rd day","4th
day","5th day"]);
plt.grid()
```

We can see that losses double over the period of five days (Figure 6-12).

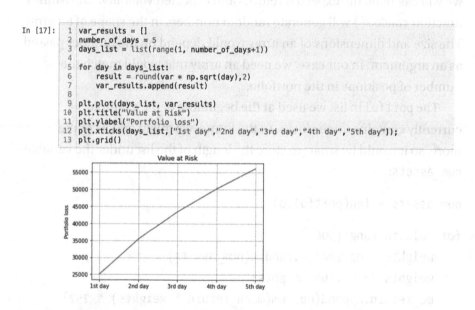

Figure 6-12.   Projecting VAR over a five-day period

Monte Carlo Simulation

Using the same historic stock prices, we can forecast the performance
of the portfolio and simulate probable outcomes using the Monte Carlo
simulation technique.

The Monte Carlo approach is to generate random outcomes for expected returns and expected volatility for the portfolio. Pretty much like rolling dice over and over again.

To save the outcomes for expected returns and expected volatility, we need to initialize two lists:

```
mc_return = []
mc_volatility = []
```

Randomly changing the percentages of each position in the portfolio, we will calculate the expected returns and expected volatility. The NumPy function random() will generate random numbers in the shape of an array. The size and dimensions of an array would depend on the number passed as an argument. In our case, we need an array that would match the number of positions in the portfolio.

The portfolio list we used at the beginning of the example currently contains three stocks. In the future, we might add a couple more, so it would be smart to store the length of the list under the variable num_assets:

```
num_assets = len(portfolio)

for roll in range(5000):
    weights = np.random.random(num_assets)
    weights /= np.sum(weights)
    mc_return.append(np.sum(mean_return * weights) * 252)
    mc_volatility.append(np.sqrt(np.dot(weights.T, np.dot
    (covar * 252, weights ))))
```

For each iteration of the for loop, the method random() generates random weights of assets in the portfolio. The total percentage of all assets always has to be exactly 100%; that is why we divide weights by sum() of weights. Next, we generate expected returns and volatility and normalize the results by the number of trading days in a year (Figure 6-13).

```
In [18]:    1  mc_returns = []
            2  mc_volatility = []
            3  num_assets = len(portfolio)
            4
            5  for roll in range(5000):
            6      weights = np.random.random(num_assets)
            7      weights /= np.sum(weights)
            8      mc_returns.append(np.sum(mean_returns * weights) * 252)
            9      mc_volatility.append(np.sqrt(np.dot(weights.T, np.dot(covar * 252, weights ))))
           10
           11  expected_returns = np.array(mc_returns)
           12  expected_volatility = np.array(mc_volatility)
```

Figure 6-13. *Running the Monte Carlo simulation on a portfolio of stocks*

We will plot the outcomes as a scatter, but before that we need to convert mc_return and mc_volatility lists into NumPy arrays:

```
expected_return = np.array(mc_return)
expected_volatility = np.array(mc_volatility)
```

In the end, we plot expected_return and expected_volatility:

```
color = expected_return/expected_volatility
plt.figure(figsize=(12,8))
plt.scatter(expected_volatility, expected_return, c=color,
marker='o')
plt.grid()
plt.title("Monte Carlo simulation")
plt.xlabel('Expected volatility')
plt.ylabel('Expected return')
plt.colorbar(label="Sharpe ratio")
plt.show()
```

The Matplotlib show() method is optional. I have included it in case you would want to run the code in Matplotlib "notebook" mode or use the operational system to generate the plot.

This example is an illustration of Harry Markowitz's Modern Portfolio Theory.[2] The higher return on investment you want to get, the higher volatility you should expect (Figure 6-14).

```
In [19]:   1  color = expected_returns/expected_volatility
           2  plt.figure(figsize=(12,8))
           3  plt.scatter(expected_volatility, expected_returns, c=color, marker='o')
           4  plt.grid()
           5  plt.title("Monte Carlo simulation")
           6  plt.xlabel('Expected volatility')
           7  plt.ylabel('Expected return')
           8  plt.colorbar(label="Sharpe ratio")
           9  plt.show()
```

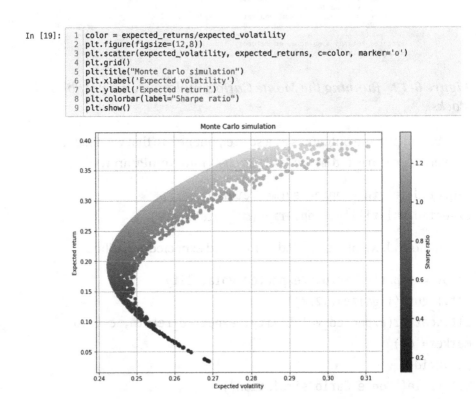

Figure 6-14. *Plotting Monte Carlo simulation results*

The curve in Figure 6-14 connects all of the most efficient outcomes, the optimal combination of risk and return, and it is called the efficient frontier.

---

[2] https://www.investopedia.com/terms/m/modernportfoliotheory.asp

Efficient Frontier

The preceding example has demonstrated that you can build any
statistical or financial model from scratch. However, if you are too busy
and require a key-turn solution, there is a professional Python package
PyPortfolioOpt that implements portfolio optimization methods, including
efficient frontier techniques and other solutions for risk management.[3]
PyPortfolioOpt comes with built-in risk models and plotting.
Unfortunately, for now PyPortfolioOpt is not a part of the Anaconda
package, and we will need to install it with the pip command. We have
gone through the installation process many times, and I am sure that by
now you know where to find the Terminal, so run

```
pip install pyportfolioopt
```

We will use PyPortfolioOpt to find the efficient frontier for our portfolio.
For the following example, you would need to open a new **Jupyter**
Notebook and import the following functions from PyPortfolioOpt:

```
import pandas as pd
import pandas_datareader.data as web
from pypfopt.efficient_frontier import EfficientFrontier
from pypfopt.cla import CLA
from pypfopt import plotting
from pypfopt.plotting import plot_weights
from pypfopt import risk_models
from pypfopt import expected_return
```

I will explain all of the imported functions as we move through
the example. Our goal is to generate and plot the efficient frontier of a

---

[3] https://pyportfolioopt.readthedocs.io/en/latest/index.html

portfolio. Also, find optimal portfolios using the Critical Line Algorithm as implemented by Marcos Lopez de Prado and David Bailey.[4]

We will be using the same portfolio from the previous example, and we will need to get the historic prices again since we are in a different notebook. At the same time, feel free to use your own favorite equities or add more stocks to the default list:

```python
portfolio = ["MSFT", "AAPL","IBM"]
prices = pd.DataFrame()
for stock in portfolio:
    prices[stock] = web.DataReader(stock, 'yahoo', '2017-01-01',
                    '2021-03-20')["Adj Close"]
```

Similar to the previous case, PyPortfolioOpt calculates the expected returns by extrapolating historic returns. There is the expected_return module, we have imported it, as the name implies it generates annualized mean returns. Run it on the historic prices we have gathered with Pandas-Datareader:

```python
mu = expected_return.mean_historical_return(prices)
```

To quantify the asset risk, PyPortfolioOpt includes risk models. One of them is the covariance matrix. Before, we have used the Pandas method cov(); this time, we will run sample_cov() from the risk_models module we have imported at the beginning of the file:

```python
sigma = risk_models.sample_cov(prices)
```

The sample_cov() function takes prices and returns annualized results. Compared to the previous example, there is no need to multiply the results by 252 trading days. It is already included in sample_cov().

---

[4]https://papers.ssrn.com/sol3/papers.cfm?abstract_id=2197616

Based on the expected returns and covariance, we can calculate the efficient frontier function we have imported, EfficientFrontier.

Besides returns and covariance, you may provide weight boundaries for all your equities in the form of a list of tuples. In the previous example, we assumed that in the portfolio we held 50% of MSFT and 25%, respectively, of AAPL and IBM. If the goal is to set the exact values, then we pass weight_bounds =[(0.5,0.5),(0.25,0.25),(0.25,0.25)] as a keyword argument. Otherwise, all positions in a portfolio would be defaulted to (0,1), meaning each asset minimum value could be 0 and maximum weight within a portfolio 100%. If a portfolio includes a short position, then weight_bounds should be set to (-1,1). I suggest we leave a default value of (0,1) and see what would be the optimal outcome:

```
efficient_front = EfficientFrontier(mu, sigma, weight_
bounds=(0,1))
```

The EfficientFrontier function always returns an object (Figure 6-15).

```
In [1]:    1  import pandas as pd
           2  import pandas_datareader.data as web
           3  from pypfopt.efficient_frontier import EfficientFrontier
           4  from pypfopt.cla import CLA
           5  from pypfopt import plotting
           6  from pypfopt.plotting import plot_weights
           7  from pypfopt import risk_models
           8  from pypfopt import expected_returns
```

```
In [2]:    1  portfolio = ["MSFT", "AAPL","IBM"]
           2  prices = pd.DataFrame()
           3  for stock in portfolio:
           4      prices[stock] = web.DataReader(stock, 'yahoo', '2017-01-01','2021-03-20')["Adj Close"]
```

```
In [3]:    1  mu = expected_returns.mean_historical_return(prices)
           2  mu
```

```
Out[3]:  MSFT     0.385396
         AAPL     0.420367
         IBM     -0.015715
         dtype: float64
```

```
In [4]:    1  sigma = risk_models.sample_cov(prices)
           2  sigma
```

Out[4]:

	MSFT	AAPL	IBM
MSFT	0.082492	0.067831	0.042270
AAPL	0.067831	0.101137	0.039950
IBM	0.042270	0.039950	0.074548

```
In [5]:    1  efficient_front = EfficientFrontier(mu, sigma, weight_bounds=(0,1))
           2  efficient_front
```

```
Out[5]:  <pypfopt.efficient_frontier.efficient_frontier.EfficientFrontier at 0x7ff8f769aa90>
```

Figure 6-15. *Generating the efficient frontier for a portfolio of stocks*

The job of PyPortfolioOpt is to optimize a portfolio of stocks. In other words, PyPortfolioOpt provides us with a guidance on how to better structure a portfolio to achieve the investment goals.

For instance, if our investment goal is to reduce volatility to a minimum, we would get the proposed allocation of assets within a portfolio with an attribute of the efficient frontier object min_volatility():

```
min_vol_weights = efficient_front.min_volatility()
```

According to PyPortfolioOpt, an allocation of 52% of all assets in IBM, 17% in AAPL, and 30% in MSFT will provide us with a maximum return at the lowest level of volatility (Figure 6-16).

```
In [6]:   1  min_vol_weights = efficient_front.min_volatility()
          2  min_vol_weights

Out[6]:  OrderedDict([('MSFT', 0.3038429749934607),
                       ('AAPL', 0.1703707960027631),
                       ('IBM', 0.5257862290037761)])
```

Figure 6-16. *Calculating weights of stocks in a portfolio to minimize volatility*

In contrast, if the goal is to drive the risk-adjusted return to a maximum, we can choose to maximize the Sharp ratio option with the max_sharp() method. By default, the risk-free rate is 2%, but you can set it to the current market:

max_sharp_weights = efficient_front.max_sharpe(risk_free_rate=0.02)

Maximizing the Sharp ratio choice will return a completely different picture and recommend to drive up MSFT and AAPL shares to 54% and 45%, respectively, and completely eliminate IBM holding (Figure 6-17).

```
In [7]:   1  max_sharp_weights = efficient_front.max_sharpe(risk_free_rate=0.02)
          2  max_sharp_weights

Out[7]:  OrderedDict([('MSFT', 0.5431272531388696),
                       ('AAPL', 0.4568727468611304),
                       ('IBM', 0.0)])
```

Figure 6-17. *Maximizing the Sharp ratio of the investment portfolio*

Depending on our assumptions and investment goals, the portfolio_ performance() method will calculate the expected return, annual volatility, and Sharp ratio. The only thing you have to keep in mind is that portfolio_performance() would return the expected returns and volatility from the last operation you have performed on a portfolio. For the clarity of the example, we would need to wipe out the memory of the notebook we are working in. You can do it by choosing the option "Restart & Clear Output" in the upper Kernel menu of a **Jupyter** Notebook. Then you would need to rerun the cells for where all the packages are imported, historic prices are gathered with Pandas-Datareader, and we had calculated expected returns and covariance matrix. Finally, you choose the scenario you want to get returns and volatility, for instance, maximizing the Sharp ratio, and run that cell. Afterward, you can get the portfolio performance by running portfolio_performance() on the instance of the efficient frontier:

```
efficient_front.portfolio_performance(verbose=True, risk_free_
rate = 0.02)
```

There are two arguments verbose and risk_free_rate we can pass into the portfolio_performance() method. The verbose argument means the returned values would be printed with explanation. By default, verbose is set to False and returns a tuple with raw numbers; a True option would print all values with explanation (Figure 6-18). The risk_free_rate argument would impact the expected return and volatility; thus, it should reflect the market rates of future assumptions.

```
In [6]:    1 max_sharp_weights = efficient_front.max_sharpe(risk_free_rate=0.02)
           2 max_sharp_weights

Out[6]: OrderedDict([('MSFT', 0.5431272531388696),
                     ('AAPL', 0.4568727468611304),
                     ('IBM', 0.0)])

In [7]:    1 efficient_front.portfolio_performance(verbose=True, risk_free_rate = 0.02)

        Expected annual return: 40.1%
        Annual volatility: 28.1%
        Sharpe Ratio: 1.36

Out[7]: (0.40137323818674575, 0.28126116543611335, 1.355939905871478)
```

Figure 6-18. *Getting the expected performance of a portfolio with a maximized Sharp ratio*

Additionally, we may plot the suggested weights from the max_sharpe() method with the plotting method we have imported, plot_weights() (Figure 6-19):

```
plot_weights(max_sharp_weights);
```

```
In [6]:    1  max_sharp_weights = efficient_front.max_sharpe(risk_free_rate=0.02)
           2  max_sharp_weights
```

```
Out[6]: OrderedDict([('MSFT', 0.5431272531388696),
                     ('AAPL', 0.4568727468611304),
                     ('IBM', 0.0)])
```

```
In [7]:    1  efficient_front.portfolio_performance(verbose=True, risk_free_rate = 0.02)
```

```
Expected annual return: 40.1%
Annual volatility: 28.1%
Sharpe Ratio: 1.36
```

```
Out[7]: (0.40137323818674575, 0.28126116543611335, 1.355939905871478)
```

```
In [8]:    1  plot_weights(max_sharp_weights);
```

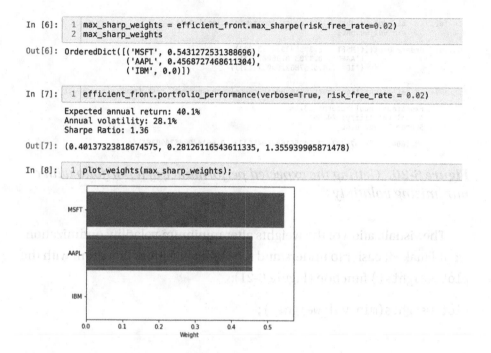

Figure 6-19. *Plotting weights of a portfolio with a maximized Sharp ratio*

Consequently, to get the expected performance of a portfolio with a low volatility, we would need to clear all outputs again and restart the Kernel. Then rerun the cells and apply the min_volatility() method to the instance of the efficient frontier. In this case, the portfolio_ performance() method returns a completely different set of performance measures (Figure 6-20).

```
In [6]:   1  min_vol_weights = efficient_front.min_volatility()
          2  min_vol_weights
```

```
Out[6]: OrderedDict([('MSFT', 0.3038429749934607),
                      ('AAPL', 0.1703707960027631),
                      ('IBM', 0.5257862290037761)])
```

```
In [7]:   1  efficient_front.portfolio_performance(verbose=True, risk_free_rate = 0.02)
```

```
Expected annual return: 18.0%
Annual volatility: 24.3%
Sharpe Ratio: 0.66
```

```
Out[7]: (0.18045535980879707, 0.24258160269458473, 0.6614490053098284)
```

Figure 6-20. *Getting the expected performance of a portfolio with a minimizing volatility*

The visualization of the weights after minimum volatility optimization would make it easier to understand the asset allocation. Plot them with the plot_weights() function (Figure 6-21):

plot_weights(min_vol_weights);

```
In [6]:   1  min_vol_weights = efficient_front.min_volatility()
          2  min_vol_weights
```

```
Out[6]:   OrderedDict([('MSFT', 0.3038429749934607),
                       ('AAPL', 0.1703707960027631),
                       ('IBM', 0.5257862290037761)])
```

```
In [7]:   1  efficient_front.portfolio_performance(verbose=True, risk_free_rate = 0.02)
```

```
Expected annual return: 18.0%
Annual volatility: 24.3%
Sharpe Ratio: 0.66
```

```
Out[7]:   (0.18045535980879707, 0.24258160269458473, 0.6614490053098284)
```

```
In [8]:   1  plot_weights(min_vol_weights);
```

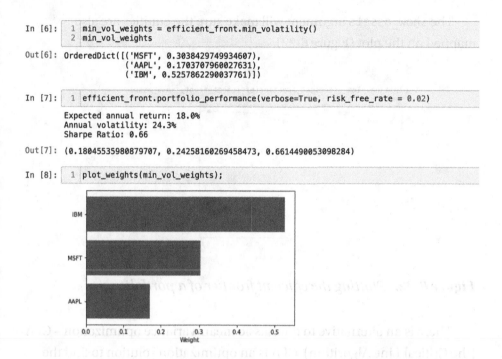

Figure 6-21. *Plotting the weights of a portfolio with a minimizing volatility*

As I have mentioned before, PyPortfolioOpt comes with plotting tools to help us visualize the entire efficient frontier. The plotting() function would not work if you had run min_volatility() or max_sharpe() methods. We would need to reinstate the instance of the original efficient frontier by clearing the memory and resetting the Kernel. After that, rerun all the cells except the ones with min_volatility() and max_sharpe() methods.

With one line of code and plotting() function we have imported before, plot the curve:

```
plotting.plot_efficient_frontier(efficient_front, show_
assets=True)
```

The show_assets argument will make sure the equities are also mapped on the plot (Figure 6-22).

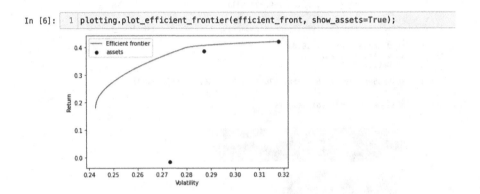

```
In [6]:    1  plotting.plot_efficient_frontier(efficient_front, show_assets=True);
```

Figure 6-22. *Plotting the efficient frontier of a portfolio*

There is an alternative to the classic mean-variance optimization – CLA (the Critical Line Algorithm). CLA is an optimization solution to find the optimal portfolio on the curve. It is quite popular in portfolio management due to the fact that it is the only algorithm specifically designed for inequality-constrained portfolio optimization. It is implemented in PyPortfolioOpt as the CLA() function. The CLA() function requires expected returns and covariance matrix to get the optimal portfolio. Pass the values we have generated before into CLA() and plot it (Figure 6-23):

```
cla = CLA(mu, sigma)
plotting.plot_efficient_frontier(cla);
```

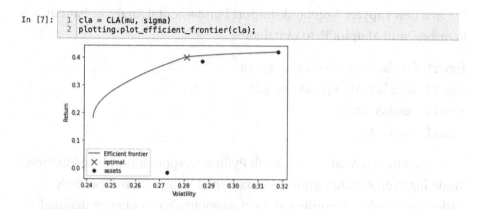

Figure 6-23. *Plotting the optimal portfolio with CLA*

The PyPortfolioOpt library is irreplaceable in investment portfolio management. It is easy to use and well documented. My advice is to keep an eye on the documentation (https://pyportfolioopt.readthedocs. io/en/latest/index.html) for new features or changes. There are some additional features we have not touched in the chapter such as implementing your own optimizers. I believe after the preceding examples, you have a better understanding of how to operate PyPortfolioOpt.

Fundamental Analysis

There are numerous ways you can access corporate financial information these days. One of them is the Alpha Vantage API we discussed in Chapter 4. Here, I would like to demonstrate another Python package Fundamental Analysis for acquiring and analyzing balance sheets, income statements, cash flows, and other substantial information of publicly traded companies.

We need to install the Fundamental Analysis library with the pip command:

```
pip install FundamentalAnalysis
```

In a new **Jupyter** Notebook, import Fundamental Analysis, Pandas, Requests, and Matplotlib to plot data:

```
import FundamentalAnalysis as fa
import matplotlib.pyplot as plt
import pandas as pd
import requests
```

Fundamental Analysis is a small Python wrapper around the Financial Modeling Prep API that gathers fundamental information of publicly traded companies. According to the documentation, it obtains detailed data on more than 13,000 companies.[5]

In order to start using the Financial Analysis package, you need to secure an API Key from `https://financialmodelingprep.com/developer/docs/`. Register and choose a free plan or a paid plan for premium APIs and 30+ years of historic data. After you select a plan, go to the dashboard in the upper menu where you can find your API Key.

We can start exploring Financial Analysis capabilities after you receive an API Key. The API Key I'll be using in this example will be disabled.

For starters, let's get the list of all available companies and ETFs (exchange-traded funds):

```
API_KEY = "1b01185c3c4ae0c8626ad15beb99a957"
companies = fa.available_companies(API_KEY)
```

The data received from the `available_companies()` function as well as all other functions comes as a DataFrame. Using the `iloc[]` method, we can move through the rows (Figure 6-24):

```
companies.iloc[5:10]
```

---

[5] `https://pypi.org/project/FundamentalAnalysis/`

```
In [1]:   1  import FundamentalAnalysis as fa
          2  import matplotlib.pyplot as plt
          3  import pandas as pd
          4  import requests
```

```
In [2]:   1  API_KEY = "1b01185c3c4ae0c8626ad15beb99a955"
```

```
In [3]:   1  companies = fa.available_companies(API_KEY)
          2  companies.iloc[5:10]
```

Out[3]:

	name	price	exchange
symbol			
GDX	VanEck Vectors Gold Miners	32.64	New York Stock Exchange Arca
GE	General Electric Co	12.66	New York Stock Exchange
BAC	Bank of America Corp	36.90	New York Stock Exchange
EEM	iShares MSCI Emerging Index Fund	52.89	New York Stock Exchange Arca
XLF	SPDR Select Sector Fund - Financial	33.16	New York Stock Exchange Arca

Figure 6-24. *Browsing through the list of available companies*

If you have a favorite company, use its exchange symbol. I'll use
Exxon Mobil Corporation. The symbol of Exxon Mobil on New York Stock
Exchange is XOM. The function profile() will get us essential information
about any publicly traded company (Figure 6-25):

```
ticker = "XOM"
profile = fa.profile(ticker, API_KEY)
```

```
In [4]:    1  ticker = "XOM"
           2  profile = fa.profile(ticker, API_KEY)
           3  profile
```

Out[4]:

	0
symbol	XOM
price	55.22
beta	1.28061
volAvg	31063027
mktCap	233774989000
lastDiv	3.48
range	31.11-62.55
changes	-0.69
companyName	Exxon Mobil Corp
currency	USD
cik	0000034088
isin	US30231G1022

Figure 6-25. *Receiving a profile of the XOM ticker*

A valuation is an important piece of information, and Financial Analysis provides it with the function `enterprise()` for the five-year period with free plans and for longer periods with a paid plan (Figure 6-26):

```
entreprise_value = fa.enterprise(ticker, API_KEY)
entreprise_value
```

```
In [6]:    1  entreprise_value = fa.enterprise(ticker, API_KEY)
           2  entreprise_value
```

Out[6]:

	2020	2019	2018	2017	2016
symbol	XOM	XOM	XOM	XOM	XOM
stockPrice	44.84	64.79	72.29	86.78	84.86
numberOfShares	4234000000	4234000000	4237000000	4256000000	4170212766
marketCapitalization	189852560000	2.74321e+11	306292734237	369335675744	3.53884e+11
minusCashAndCashEquivalents	4364000000	3089000000	3042000000	3177000000	3657000000
addTotalDebt	65960000000	26373000000	23305000000	27845000000	30667000000
enterpriseValue	251448560000	297604864234	326555734237	394003675744	3.80894e+11

Figure 6-26. *Valuation of Exxon Mobil Corp*

They called it Fundamental Analysis for a reason; with the function `balance_sheet_statement()`, we can fetch balance sheets of a publicly traded company for a several year period (Figure 6-27). The keyword argument `period` could be set either to the `"annual"` or `"quarter"` option. Besides the assets and liabilities, `balance_sheet_statement()` returns the links to SEC (US Securities and Exchange Commission) filings so you could go right to the source.

```
In [8]:   1  balance_sheet_annually = fa.balance_sheet_statement(ticker, API_KEY, period="annual")
          2  balance_sheet_annually
```

Out[8]:

	2020	2019	2018
	USD	USD	USD
	2021-02-24	2020-02-26 00:00:00	2019-02-27 00:00:00
	2021-02-24 17:01:02	2020-02-26 16:15:19	2019-02-27 16:19:37
	FY	FY	FY
	4364000000	3089000000	3042000000
	0	0	0
	4364000000	3089000000	3042000000
	20581000000	26966000000	24701000000

Figure 6-27. *Balance sheets of Exxon Mobil Corp*

Along with a balance sheet, you can get an income statement and a cash flow statement:

```
income_statement_annually = fa.income_statement(ticker,
API_KEY, period="annual")
cash_flow_statement_annually = fa.cash_flow_statement(ticker,
API_KEY, period="annual")
```

We can visually analyze the data with Matplotlib. Gross profit is an important component of a Fundamental Analysis, and we will visualize it by plotting the revenue and cost of revenue numbers as bars.

On the x axis of the graph, we will plot years:

```
x = income_statement_annually.columns
```

and we will grab the numbers from the income statement for the
revenue and cost of revenue:

revenue = income_statement_annually.loc["revenue"]

cost = income_statement_annually.loc["costOfRevenue"]

The bar chart as other Matplotlib figures requires coordinates for x and
y axis arguments. Along with that, we will specify the color and width of
bars arguments:

```
plt.bar(x, revenue, color ='maroon', width = 0.6)
plt.bar(x, cost, color ='blue', width = 0.6)
plt.title("Exxon Mobil Corp Revenue/Cost of Revenue");
```

Based on the visual analysis, we see that 2020 was a tough year for
Exxon Mobil Corp (Figure 6-28).

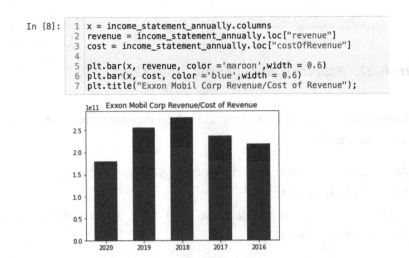

Figure 6-28. *Visualization of gross profit*

With Financial Analysis, you can get the raw data from the US
Securities and Exchange Commission (SEC) or key financial ratios.

The function key_metrics() will deliver all the main measures like the current ratio of return on equity:

```
ratios = fa.key_metrics(ticker, API_KEY)
```

Using the subplot() function from Matplotlib, we will plot the return on investment capital and return on equity from ratios on the same figure but in the separate windows. We set the x axis as years from ratios.columns and y values will be roic and roe from the rows. We get the rows by labels with the DataFrame method loc[]:

```
x = ratios.columns
roic = ratios.loc["roic"]
roe = ratios.loc["roe"]

plt.subplot(211)
plt.plot(x, roic, color="blue", marker="o", label="ROIC")
plt.legend()
plt.subplot(212)
plt.plot(x, roe, color="green", linestyle='--', label="ROE")
plt.legend();
```

The numbers 211 and 212 in the method subplot represent the grids, where the first number 2 means the number of rows, and the second number 1 is the number of columns; each subplot has just one column. The last number shows a position of a subplot within the whole figure.

The plot gets us two subplots on the same figure where each graph displays separate values (Figure 6-29).

```
In [11]:    1  x = ratios.columns
            2  roic = ratios.loc["roic"]
            3  roe = ratios.loc["roe"]
            4
            5  plt.subplot(211)
            6  plt.plot(x, roic, color="blue", marker="o", label="ROIC")
            7  plt.legend()
            8  plt.subplot(212)
            9  plt.plot(x, roe, color="green", linestyle='--', label="ROE")
           10  plt.legend();
```

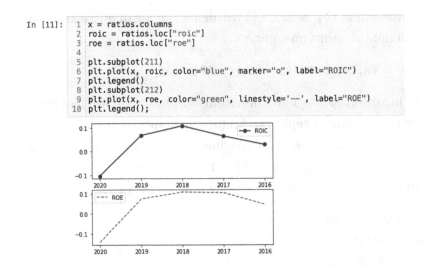

Figure 6-29. *Plotting ROIC and ROE ratios*

Financial Ratios

Another set of ratios are financial ratios. Fiancial ratios help investors important information about a company health and help to compare companies performance within an industry. We can get them with the function `financial_ratios()`:

`fin_ratios = fa.financial_ratios(ticker, API_KEY)`

One of the financial ratios we have received that I want to plot is the inventory turnover.

In [13]:
```
1  x = fin_ratios.columns
2  it = fin_ratios.loc["inventoryTurnover"]
3  plt.grid()
4  plt.plot(x, it, marker="p" )
5  plt.title("Exxon Mobil Corp Inventory Turnover");
```

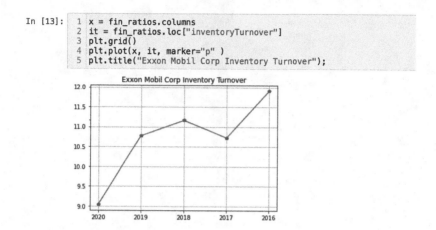

Figure 6-30. *Plotting the inventory turnover ratio*

An inventory turnover shows how fast a company sells its inventory. The high inventory turnover ratio in 2016 points to higher sales, which probably reflects high oil prices (Figure 6-30).

Financial Analysis is a very convenient package to grab financial information with just a few lines of code.

As we have seen in this chapter, you can build a solution from scratch or use a third-party library with Python. It is entirely up to you what road to take. If you are an algorithmic trader, you would probably prefer a custom-built high-tuned solution. On the other hand, if you need to get the numbers fast, then you can always find a Python package that does the job. In my opinion, Python is a great tool for any kind of financial analysis.

CHAPTER 7

Essential Digital Marketing Tasks Done with Python

Digital marketing requires digital tools to work with social media, send sales emails, and acquire clients in the World Wide Web. There are numerous marketing applications helping digital marketeers to run, test, and analyze promo campaigns, but some of them are ridiculously expensive, and others are not customizable and require additional work to get needed results.

Would it be great if with a few lines of code, you could've run and evaluate any custom scenario for free? You can build your own marketing tools with Python. All big tech giants provide free and easy-to-use APIs to automate tasks and manage the information.

In this chapter, we will take a look at the most popular marketing services from Google, Twitter, and Mailgun. Using their APIs and Python, we will robotize many tedious tasks. Besides, we will learn how to get the marketing data in Python-readable format to examine it with Pandas.

We will start with the most essential digital marketing instrument – Google Analytics. Google is a Python-friendly company, and Python's inventor Guido van Rossum had work at Google for a while. Many Google services run on Python, and almost all of them can be

© Art Yudin 2021
A. Yudin, *Basic Python for Data Management, Finance, and Marketing*,
https://doi.org/10.1007/978-1-4842-7189-6_7

accessed through APIs. Google even has its own Python library to make a connection to its services as simple as possible.

Getting Started with Google API Client

I want to start with a quick introduction to the Google API Client package. The Google API Client libraries provide an entry point to all essential Google products. Whether you want to send or read email from a Gmail account or access Google Maps with Python, you would need to have Google API Python Client installed on your machine.

The installation process is seamless with a Python package manager pip. Open Terminal in Anaconda Navigator ➤ Environments ➤ base ➤ Terminal, and using the *pip* command, install the Google API Client package:

```
pip install google-api-python-client
```

All Google services require authentication and enabling the API.[1] The process I am about to describe here would be a generic scenario for any Google API service.

Google recommends managing your projects and monitoring API usage in one place, Google Cloud Platform (`https://cloud.google.com/`). Some of Google services are free, some require payments, but regardless of that, for new developers Google offers a $300 credit which is more than enough to try the APIs. If you do not have a Google account yet, create one at `https://accounts.google.com` and log in to Google Cloud Platform.

The dashboard of Google Cloud Platform might be a bit intimidating for a newcomer because of too much information and unknown abbreviations. We need to create a new project for an API.

---

[1] `https://developers.google.com/analytics/devguides/reporting/data/v1/quickstart-client-libraries`

Step 1: Look for **"create project"** right next to the Google Cloud Platform logo on top or simply jump to the Manage resources page (`https://console.cloud.google.com/cloud-resource-manager`).

On the Manage resources page, you will see the "create project" button on top (Figure 7-1).

Figure 7-1. *Google Cloud Platform Manage resources page*

Click **"create project"** and assign a project name in the new project prompt. The name could be anything, and the location field could be left with a default "No organization" value. Step 2: After you click the blue create button, you should see the newly created project in the dashboard. If you have another project on the home page of Google Cloud Platform, in the top menu choose the one you want to use. Step 3: The dashboard consists of many cards; choose the one that says API. On the bottom of the API's card, you will see a **"Go to APIs overview"** arrow. As you may recall from Chapter 4, pretty much any API requires authentication in the form of an API Key. The API overview link should take you to the API & Services page where you can see all usage information and establish credentials. Step 4: On the top of API & Services, click the plus sign **"ENABLE APIS AND SERVICES".**

This will take you to the API Library where you could choose any Google service you want to get connected to. In the current case, type Google Analytics API in the search prompt on the page. Besides the Google Analytics API, we also filtered all other Google analytical services such as the Google Analytics Reporting API and YouTube Analytics. Choose the Google Analytics Reporting API (Figure 7-2).

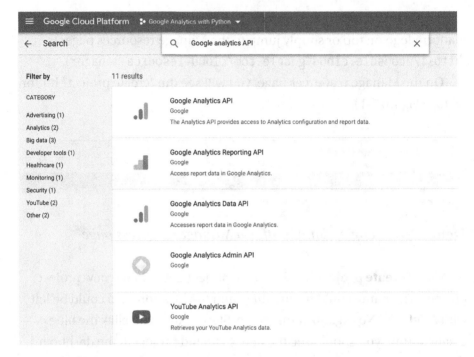

Figure 7-2. Searching for Google Analytics Reporting API services

The Google Analytics Reporting API page provides all information about the service. Also, you could find a link to tutorials and documentation. I would recommend keeping an eye on the documentation as they might change something going forward.

Our goal is to invoke the Google Analytics Reporting API; on the page, look for the blue "ENABLE" button and click it. After that, you should be redirected back to the APIs & Services page. One last step left to have a fully functional app service with Google is receive an API Key for the service. In the left-hand menu, click the credentials option with a key. The credentials page lets you to initialize, manage, and change API Keys. On the top of the credentials page, you should see the plus sign create credentials button. Click it and choose the API Key option. The API Key created card will pop up upon creation of an API Key (Figure 7-3).

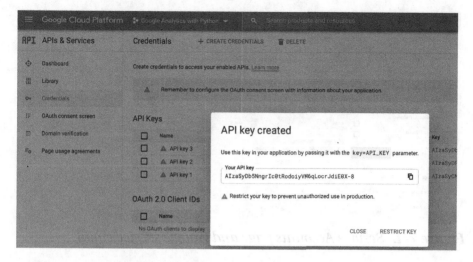

Figure 7-3. *Generating an API Key for a Google Analytics service*

Most Google API services require an API Key. Save that key for later.

Google Analytics with Python

We are one step away from placing our first Google Analytics API call; Google Analytics requires an API Key to be provided in JSON format. The easy way to generate a JSON file with a key would be to open the **Service Accounts** page in Google Cloud Platform. You can search for it in a prompt on top or navigate to **IAM & Admin** in the left menu. From **IAM & Admin**, choose the **Service Accounts** option; it should take you to the https://console.cloud.google.com/iam-admin/serviceaccounts page. If you have multiple projects, click the one for Google Analytics. There you should see the project email Google has created for the service (Figure 7-4).

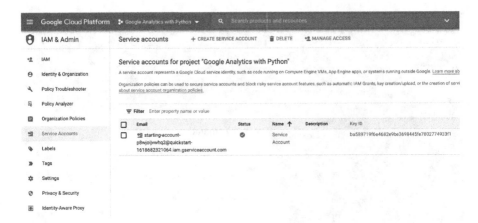

Figure 7-4. *Service Accounts page and Google service email*

Click the email and navigate to the **Keys** tab. There you'll see the **Add Key** button. Click **Add Key** and choose the **Create New Key** option. The pop-up window will offer to generate a JSON Key file (Figure 7-5); click the **Create** button and save it to your machine.

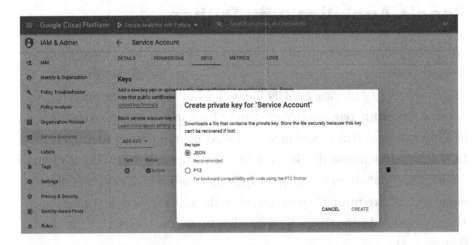

Figure 7-5. *Generating a key and saving it as a JSON file*

Finally, after we have generated an API Key as a JSON file, we can write some code to use Google Analytics. It is time for Python code; open a new **Jupyter** Notebook and move the downloaded JSON Key file to the same working directory. Also, it would be a good idea to rename the JSON file to client_secret_api.js.

To get authenticated, we would need to install the Oauth2client library. You know where to find a Terminal window, so just run the pip command and install the library:

```
pip install oauth2client
```

On top of a new **Jupyter** Notebook, import

```
from oauth2client.service_account import
ServiceAccountCredentials
from apiclient.discovery import build
```

At the beginning of the script, we need to define the credentials. SCOPES will be the same for everybody trying to get access to Google Analytics. KEY_FILE_LOCATION should provide a path to the downloaded JSON file with the API Key. I have renamed my file to *client_secret_api.json*. Finally, VIEW_ID should hold your View ID for your Google Analytics project. You can find VIEW_ID on your analytics.google.com page. VIEW_ID is assigned to the .\ Web resource you track if you have activated the **"Create a Universal Analytics property"** option in Google Analytics. Go to **Admin** settings on the bottom left and look for View Settings. There in **Basic Settings**, you'll find the **View ID** number for your website. While you are in Google Analytics, add the email from Service Accounts (Figure 7-4) to the list of users allowed to generate reports in Account User Management.

```
SCOPES = ['https://www.googleapis.com/auth/analytics.readonly']
KEY_FILE_LOCATION = 'client_secret_api.json'
VIEW_ID = '123415356'
```

To initialize credentials, we will use imported *ServiceAccountCredentials* and pass `KEY_FILE_LOCATION` and `SCOPES` as arguments:

```
credentials = ServiceAccountCredentials.from_json_keyfile_
name(KEY_FILE_LOCATION, SCOPES)
```

Next, we will need to connect the Google API Client library via the function *build()*. As I have mentioned before, the Google API Client package is generic and works with all Google services. In the function build(), you need to specify a service you want to get connected to and a version of the package:

```
analytics = build('analyticsreporting', 'v4', credentials=
credentials)
```

The Google Analytics report requires a period range. We can set `start_date` and `end_date`:

```
start_date = "2020-01-01"
end_date = "2021-04-23"
```

Also, we would need to specify dimensions and metrics for the Google Analytics report. You can find the list of all available metrics here: `https://ga-dev-tools.appspot.com/dimensions-metrics-explorer/`.

For my first report, I'll use very popular `users` and `sessions` metrics. To send a request for this report, we need to use the *analytics.reports()* function, and in the body specify `VIEW_ID`, dates, metrics, and dimensions:

```
response = analytics.reports().batchGet(body={
    'reportRequests': [{
        'viewId': VIEW_ID,
        'dateRanges': [{'startDate': start_date, 'endDate':
        end_date}],
        'metrics': [
```

```
        {"expression": "ga:users"},
        {"expression": "ga:sessions"}
    ]
}]}).execute()
```

Users and sessions metrics arguments should be passed into the function as array keys and values where "expression" followed by metrics.

Print the response in a new cell, and you'll see a generated report from Google Analytics come in JSON format (Figure 7-6).

```
In [1]:  1  from oauth2client.service_account import ServiceAccountCredentials
         2  from apiclient.discovery import build

In [2]:  1  SCOPES = ['https://www.googleapis.com/auth/analytics.readonly']
         2  KEY_FILE_LOCATION = 'client_secret_api.json'
         3  VIEW_ID = '123415356'

In [3]:  1  credentials = ServiceAccountCredentials.from_json_keyfile_name(KEY_FILE_LOCATION, SCOPES)
         2  analytics = build('analyticsreporting', 'v4', credentials=credentials)

In [4]:  1  start_date = "2020-01-01"
         2  end_date = "2021-04-23"

In [5]:  1  response = analytics.reports().batchGet(body={
         2      'reportRequests': [{
         3          'viewId': VIEW_ID,
         4          'dateRanges': [{'startDate': start_date, 'endDate': end_date}],
         5          'metrics': [
         6              {"expression": "ga:users"},
         7              {"expression": "ga:sessions"}
         8          ]
         9      }]}).execute()

In [6]:  1  response

Out[6]: {'reports': [{'columnHeader': {'metricHeader': {'metricHeaderEntries': [{'name': 'ga:users',
           'type': 'INTEGER'},
          {'name': 'ga:sessions', 'type': 'INTEGER'}]}},
         'data': {'rows': [{'metrics': [{'values': ['308074', '363017']}]}],
          'totals': [{'values': ['308074', '363017']}],
          'rowCount': 1,
          'minimums': [{'values': ['308074', '363017']}],
          'maximums': [{'values': ['308074', '363017']}]}}]}
```

Figure 7-6. *Generating a Google Analytics report for users and sessions metrics*

We have dealt with JSON before and know that it works like a Python dictionary.

The response contains an array under the key `"reports"`. We can fetch the array and grab the first item:

```
response['reports'][0]
```

The information we are looking for is stored under the `data` key. The `data` holds another dictionary, and we can see all the keys by applying a dictionary method `keys()`:

```
response['reports'][0]["data"].keys()
```

The options we receive are

```
dict_keys(['rows', 'totals', 'rowCount', 'minimums',
'maximums'])
```

The `totals` key is holding the information we want to use. We will get the values for `users` and `sessions`:

```
report = response['reports'][0]["data"]['totals'][0]
users = report['values'][0]
sessions = report['values'][1]
```

In Figure 7-7, we can see that unique users 308087 visited the site with a total of 363031 sessions.

```
In [6]:    1  response
Out[6]: {'reports': [{'columnHeader': {'metricHeader': {'metricHeaderEntries': [{'name': 'ga:users',
                'type': 'INTEGER'},
              {'name': 'ga:sessions', 'type': 'INTEGER'}]}},
            'data': {'rows': [{'metrics': [{'values': ['308087', '363031']}]}],
            'totals': [{'values': ['308087', '363031']}],
            'rowCount': 1,
            'minimums': [{'values': ['308087', '363031']}],
            'maximums': [{'values': ['308087', '363031']}]}}]}

In [7]:    1  report = response['reports'][0]["data"]['totals'][0]

In [8]:    1  users = report['values'][0]
           2  users
Out[8]: '308087'

In [9]:    1  sessions = report['values'][1]
           2  sessions
Out[9]: '363031'
```

Figure 7-7. *Fetching users and sessions values from a JSON response*

To visualize how engaged users are with the site, we can plot new and returning users. The sessions includes all visitors, new and returning. The users on the other hand represent new visitors.

We need to import Matplotlib in the first cell where we keep all our imports:

```
import matplotlib.pyplot as plt
```

The percentage of new visitors can be calculated as users divided by sessions. Do not forget that JSON comes as a string, and all values have to be converted to numeric data types:

```
new_visitors = int(users)/int(sessions)
returning_visitors = 100 - new_visitors
```

We will plot these numbers as a donut chart. A donut chart is a combination of a pie chart and a circle (Figure 7-8):

```
metrics = [new_visitors, returning_visitors]
plt.pie(metrics, shadow=True, colors=["#E74C3C","#27AE60"],
labels=["New Visitors", "Returning Visitors"])
```

```
donut = plt.Circle( (0,0), 0.5, color='white')
p = plt.gcf()
p.gca().add_artist(donut);
```

```
In [10]:   1  new_visitors = int(users)/int(sessions)
           2  returning_visitors = 100 - new_visitors
           3  new_visitors

Out[10]:   0.848651790313384

In [11]:   1  metrics = [new_visitors,returning_visitors]
           2  plt.pie(metrics,shadow=True,colors=["#E74C3C","#27AE60"], labels=["New Visitors","Returning Visitors"])
           3  # add a circle at the center to transform it in a donut chart
           4  donut = plt.Circle( (0,0), 0.5, color='white')
           5  p = plt.gcf()
           6  p.gca().add_artist(donut);
```

Figure 7-8. *Plot of new users and returning users based on metrics values*

Another popular Google Analytics report is pageviews and session duration.

Dates and VIEW_ID will be the same as we used in the previous example. This time, we can structure the received data as a DataFrame. In the first cell, add Pandas to the imported libraries:

import pandas as pd

According to the Google Dimensions & Metrics Explorer,[2] we will need to pass ga:pageviews and ga:avgSessionDuration as metrics and ga:deviceCategory as dimensions. Let's compile an analytics report request like this:

---

[2]https://ga-dev-tools.appspot.com/dimensions-metrics-explorer/

```
response = analytics.reports().batchGet(body={
    'reportRequests': [{
        'viewId': VIEW_ID,
        'dateRanges': [{'startDate': start_date, 'endDate':
        end_date}],
        'metrics': [
            {"expression": "ga:pageviews"},
            {"expression": "ga:avgSessionDuration"}
        ], "dimensions": [
            {"name": "ga:deviceCategory"}
        ]
}]}).execute()
```

The response you receive should look like the one in Figure 7-9.

```
In [12]:     1  response = analytics.reports().batchGet(body={
             2      'reportRequests': [{
             3          'viewId': VIEW_ID,
             4          'dateRanges': [{'startDate': start_date, 'endDate': end_date}],
             5          'metrics': [
             6              {"expression": "ga:pageviews"},
             7              {"expression": "ga:avgSessionDuration"}
             8          ], "dimensions": [
             9              {"name": "ga:deviceCategory"}
            10          ]
            11  }]}).execute()

In [13]:     1  response

Out[13]: {'reports': [{'columnHeader': {'dimensions': ['ga:deviceCategory'],
            'metricHeader': {'metricHeaderEntries': [{'name': 'ga:pageviews',
             'type': 'INTEGER'},
            {'name': 'ga:avgSessionDuration', 'type': 'TIME'}]}},
          'data': {'rows': [{'dimensions': ['desktop'],
            'metrics': [{'values': ['689331', '47.1034009002383']}]},
           {'dimensions': ['mobile'],
            'metrics': [{'values': ['48839', '61.065466666666666']}]},
           {'dimensions': ['tablet'],
            'metrics': [{'values': ['1571', '74.28005657708628']}]}],
          'totals': [{'values': ['739741', '48.021453140447846']}],
          'rowCount': 3,
          'minimums': [{'values': ['1571', '47.1034009002383']}],
          'maximums': [{'values': ['689331', '74.28005657708628']}],
          'isDataGolden': True}}]}
```

Figure 7-9. *Requesting a Google Analytics report for pageviews and session duration*

As in the previous example, we would need to fetch the values out of the response. In most APIs, all information is stored under the `"data"` key. Using a dictionary notation, we can unpack the response and get to "data":

```
response['reports'][0]["data"]
```

Since we have asked for dimensions values, the data contains another key `"rows"`. We can store that path under a new variable `report_two`:

```
report_two = response['reports'][0]["data"]["rows"]
```

If you run the function `type()` on the `report_two` object, you'll see that it is a list data structure. The `report_two` list contains three dictionaries with `"dimensions"` and `"metrics"` keys. At the same time, `"metrics"` leads to another list with one dictionary and the key `"values"` (Figure 7-10).

```
In [14]:    1  report_two = response['reports'][0]["data"]["rows"]
            2  report_two

Out[14]:  [{'dimensions': ['desktop'],
            'metrics': [{'values': ['689331', '47.1034009002383']}]},
           {'dimensions': ['mobile'],
            'metrics': [{'values': ['48839', '61.065466666666666']}]},
           {'dimensions': ['tablet'],
            'metrics': [{'values': ['1571', '74.28005657708628']}]}]
```

Figure 7-10. *Unpacking the response*

Our goal is to grab the values and to store them in a DataFrame. Due to the fact that `report_two` is a list, we can iterate through it and fetch the values using a dictionary notation:

```
for item in report_two:
    print(
        item["dimensions"][0], item["metrics"][0]["values"][0],
        item["metrics"][0]["values"][1]
    )
```

I know that the print() part of the for loop is a little bit messy and confusing. I'll explain what is going on there. We will start with item["dimensions"][0]. In Figure 7-10, we see that the "dimensions" key holds a list with one value; to get that value, we would need to index it [0]. In the for loop, the item variable represents each dictionary from the report_two list. item["dimensions"] gets us another list, and then we index it to fetch the first and the only value item["dimensions"][0]. Using the same logic, we can fetch the pageviews values. item["metrics"] gets us a list; we index it [0] and see another dictionary like this one: {'values': ['689331', '47.1034009002383']}. The key "values" item["metrics"][0]["values"] leads us to another list with two values. One for the pageview and the other one for session duration. The first value from that list can be indexed as [0] and the second as [1]. The bottom-line item["metrics"][0]["values"][0] fetches us a value for pageview and item["metrics"][0]["values"][1] for session duration.

In order to store all these values as a DataFrame, we need to place them into Python lists.

Initialize three empty lists:

```
devices = []
pageviews = []
session_duration = []
```

As we iterate through the report_two list, we append the values to each list. As always, keep in mind that down the road you would want to do something with these values. Maybe filter or compare them. The response came as a string, and we will convert the values into integers and floats:

```
devices = []
pageviews = []
session_durations = []

for item in report_two:
    device = item["dimensions"][0]
    page = int(item["metrics"][0]["values"][0])
```

```
session = round(float(item["metrics"][0]["values"][1]),2)
devices.append(device)
pageviews.append(page)
session_durations.append(session)
```

After we have grouped all values in the lists, we will construct a DataFrame:

```
data = pd.DataFrame()
```

Add the lists as columns:

```
data["Page_views"] = pageviews
data["Session_duration"] = session_durations
data.index = devices
```

At the end of the day, the received report boils down to clean values stored in a DataFrame and ready to be analyzed (Figure 7-11).

```
In [15]:    1  devices = []
            2  pageviews = []
            3  session_durations = []
            4
            5  for item in report_two:
            6      device = item["dimensions"][0]
            7      page = int(item["metrics"][0]["values"][0])
            8      session = round(float(item["metrics"][0]["values"][1]),2)
            9      devices.append(device)
           10      pageviews.append(page)
           11      session_durations.append(session)

In [16]:    1  data = pd.DataFrame()
            2
            3  data["Page_views"] = pageviews
            4  data["Session_duration"] = session_durations
            5  data.index = devices
            6
            7  data

Out[16]:
                    Page_views   Session_duration
         desktop      689331           47.10
          mobile       48839           61.07
          tablet        1571           74.28
```

Figure 7-11.   The values from the Google Analytics report stored as a DataFrame

With one line of code, we can visualize the data. This time, we will be using Pandas built-in `plot()` and `pie()` methods:

```
data.plot.pie(figsize=(18, 12), subplots=True, colors=["#FF0000",
"#00FF00","#0000FF"]);
```

Our graph for the pageviews vs. session duration report will look like in Figure 7-12.

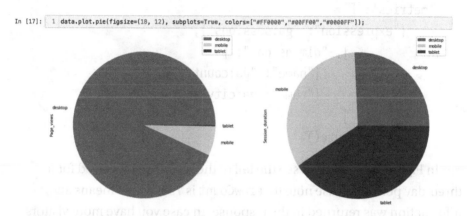

Figure 7-12. *Visualization of pageviews and session duration values from the Google Analytics report*

Every time I check my Google Analytics, I wonder where people visiting my site are from. With the same template for the Google Analytics request, we will get the location of sessions using the country and city.

This time, I will decrease the date range and set it to a three-day period. With a larger time period, you will get more information. Each Google Analytics response contains a thousand of rows, and to fetch all data, you would need to use a `while` loop to send an API request over and over again till you get all the rows. For the dimensions, I'll use `ga:country` and `ga:city`. Another way to track the site visitors would be `ga:latitude` and ga:longitude. Besides the date range and dimensions, my Google Analytics request will be the same:

```
response = analytics.reports().batchGet(body={
    'reportRequests': [{
    'viewId': VIEW_ID,
    'dateRanges': [{'startDate': "2021-04-20",
                'endDate':"2021-04-23"}],
    'metrics': [
        {"expression": "ga:sessions"},
            ], "dimensions": [
                {"name": "ga:country"},
                {"name":"ga:city"}
            ]
    }]}).execute()
```

In Figure 7-13, you can see the tail of the response I received for a three-day period. Please note that rowCount is 758, which means all information was returned in the response. In case you have more visitors or take a larger timeframe, a response would contain nextPageToken. Then you would need to send another request for the next 1000 rows.

```
In [18]:    1  response = analytics.reports().batchGet(body={
            2      'reportRequests': [{
            3      'viewId': VIEW_ID,
            4      'dateRanges': [{'startDate': "2021-04-20", 'endDate':"2021-04-23"}],
            5      'metrics': [
            6          {"expression": "ga:sessions"},
            7              ], "dimensions": [
            8                      {"name": "ga:country"},
            9                      {"name":"ga:city"}
           10              ]
           11          }]}).execute()
```

```
In [19]:    1  response
```

```
{'dimensions': ['United States', 'Woodstock'],
 'metrics': [{'values': ['1']}]},
{'dimensions': ['Uruguay', 'Montevideo'], 'metrics': [{'values': ['1']}]},
{'dimensions': ['Uzbekistan', 'Tashkent'],
 'metrics': [{'values': ['6']}]},
{'dimensions': ['Venezuela', 'Caracas'], 'metrics': [{'values': ['3']}]},
{'dimensions': ['Vietnam', '(not set)'], 'metrics': [{'values': ['2']}]},
{'dimensions': ['Vietnam', 'Da Nang'], 'metrics': [{'values': ['1']}]},
{'dimensions': ['Vietnam', 'Di An'], 'metrics': [{'values': ['12']}]},
{'dimensions': ['Vietnam', 'Hanoi'], 'metrics': [{'values': ['6']}]},
{'dimensions': ['Vietnam', 'Ho Chi Minh City'],
 'metrics': [{'values': ['7']}]},
{'dimensions': ['Vietnam', 'Tay Ninh'], 'metrics': [{'values': ['2']}]},
{'dimensions': ['Vietnam', 'Vinh Yen'], 'metrics': [{'values': ['1']}]}],
'totals': [{'values': ['1650']}],
'rowCount': 758,
'minimums': [{'values': ['1']}],
'maximums': [{'values': ['41']}],
'isDataGolden': True}}]}
```

Figure 7-13. *Calling the Google Analytics API to see visitors of the site by country and city dimensions*

The raw response data has to be converted to an analysis-friendly DataFrame. The routine will be similar to what we did in the previous examples.

We need to grab the information out of the response. I'll save the information as a list under the variable name report_three:

```
report_three = response['reports'][0]["data"]["rows"]
```

Then we need to initialize three Python lists to hold our data:

```
countries = []
cities = []
sessions = []
```

To iterate through report_three and get country, city, and sessions out of each row, we will use the for loop:

```
for item in report_three:
    country = item["dimensions"][0]
    city = item["dimensions"][1]
    session = item["metrics"][0]["values"][0]
    countries.append(country)
    cities.append(city)
    sessions.append(session)
```

After we have all data in the lists, we can construct a DataFrame out of them.

Initialize a new DataFrame:

```
location = pd.DataFrame()
```

Assign the lists as values to columns in the DataFrame location:

```
location["Country"] = countries
location["City"] = cities
location["Sessions"] = sessions
```

Some of the values in the DataFrame location contain (not set) (Figure 7-14). That simply means Google Analytics could not identify a visitor by location.

```
In [20]:   1  report_three = response['reports'][0]["data"]["rows"]
           2
           3  countries = []
           4  cities = []
           5  sessions = []
           6
           7  for item in report_three:
           8
           9      country = item["dimensions"][0]
          10      city = item["dimensions"][1]
          11      session = item["metrics"][0]["values"][0]
          12      countries.append(country)
          13      cities.append(city)
          14      sessions.append(session)
          15
          16
          17  location = pd.DataFrame()
          18  location["Country"] = countries
          19  location["City"] = cities
          20  location["Sessions"] = sessions
```

```
In [21]:   1  location
```

Out[21]:

	Country	City	Sessions
0	(not set)	(not set)	2
1	Albania	Tirana	1
2	Algeria	(not set)	3
3	Algeria	Oran	1

Figure 7-14. *Constructing a DataFrame with values from the response received from the Google Analytics API*

For me, the most important market is the United States, and I can sort the DataFrame by the Country column:

```
market = location[location.Country=="United States"]
```

Also, I want to see the cities with most sessions during this three-day period. I'll sort market data by the number of sessions:

```
market.sort_values(by="Sessions", ascending=False,
inplace=True)
```

This operation might get you a warning that you are trying to save sorting values on a slice of the main DataFrame (Figure 7-15). That is because I use inplace=True. The inplace argument saves the changes.

That is OK; it is just a warning. To get three cities with the most sessions, I can slice the market DataFrame:

```
market.iloc[0:3]
```

```
In [22]:   1  market = location[location.Country=="United States"]

In [23]:   1  market.sort_values(by="Sessions", ascending=False, inplace=True)
           <ipython-input-23-9c0bccb3be1d>:1: SettingWithCopyWarning:
           A value is trying to be set on a copy of a slice from a DataFrame

           See the caveats in the documentation: https://pandas.pydata.org/pandas-docs/stable/user_guide/indexing.html#returni
           ng-a-view-versus-a-copy
             market.sort_values(by="Sessions", ascending=False, inplace=True)

In [24]:   1  market.iloc[:3]
Out[24]:
```

	Country	City	Sessions
720	United States	San Jose	9
641	United States	Houston	8
580	United States	Boston	7

Figure 7-15. *Sorting the DataFrame by values in the Session column*

I think the Google Analytics example gave you a sense of how to work with the Google API. All other Google API packages would require the same authentication, and the process of obtaining an API Key would be pretty much the same as we did at the beginning of this chapter.

Twitter Bot

Another practical application of Python is building bots for social media and chats. Here, we will build a simple Twitter bot. It will post content on a Twitter account.

I'll be honest with you; lately, it became more difficult to get your bot registered with Twitter and get API Keys. I hope by the time the book is published, the Twitter authentication process will be the same as I describe it here.

As a developer, you should start your API registration process with the Twitter developer docs here: https://developer.twitter.com/en. There you'll find a lot of information how to automate your Twitter account. Besides, they have a developer Q&A blog where you can find tons of useful information and get answers to any Twitter-related questions.

Before we start coding, we need to register our future app and obtain API Keys on https://developer.twitter.com/en/portal/dashboard. But even before that, you should be a Twitter user and have an active account.

The process of obtaining Twitter API Keys is the following. With your Twitter account, log in to the Twitter developer portal. There you would need to click the central button **"Create Project"** to launch a new app. Be prepared to provide your phone number. Twitter will not allow you to create an app without a phone number on your profile.

To obtain API Keys, you would need to provide the name of your project and shortly explain the purpose of your bot (Figure 7-16).

Figure 7-16. *Regestering a new Twitter App*

After you answer all questions, Twitter will provide you the API Key, API Secret Key, and Bearer Tokens. These are three keys we will need for our bot to get authenticated with Twitter. Besides these keys, you'll need to generate an Access Token and a Secret Token. To generate tokens, in

the left-side menu under **Projects & Apps**, click your app name. After
you clicked the app, you should see the **App Details** information. Scroll
down and look for the **App permissions** section. In the **App permissions**
section, click the **Edit** option and switch to **Read and Write** mode. This
operation is necessary for the bot to be able to post tweets. On top of the
same page on the **Keys and tokens** section, you need to generate the
Access Token and Secret token. Click the **Regenerate** button and store
the tokens in a secure place (Figure 7-17).

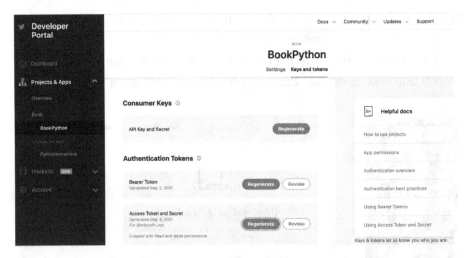

Figure 7-17. *Generating Access Token and Secret*

Right after you have all API Keys and Access tokens on hand, you are
ready to build a Twitter bot.

There are several Python Twitter libraries. I personally prefer Tweepy
for its simplicity. If later you decide to build something more sophisticated
than what we go over here, you can always refer to the Tweepy
documentation (`https://docs.tweepy.org/en/latest/`).

Tweepy is not a part of Anaconda, and you need to install it separately. In a Terminal window, run

```
pip install tweepy
```

In a new **Jupyter** Notebook, import Tweepy, the library we would need to send tweets:

```
import tweepy
```

The next step would be to define the API Keys and tokens Twitter provided us with:

```
API_KEY = 'Q88uOKvQK4f7fGfqO43SxVbcE'
API_SECRET = 'ahQk6VKzjuF5eucS6a6DJT3LubBqnBTj5JxT2BvBTaIDMKkZhO'
ACCESS_TOKEN = '797271725629173762-3etBbFChCjbQFCYYKf9oq5HtvMqmha9'
SECRET_TOKEN = 'apXizrBPPE7TqqW7OAhnBx1DzetrUpqNbPS1PoRzTZKjF'
```

First of all, we need to get authenticated by Twitter. Using Tweepy methods OAuthHandler and set_access_token, we pass the API Keys as arguments. Using these API Keys and tokens, you get authenticated and establish a connection with Twitter:

```
auth = tweepy.OAuthHandler(CONSUMER_KEY, CONSUMER_SECRET)
auth.set_access_token(OAUTH_TOKEN, OAUTH_TOKEN_SECRET)
api = tweepy.API(auth)
```

Our goal is to generate and send a tweet with an image and some text. Prepare an image and store it in the same directory where your **Jupyter** file is, or make sure you know the relative path to the image file.

Define the path to the file you want to upload with the image_path variable:

```
image_path = "/Users/programwithus/Chapter7/fortweeter.png"
```

After the bot has got authenticated, we are ready to post tweets with media files. The special Tweepy method `update_with_media()` posts media and adds a message. According to the documentation, too long messages or duplicating messages will be ignored. The message should be passed with the keyword `status`:

```
api.update_with_media(image_path, status="Python Rules! Learn
Python")
```

If the tweet was sent successfully, you should see the `Status` message with all details returned as in Figure 7-18 and the actual tweet (Figure 7-19).

```python
In [1]:    1  import tweepy
           2
           3  # personal information
           4  API_KEY = 'CxqpRJp1ZnhAUvCtnAF9wq43R'
           5  API_SECRET = 'fXvoPjSdc12qUDJi8UfAAX3d20jDbaFH2sgzDCu51sP20lTivU'
           6  ACCESS_TOKEN = '1152666427645726720-lqGcuwXjfRDqsc5YLVde9uCsQqoRGg'
           7  SECRET_TOKEN = 'R7rAw3UzBMJVmRQdujXCVKj6hoiXKORpc4wGoTMvbXqsn'
           8
           9
          10  auth = tweepy.OAuthHandler(API_KEY, API_SECRET)
          11  auth.set_access_token(ACCESS_TOKEN, SECRET_TOKEN)
          12  api = tweepy.API(auth)
          13
          14  image_path = "/Users/programwithus/Chapter7/fortweeter.png"
          15  api.update_with_media(image_path, status="Python Rules! Learn Python")
```

```
Out[1]:    Status(_api=<tweepy.api.API object at 0x7f968e484460>, _json={'created_at': 'Thu May 06 03:17:14 +0000 2021', 'id':
           1390143593369772037, 'id_str': '1390143593369772037', 'text': 'Python Rules! Learn Python https://t.co/U5ZePKsqdz',
           'truncated': False, 'entities': {'hashtags': [], 'symbols': [], 'user_mentions': [], 'urls': [], 'media': [{'id': 1
           390143591503351808, 'id_str': '1390143591503351808', 'indices': [27, 50], 'media_url': 'http://pbs.twimg.com/media/
           E0rIOy5X0AAkL4n.jpg', 'media_url_https': 'https://pbs.twimg.com/media/E0rIOy5X0AAkL4n.jpg', 'url': 'https://t.co/U5
           ZePKsqdz', 'display_url': 'pic.twitter.com/U5ZePKsqdz', 'expanded_url': 'https://twitter.com/artyudin_nyc/status/13
           90143593369772037/photo/1', 'type': 'photo', 'sizes': {'small': {'w': 680, 'h': 340, 'resize': 'fit'}, 'thumb': {'w
           ': 150, 'h': 150, 'resize': 'crop'}, 'medium': {'w': 1024, 'h': 512, 'resize': 'fit'}, 'large': {'w': 1024, 'h': 51
           2, 'resize': 'fit'}}}]}, 'extended_entities': {'media': [{'id': 1390143591503351808, 'id_str': '1390143591503351808
           ', 'indices': [27, 50], 'media_url': 'http://pbs.twimg.com/media/E0rIOy5X0AAkL4n.jpg', 'media_url_https': 'https://
           pbs.twimg.com/media/E0rIOy5X0AAkL4n.jpg', 'url': 'https://t.co/U5ZePKsqdz', 'display_url': 'pic.twitter.com/U5ZePKs
           qdz', 'expanded_url': 'https://twitter.com/artyudin_nyc/status/1390143593369772037/photo/1', 'type': 'photo', 'size
           s': {'small': {'w': 680, 'h': 340, 'resize': 'fit'}, 'thumb': {'w': 150, 'h': 150, 'resize': 'crop'}, 'medium': {'w
           ': 1024, 'h': 512, 'resize': 'fit'}, 'large': {'w': 1024, 'h': 512, 'resize': 'fit'}}}]}, 'source': '<a href="https
           ://help.twitter.com/en/using-twitter/how-to-tweet#source-labels" rel="nofollow">BookPython</a>', 'in_reply_to_statu
```

Figure 7-18. *The code to automatically send tweets with media files*

Figure 7-19. *Tweet sent by the Tweepy library*

In case you want to run a Twitter campaign and send tweets every day, you would need to store the content somewhere. Obviously, the best place would be a database with prepared text and paths to the images. Python works with any type of relational databases. The easiest option would be to use the Sqlite3 database. The Sqlite3 module comes with a standard Python distribution.

If you are not familiar with relational databases, a simple text or CSV file might be an alternative. The content and image links could be read from a file and then tweeted with Tweepy. The information about to be sent would be held in a list of lists and later dispended with the code we just created running in the for loop.

Email Marketing with Python

Sending an email with Python is quite an easy task. Python has Email and Smtplib modules to compose and send messages. The process is very well documented here: `https://docs.python.org/3/library/email.examples.html`. You need to simulate a server with the Smtplib package on your computer, and it will dispatch the email.

Regardless of its easiness, I do not find the process to be convenient for marketing purposes, especially when you want to reach 10,000 or even 100,000 recipients. For serious marketeers, I would recommend the Mailgun service. Mailgun gives you more flexibility using your own Python code with the comfort of an analytic dashboard.

Mailgun provides a Python API and could be easily integrated in any web application or used in a Python script. The Mailgun API is easy to use even for Python beginners. Also, the Mailgun service allows to use HTML templates and provides analytics on the performance of your email campaigns.

If you currently use one of the email marketing services, you should definitely compare the pricing and see if it would make sense to switch to Mailgun. In this book, we will use the Mailgun free trial.

Any marketing professional knows that branding is a key to gain customer trust. People these days will not open just any email. Potential customers will not click unless an email comes from a reliable source or clearly shows whom it's from. Mailgun gives you an option to add your domain name and make emails look professional. Although it is not necessary to add a domain name for testing purposes, Mailgun provides a sandbox domain, I will set up my domain artyudin.com to illustrate the process. In case you want to follow my code but do not have a domain name, you can get one at godaddy.com or namecheap.com as cheap as a dollar a year.

Open `www.mailgun.com/` in a browser and sign up for free to obtain an API Key. After the registration is completed, log in. You will see the dashboard; there you should see the **Sending** option in the left-side menu. Click **Sending**. Choose the **Domains** option from the menu, and if you want to add an existing domain, click the green **Add New Domain** button in the upper-left corner. In case you just want to try Mailgun, you can stick to the sandbox domain provided by Mailgun by default. The major disadvantage of using the sandbox domain is Mailgun allows to send messages to authorized recipients only. That means you would need to send them an invitation and ask to agree to receive emails from the Mailgun server.

After you clicked the green **Add New Domain** button, you should see a prompt asking for a domain you want to use. Before you click **Add Domain**, choose one of the regions **US** or **EU** where the domain was originated. The next step is to set up your domain and verify the ownership of it.

Figure 7-20. *Adding a domain to the Mailgun server*

I know all these DNS settings (Figure 7-20) sound confusing and complicated at first. But on the same page, you'll find a video and step-by-step instructions for all major domain sellers and providers. All you have to do is to log in to your domain provider and manage DNS right next to your domain name. In the DNS records, add TXT and MX records as in the Mailgun guide. All you have to do is to copy the values from the Mailgun page and paste them into the domain DNS records. To make sure your settings are correct, click Verify DNS Settings, and if you see green marks right next to DNS Types, then everything is working, and you are ready to send emails (Figure 7-21). In case something is not working, and you still see red and yellow crosses, watch the video one more time and try again.

Figure 7-21. *Added domain name was successfully verified*

Mailgun works as a regular API and requires the Requests library to send a message to a server and an API Key. Open the Mailgun Dashboard and select the option *Settings* from the left menu and then find the option *API Keys*. Also, API Keys can be found in your personal settings (Figure 7-22).

Figure 7-22. *Mailgun API Keys*

To send an email, open a new **Jupyter** Notebook and import the Requests library on top of the file:

```
import requests
```

As in previous API examples, we will define the API_KEY variable to hold the API Key. Also define the DOMAIN variable for your domain name:

```
API_KEY = "9514cb771d5da80eb6"
DOMAIN = "artyudin.com"
```

The Requests library has functions that match major HTTP methods get(), post(), put(), and delete(). The get() method sends a request to obtain data from a server, and the post() method delivers the data to a server. Since we want to deliver information, we will use the post() method.

We will need to pass a few parameters into the post() method. I'll break it down and define each information piece separately to make it clear.

First of all, the Requests method post() requires the HTTP address we are trying to reach. We will define it as url and use the template from the Mailgun documentation.

Our goal is to reach many potential customers, so I'll set recipients as a list of email addresses. In real life, you will probably be fetching emails and names from a file or a database. In any case, you would need to provide all emails as a Python list:

```
recipients = ["anna@example.com", "sherlock@example.com"]
```

I'll set the subject as the subject_matter variable:

```
subject_matter = "Hello there"
```

The message itself I'll assign as a string to the message variable:

```
message = "I am sending this email with Python!"
```

Finally, I'll define who I am sending the message as `sender`. If you have not added a domain name, then you'll have to use the verified email address.

In the `post()` method, we will pass `url`, authentication as `auth`, and information as `data`. For authentication in the `auth` tuple, we need to set the `API_KEY`:

```
auth=("api", API_KEY)
```

The keyword argument `data` will contain all the information we have defined before:

```
data = {"from": sender, "to": recipients, "subject": subject_
matter, "text": message}
```

The whole Requests method `post()` would look like this:

```
requests.post(
        url,
        auth=("api", API_KEY),
        data={"from": sender,
            "to": recipients,
            "subject": subject_matter,
            "text": message}
        )
```

Every time we send a request to a server, the Requests package returns a code. Anything in the range from 200 to 300 means that the operation was completed successfully. In case you see 400, check your code. You might have missed a closing bracket or provided a wrong API or domain name.

In our example, we have received 200 (Figure 7-23). Since the email was successfully sent, start looking for it in a mailbox.

```
In [1]: import requests

In [2]: API_KEY = "9514771d5da80eb6"
        DOMAIN = "artyudin.com"

In [3]: url = "https://api.mailgun.net/v3/{}/messages".format(DOMAIN)
        recipients = ["anna@example.com", "sherlock@example.com"]
        subject_matter = "Hello there"
        message = "I am sending this email with Python!"
        sender = "Art Yudin <art@artyudin.com>"

In [4]: requests.post(
                url,
                auth=("api", API_KEY),
                data={"from": sender,
                    "to": recipients,
                    "subject": subject_matter,
                    "text": message}
                )

Out[4]: <Response [200]>
```

Figure 7-23. *Successfully sent an email with Python*

As you can see, the process of using the Mailgun API is not difficult at all. Wrapping the API into your own Python script gives you flexibility to add a bunch of other tasks along with sending emails. For example, scheduling email campaigns or maybe scraping data from the Internet and then emailing that information. In any case, using Python and Mailgun services gives you more room for automation. Our goal is to automate tedious marketing tasks with Python.

You should regard this chapter as a trampoline for using the Python programming language for marketing. All the big companies provide useful APIs that you can use to make your work process faster and efficient. I believe that by now you have a strong understanding of how to retrieve information from APIs with the Requests library and how to manipulate received data with Python.

Index

A, B

Anaconda package
  data analysis tools, 3
  graphical installation, 3, 4
  installation process, 3
  Jupyter Notebook file, 5, 6
  Kernel operation, 8
  navigator menu, 4, 5
  print() command, 7, 8
  PyCharm, 4
  run play icon button, 7
  untitled file, 6
Application programming
      interfaces (APIs)
  accessing values, 197
  Alpha Vantage services, 194
  built-in method, 199
  client/browser, 192
  client libraries
    authentication, 278
    Cloud Platform, 278
    installation process, 278
    key option, 280
    reporting process, 279, 280
    resources page, 279
  device sending, 193
  dictionary object, 198

Google analytics, 193
libraries, 194
plotting data, 200
receiving data, 196
registration, 193
requests.get() method, 195
transpose() method, 198
type() function, 196
applymap() method, 199

C

Comma-separated values (CSV)
  aggregation methods, 132
  apply()/lambda() method,
    138, 139
  converting strings, 131
  delete option, 129
  dictionary notation, 129
  exchange-traded fund, 124
  financial companies fund, 125
  info() method, 128
  lambda expression, 136
  min() and max() methods, 132
  numeric type, 137
  online location, 127
  read_csv() function, 125
  Sectorspdr website, 126

Comma-separated
    values (CSV) (*cont.*)
  series method, 130
  skiprows keyword, 127
  smallest and largest shares, 133
  str methods, 138
  strip() and str.strip() method, 130
  str_to_num() function, 135, 136
contains() method, 133, 134
Critical Line Algorithm (CLA), 266

D

DataFrame
  constructing file
    attributes, 102, 103
    portfolio variable, 100, 101
    scratch creation, 102
  filtering process, 114–117
  slicing approach
    attributes, 104, 107
    column name, 103
    column names, 104
    dir() function, 104
    intermediatory structure, 106
    loc and iloc method,
      112–114
    reassignment, 106
    square brackets method,
      104, 105
    stock symbols, 108
    string, 103
    symbol column, 108,
      110, 111

    vectorized operation, 107
  two-dimensional structure, 100
Data structure
  close() function, 82
  dictionary, 49, 74–80
  loop/for loop, 49–53
  functions
    add() function, 61, 63
    definition, 59
    docstring, 63
    error message, 60
    help() function, 63
    indentation, 60
    parentheses, 60
    print() function, 61
  get() method, 78
  indefinite loops, 71–74
  items() method, 77
  multiplication table, 59
  nested for loops, 57–59
  open() function, 81, 82
  program structure
    grabbing code, 65
    input() function, 68
    is_vowel() function, 68, 70
    lowercase function, 70
    pseudocode code solution,
      64–67
    refactored code, 71
  range function, 54–57
  reading data
    dictionary, 88
    FileNotFoundError, 84
    frequent words, 90

open() function, 84
parsing information, 85
read() method, 84
remote text file, 86
sort() method, 89
split() function, 85, 87
urllib, 85
urlopen() function, 86
writing information (text files), 81–84
Definite/indefinite loops, 71–74
Dictionary, 74–80
Digital marketing tasks
analytics, 281–298
client libraries, 278–281
definition, 277
email marketing, 304–309
Twitter bot, 298–303
drop() method, 128

E

Efficient frontier techniques
classic mean/variance optimization, 266
definition, 257
investment portfolio, 261
max_sharp() method, 261
min_volatility() function, 260
optimal portfolios, 258
plotting() function, 265, 266
plot_weights() function, 264
portfolio_performance() method, 262

PyPortfolioOpt, 257
sample_cov() function, 258
sharp ratio, 262, 263
visualization, 264
volatility, 261, 264
Email marketing
API Keys, 306
delete() method, 307
documentation, 304
domain option, 305, 306
mailbox, 308
Mailgun service, 304
post() method, 308
sending/domains option, 305
Smtplib package, 304

F

Filtering process, 114–117
Financial tasks
definition, 231
efficient frontier, 257
fundamental analysis, 267–277
future value fv(), 233, 234
inventory turnover, 275
Monte Carlo simulation, 253–256
net present value, 235–242
Numpy, 231–233
present value, 234, 235
ratios, 274, 275
value at risk, 243–253
Loop/for loop
append() method, 53

Loop/for loop (*cont.*)
    definition, 49
    design pattern, 52
    format() function, 51
    if statement, 51
    iteration, 50
    list variables, 51
    translation, 50
Fundamental analysis
    balance sheets, 271
    bar chart, 272
    capabilities, 268
    cash flow statement, 271
    companies, 269
    definition, 267
    enterprise() function, 270
    exchange-traded funds, 268
    pip command, 267
    plotting data, 268
    profile() function, 269
    revenue numbers, 271
    ROIC and ROE ratios, 273, 274
    subplot() function, 273
    valuation, 270
    visualization, 272
Future value (fv() function),
    233, 234

G

Gathering data
    application programming
        interfaces, 192–200
    information, 151
    list comprehension, 165–171
    Pandas-Datareader, 200–205
    Selenium, 175–192
    web scraping (*see* Web scraping
        process)
Google Analytics
    account user management, 283
    build() function, 284
    constructing option, 296, 297
    DataFrame, 292
    dictionary notation, 290
    email/navigation, 282
    fetching option, 287
    for loop, 296
    integers and floats, 291
    JSON files, 281
    libraries, 288
    metrics values, 287, 288
    pageviews and session
        duration, 289
    pip command, 283
    plot()/pie() methods, 293
    request method, 294
    response method, 295
    service accounts page, 282
    sorting, 298
    source code, 288
    unpacking process, 290
    users and sessions metrics, 285
    values, 292
    visualization, 293
Groupby, 147–150

H, I

Histogram graph, 216–218
Hypertext Markup
    Language (HTML), 152

J

JavaScript Object
    Notation (JSON), 193

K

keys() method, 76, 196, 286

L

Line chart
    grid() function, 214
    HEX/RGB formats, 210
    legend() function, 211
    plot() function, 208, 210
    plotting statement, 212
    plt.grid() function, 208
    plt.legend() function, 211, 213
    plt.plot() function, 209
    plt.style.use() method, 215
    plt.title() function, 212
    pyplot modules, 208
    title/legend, 214
List comprehension
    append() method, 165, 166
    final_list, 169
    gathering data, 165
    list_article, 167

mega_list, 167
open() function, 170
parsing and cleaning
    information, 168
string template, 168
syntax, 165
text formation, 170
web scraping operation, 171
zip() function, 168

M

Matplotlib
    library, 207
    line chart, 208–216
    pie chart, 227–230
    scatter plot, 219–227
Monte Carlo simulation
    definition, 253
    NumPy arrays, 255
    plotting option, 256
    portfolio list, 254
    random() function, 254
    show() method, 255
    volatility, 254

N

Net present value (NPV)
    assumptions, 236
    calculating/plotting projects,
        241, 242
    company planning, 235
    crossover rate, 242

Net present value (NPV) (*cont.*)
    definition, 235
    discount_rates, 237
    geometrical object, 239
    hline()/vline() functions, 241
    intersection() method, 238
    LineString operation, 240
    plot() function, 240
    project creation, 236, 237
    scenario analysis, 237
    xlim() method, 238
    ylim() method, 239
    zip() function, 239
Numpy-Financial package,
    231–233

O

Object-oriented
    programming (OOP), 31

P, Q

Pandas
    CSV (*see* Comma-separated
      values (CSV))
    DataFrame, 100–117
    Datareader
      DataReader() function,
        201, 203
      definition, 200–205
      Gross Domestic Product, 204
      IEX, 202
      nonfarm payrolls, 205

      pip command, 201
      plot.line() method, 204
      receiving data, 203
    data sets
      combination, 139
      concatenation, 140–144
      drop keyword, 143
      groupby() method, 147–150
      zip() function, 140
    definition, 93
    logical operations
      anonymous function, 118
      apply() method, 118,
        119, 121
      double function, 119, 120
      if and else conditions, 121
      lambda syntax, 120
      logical operation, 122
      np.where function, 123
      NumPy function, 122
      where() function, 123, 124
    merging function, 145–147
    panel data, 93
    plotting tools, 150
    series (*see* Series)
    sophisticated data structures, 93
Pie chart, 227–230
post() method, 307
Python
    Anaconda (*see* Anaconda)
    concepts, 2
    error message, 18, 22
    first program creation, 20–23
    float() function, 18

if, Elif/Else statements
   boolean data type, 23
   comparison operators, 24, 25
   documentation, 25
   Elif keyword, 27, 28, 30
   Else statement, 26
   if statement, 25
   logical operators, 29, 30
   structuring decision
     structures, 29
indexing/slicing
   element/character, 44
   fetching elements, 42
   insert() method, 42
   list storage, 41
   negative index, 43
   negative step, 45
   ordered collections, 41
   skipping option, 45
   string/element, 44
installation process, 3
int() function, 18
learning process, 2
lists/tuples
   append() method, 36
   ascending order, 38
   conditions, 39
   container, 35
   data structure, 35, 39
   help() function, 36
   list methods, 36
   numbers, 37
   operators, 40
   remove() method, 38

   sort() function, 37
   tuple() function, 40
   type() function, 38
   vowel/consonant, 40
methods
   concept, 31
   dir() function, 31, 32
   len() function, 33
   lowercase strings, 35
   string methods, 32
   upper() method, 34
ord() function, 16, 17
print() statement, 22
routine tasks, 1
str() function, 19
strings, 16–19
tax and tip calculator, 21
variables/numeric types
   area calculation, 15
   arithmetic operators,
     11, 12
   built-in functions, 13
   case sensitive, 11
   data types, 10
   expression, 14
   floats, 11
   integers, 11
   memory, 9
   naming conventions, 10
   plastic bottle/glass, 10
   reserved words/keywords, 10
   source code, 15
   store information, 9
   type() function, 13

R

Range function
    descending order, 55
    index value, 56
    len() function, 56
    parameters, 54–57
    range() function, 54
requests.get() method, 153, 159,
    160, 164

S

Scatter plot
    annotate() function, 225
    annotating values, 226
    colorbar scale, 223, 224
    enumerate() function, 225
    insert statement, 224
    interactive graph, 221, 222, 226
    magic function, 219
    inline format, 219
    notebook mode, 219
    read_excel() function, 220
Selenium
    Amazon landing page, 181
    automation solution, 181
    BeautifulSoup() function, 176
    browser window, 190
    category name, 183
    Chrome() function, 176
    ChromeDriver, 175
    dir() function, 179
    div container, 184
    excel file, 190

    exception handling, 187
    fetching option, 180
    find_element_by_id()
        method, 180
    get() method, 177
    input prompt, 181
    inspect option, 182
    Keys module, 181
    page.get() method, 187
    product page, 178
    productTitle, 188
    try and except blocks, 187–189
    source code, 190–192
    text method, 185
    web page, 183, 185
    web scraping
        command prompt window,
         172–174
        documentation, 174
        get-pip.py file, 174
        installation, 173
        Sudo command, 172
        Terminal window, 172
        web development, 171
    write() method, 189
Series
    advantages, 97
    attributes, 99
    data type identifier, 96
    definition, 94
    dictionary, 99, 100
    differences, 95
    division operation, 98
    homogeneous, 96

one-dimensional structure, 94
pd variable, 94
relational database, 95
round() function, 98
string keys, 99
vectorization, 97, 98

T

Twitter bot
  account creation, 299
  API registration process, 298
  image_path variable, 301
  media files, 302
  OAuthHandler method, 301
  session column, 299
  Terminal window, 301
  token/secret access, 300
  Tweepy documentation, 300
  Tweepy library, 303

U

Uniform Resource Locator (URL),
  85, 125, 152

V

Value at risk (VAR)
  covariance matrix, 250
  cov() function, 249
  pct_change() method, 246
  DataFrame, 244
  definition, 243

describe() method, 248, 249
dot() method, 250
dropna() method, 247
head() method, 244
Jupyter Notebook, 243
normalized historic
    prices, 246
NumPy array, 250
plotting historic stock, 248
ppf() method, 251
projecting value, 253
retrieving historic prices, 244
risk calculation, 252
shift() method, 246
sqrt() method, 250
string format, 244
Visualization
  definition, 207
  histogram, 216–218
  line chart, 208–216
  Matplotlib library, 207
  pie chart, 227–230
  scatter plot, 219–227

W, X, Y, Z

Web scraping process
  BeautifulSoup() function, 160
  Chrome browser, 152
  definition, 152–165
  find()/find_all() method,
      155, 156
  get() method, 153
  get_text() method, 159

Web scraping process (*cont.*)
  hrefs, 162
  HTML markup, 154
  information, 152
  inspect option, 161, 163
  investing.com, 159
  locating/inspecting line, 158

inspect option, 155
requests method, 152
Selenium, 171–175
text elements, 157
variable titles, 162, 163
URL site, 164
web links, 159

Printed in the United States
by Baker & Taylor Publisher Services

Printed in the United States
by Baker & Taylor Publisher Services